The Secret War in Tibet

The Secret War in Tibet

Michel Peissel

illustrated

Little, Brown and Company
Boston · Toronto

FIRST AMERICAN EDITION

T 07/73

First published in England in 1972 under the title
Cavaliers of Kham.

Library of Congress Cataloging in Publication Data

Peissel, Michel, 1937-
   The secret war in Tibet.

   Bibliography: p.
   1. Tibet--Politics and government--1951-
2. Guerrillas--Tibet.   I. Title.
DS786.P38 1973   320.9'51'505   73-4986
ISBN 0-316-69790-7

PRINTED IN THE UNITED STATES OF AMERICA

Silence is consent

Contents

Illustrations

———◆●◆———

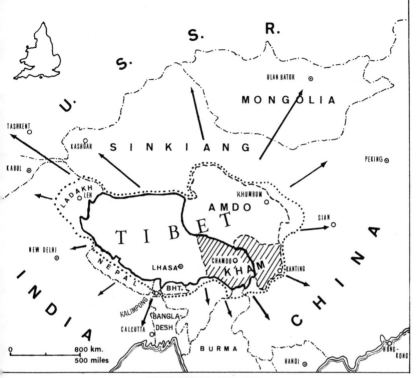

GREATER TIBET

→ Limits of Songtsen Gampo's conquests and empire.
···· Limits of ethnic, linguistic, and cultural Tibet in 1970 and of political Tibet until 1850.
– – – Boundaries of Greater Tibet, 1914.
—— Tibet of Dalai Lama, 1950.

Ulan Bator (Urga). Capital of Mongolia and seat of the Urga Lama, religious head of the Mongolians, who until 1924 was a Tibetan.
Sian. Ancient capital of China, conquered in 763 by the Tibetan King Tri-song De-tsen, great-grandson of Songtsen Gampo.
Khumbum. Largest monastery of eastern Tibet, close to birth place of present Dalai Lama.
Kanting. Better known by its Tibetan name Tachenlu. Trade centre and Kham's door to China.
Kalimpong (Kalemphu). Tibetan village incorporated into West Bengal, market town and India's door to Tibet.
Tashkent. Western limit of advance of Tibetan soldiers of Songtsen Gampo.
Calcutta. Southern limit of Tibetan conquest.
Leh. Capital of western Tibet and of Tibetan realm of Laddak; often called Little Tibet.
The distance between Leh and Kanting or Leh and Khumbum is equal to the distance between Paris and Moscow.

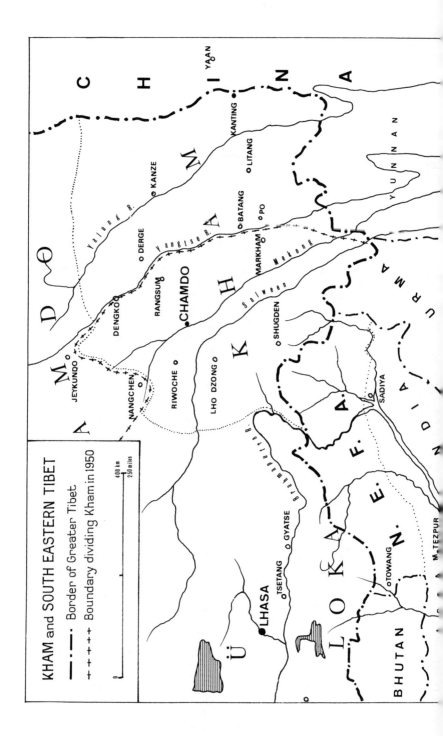

KHAM and SOUTH EASTERN TIBET

— · — · — Border of Greater Tibet

+ + + + + Boundary dividing Kham in 1950

0   400 km
         250 miles

C   H   I   N   A

A   M   D   O

K   H   A   M

YAAN

KANTING

LITANG

KANZE

BATANG

PO

DERGE

MARKHAM

RANGSUM

CHAMDO

DENGKO

SHUGDEN

JEYKUNDO

NANGCHEN

RIWOCHE

LHO DZONG

Yalung R.

Yangtse R.

Mekong

Salween

YUNNAN

BURMA

SADIYA

N. E. F. A.

INDIA

M. TEZPUR

TOWANG

L O K A

Ü

LHASA

TSETANG

GYATSE

Brahmaputra R.

BHUTAN

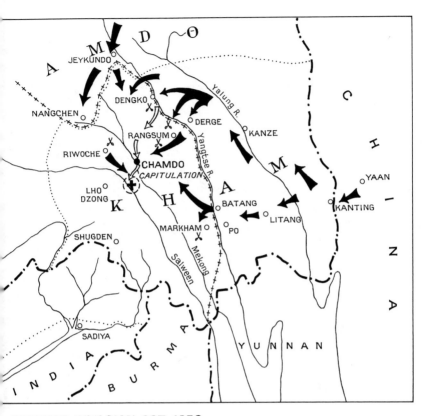

CHINESE INVASION OCT. 1950

➤ Chinese advance
⇨ Tibetan retreat
✗ Battles

0 ——————————————— 400 km
——————————————— 250 miles

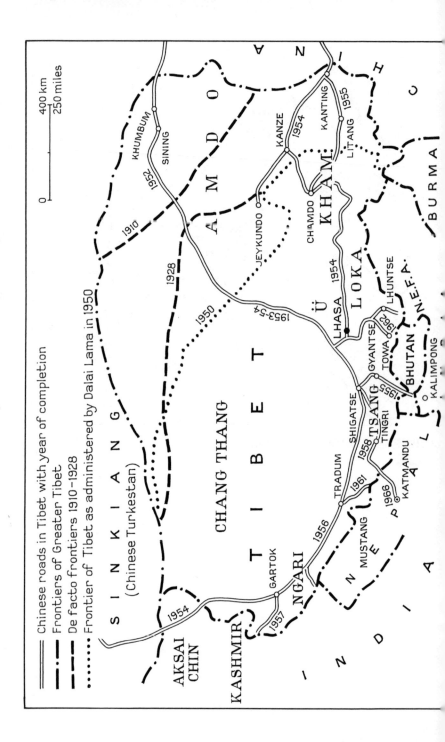

Chinese roads in Tibet with year of completion

Frontiers of Greater Tibet

De facto frontiers 1910–1928

Frontier of Tibet as administered by Dalai Lama in 1950

400 km
250 miles
0

The Secret War in Tibet

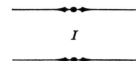

A War Called Genocide

As nobody cares, I think it may be wise to write what I have seen and heard. Betty-la in tears as she wondered whether to abandon her children or leave her husband; whether to risk being imprisoned and possibly killed, or to remain with the man who had four times given her those pregnancies so much desired when one is a young Tibetan girl, even a princess.

Along with her children, Betty-la eventually had to leave everything, even down to the old beggar who used to argue with her on the doorstep of her home. None of the 35,000 inhabitants of the most mysterious capital in the world was unaware of who she was; Betty-la, the daughter of the great Tsarong of Lhasa.

I, of course, had never heard of her, or of her famous father when, walking up a country lane bordered with flowers, I went to Tashiding for the first time in 1959. I had some trouble finding the villa, and had entered two others by mistake. Each was a little bit of England set in the Himalayan foothills, houses surrounded by lawns and flowering gardens where one rapidly forgot the bustle of Kalimpong's bazaar with its dirty stalls stretching along either side of one long trail leading to Tibet.

When I first arrived in Kalimpong, twelve years ago, I knew little or nothing of the war in Tibet. In fact I possessed only the vaguest knowledge of the land of the snows, information gleaned from all those books praising the saintly sages of what seemed to me a never-never land, a strange Shangri-la populated by floating monks, a country where people never grew old.

Like most people, I believed then that with the recent flight of the Dalai Lama to India, the Tibetan revolt was over, that it had been nothing more than a short, unsuccessful uprising, an isolated unfortunate incident. Few indeed were those who understood the true nature of the crisis. This was because India, siding with the Government of Mao, made certain that little or no information was allowed to filter through the 'inner line', a border sealing off the Indo-Tibetan frontier to all foreigners.

The truth on Tibet lay concealed from the world, masked by Chinese propaganda, Indian complicity, Western indifference, and the docile resignation of the young Dalai Lama who at best was merely an unhappy puppet caught in the conflicting seas of an incredible upheaval.

I could hardly have guessed, in that spring of 1959, that the key to what was happening in Tibet lay not with the Dalai Lama but in the hands of warriors from a practically unknown tribe, the tribe of such men as Osher and Tsering whom I was about to meet; still less could I have imagined that in the years to come I would myself become involved with these Tibetan guerrillas of despair, the last cavaliers of the fierce warrior tribes of Central Asia, men who still, today, in 1972, are holding the Chinese forces at bay.

With the tears of Betty-la in the Indian Tibetan border town of Kalimpong there began for me a long and tragic adventure which in the next twelve years was to lead me deep into the secrets of those anonymous guerrillas who, even now, are still fighting and dying in Tibet.

It is because of Osher, because of Betty-la, Tsering and all the others whom I met in the course of twelve years in the Himalayas that I have decided to write this book, so that, perhaps in another life, they may know that somewhere out there in the lowlands, beyond the great desert plains, below the ocean of snow-covered peaks, at least someone cared, so that they may know that they have not all suffered or died in vain, those countless victims of a war that lawyers have called genocide.

I wish I could describe all the phases of this war, and follow all its actions, both in the field and in the minds of the people. I would like to write the epic history of these warriors who on horseback charged the armoured cars of the Chinese. But who am I to speak? I was not there when Litang was bombed, or Lhasa mortared, nor was I there when Tsering's children had died one by one in the Chang Thang. It was not so much their dying that was unbearable, Tsering explained to me, not so much their dying as seeing them go, slowly, inevitably, one after the other: 'You have to have seen your four children die slowly before your eyes to understand what went on.' And although Osher was to die in my own arms in May 1964 Tsering was right. I could never bear witness to what I had not seen, nor could I feel what he had felt, or understand the grief of Betty-la who had left all her small children behind for ever.

I can therefore only report here what I myself have witnessed, the desperate, courageous struggle of the guerrillas, the secret military feats of the soldiers of the 'Fortress of Religion', the silent tears of those who, like Tsering, have subsided into despair, the tragedy of those who, like Osher, have died anonymous deaths, and the foolhardy courage of those who continue to struggle.

I have seen and heard much in the years since that morning when I entered that flowered villa called 'Tashiding' for the first time; and twelve years have been too many for me to keep the silence of cowardice any longer. Little do I care what embarrassment my meagre testimony may cause to the governments of Nepal, India, Russia, Formosa, China, or the United States who, like the British, who, like too many of us, must bear the real responsibility for what has happened out there above the great Himalayas that stand today like a wall, a wall of deeper shame than Berlin's.

It is to Betty-la, to Tsering, and to the memory of Osher, that I dedicate this book.

Tonight, as almost every night for the past fifteen years, out in the nameless wilds of Tibet, men are questioning the silence, waiting in ambush, waiting for the distant whine of a truck whose driver, lulled by the roar of his engine, scans in fear the bleak horizon. Tonight that driver will die.

The victim is Chinese. The attackers are members of a tribe unknown to the world, although in Tibet its very name has been for centuries synonymous with fear: men whose bullets echo the rhythm of their horses' hooves, as their war cries ring out upon the hills when, with swords flashing, they ride in to kill. One more convoy is being attacked, one more garrison assailed, one more victory registered by the cavaliers of Kham, the soldiers of the Fortress of Religion.

This is an account of the as-yet-unrecorded and highly secret actions of a small group of Tibetans from the province of Kham, a land described by one of the very few westerners ever to go there as a country of 'Gentlemen Robbers', a land inhabited by a fierce race whose emergence into the complex world of international politics teaches us that in our age of atomic bombs there still exists a force far greater than machines: the power of courage and determination. This is the force by which these men, against all probability, and facing incredible odds, have succeeded in changing the history of our modern world, not only by opposing, with success, the world's greatest army, that of China, but also by affecting the policies of other great nations against which they had also to battle.

Who are these men? According to the Chinese Communists: 'The Khambas are cavaliers, wild, undisciplined, and accustomed to living by loot.' While to quote the Dalai Lama: 'The Khamba's most precious possession is a gun'; even the reserved Scotsman Hugh Richardson, one-time British resident in Lhasa, calls them in his History of Tibet 'a wild, war-like feuding sort of people'. As a consequence few westerners have ever set foot in their land and even fewer have survived to tell the tale.

Yet Kham is larger than Spain; a rectangle of approximately 160,000 square miles lying between central Tibet and China, it is part of what is known as greater Tibet. Cut by tremendous gorges and high passes, Kham's altitude, weather and aggressive population have always united to deny entry to the foreigner, and if the central portion of Tibet, ruled by the Dalai Lama, was for generations considered inaccessible to westerners, Kham was beyond such qualification. Even today, there are no accurate maps to define its contours, to record its villages and monasteries and trace the secret routes by which its nomads migrate from north to south, from east to west over its vast expanse.

Kham is the great high plateau of south-eastern Tibet, a region from which three of the world's largest rivers flow: the Dre Chu, the Dza Chu and the Dri Chu, better known as the Yangtse, the Mekong and the Salween, to use the names they take when emerging from Kham.

To Europeans, to the Chinese, and even to the inhabitants of Lhasa, Kham has always been a vast no-man's-land. To the south it is bounded by the Himalayas of Assam and the mighty bend of the Brahmaputra (which allowed the Khambas to claim that the entire world drank from their rivers), to the north Kham's limits are lost somewhere in the wilds of the immense Amne Machin range, which separates Kham from the further deserts of another vast, little-known Tibetan region called Amdo which stretches northwards to mighty Lake Kokonor and the limits of the Gobi.

To the east Kham is two months' journey from Lhasa, across the eastern extremity of the fearful Chang Thang, the most frightening desert in the world. A plateau whose mean altitude is 16,000 feet, this desert is as large as the Gobi, more parched than the Sahara and as cold as the Arctic.

Only to the west are Kham's borders well defined, marked by the last ridges from which one may glimpse the first lowlands of Szechwan, the birthplace of China's great plains.

For Osher and for Tsering, as for all Khambas, their land was a land of happiness, one with 'more yaks than virtues to Buddha, more grass than in the rest of the world'. The country, they all agreed, 'was a pleasure to behold'. 'A great desert void' retorted those few westerners who, coming from China, had set eyes upon the endless barren mountains stretching westward beyond the Chinese province of Szechwan. Yet here, scattered over this immensity, lived over two million people, nearly a third of the population of greater Tibet, centred around the area's five largest monasteries in the towns of Chamdo, Dergue, Batang, Kandze and Litang.

It is hardly surprising that here in this wild, forgotten land, should be found the most rugged race of our planet in this second half of the twentieth century, or that this was the region of Tibet where the fighting spirit of independence which had once forged the great Tibetan Empire of Songtsen Gampo burned strongest.

Who in the West today has ever heard of Songtsen Gampo, any more than they have of Kham? Yet his name deserves to stand beside those of Alexander, Caesar, Genghiz Khan and Napoleon as one of the greatest conquerors of all times.

The issues of the Tibetan crisis can only be wholly understood in terms of Songtsen Gampo's strange and mysterious Empire, an empire forgotten perhaps in the West, but which is still very much alive.

Songtsen Gampo was a Tibetan chieftain who, in A.D. 630, set out on horseback to unify the wild tribes of central Asia.

Twenty years after taking up arms, this man had raised one of the fiercest armies of all time and had extended his dominion over most of central Asia and well into China. From the frightened Chinese emperor he demanded a daughter in marriage. The emperor was obliged to comply and also to pay tribute to the fierce Tibetan warrior.

After seizing a large area of China, Songtsen Gampo marched south over the Himalayas. Here he acquired a second wife, a Nepalese princess, thereby assuring himself dominion over the hill tribes of Nepal. From there, his horsemen carried on right down to the rich plains of the Ganges. Then, once in India, some of his men penetrated as far south as the great Delta of the Brahmaputra and gave the Bay of Bengal the surprising name of the 'Tibetan Ocean'!

To the north the Tibetan conqueror established control over the vast steppes of the Mongolians whence, seven centuries later, there emerged another great soldier, Ghengiz Khan.

To the west the 'Noble Tibetan King', as he is often called, conquered Swat and reached out as far as Samarkand. Years later his descendants so greatly frightened the all-powerful Caliph of Bagdad, Harun-al-Rashid, of *The Thousand and One Nights,* that the Caliph was obliged to send his best armies in an attempt to contain those of the Tibetan kings.

So powerful was the Tibet of those times that when, in 763, the Chinese emperor refused to pay the fifty thousand rolls of silk owed in tribute to the Tibetan court, Songtsen Gampo's great-great-grandson invaded China and captured the very capital of the Celestial Empire (then Chang'an (Sian)). The Tibetan king then deposed the Chinese emperor and replaced him temporarily with his own brother-in-law.

Thus it came about that from northern Burma to Afghanistan, from Siberia to India, from what is today Russian Turkestan to well inside China. Songsten Gampo and his descendants ruled for four hundred years over the greatest empire of central Asia, an empire called Tibet. Of *all* the great conquerors of history, Songtsen Gampo is perhaps the one who has left the most lasting imprint on the world. This is because he not only established military control over territories vaster than Europe but also spread there his culture and language, along with the Buddhist religion he adopted from his

Chinese and Nepalese wives, and which in his domains took a special form known as Lamaism.

But what is most remarkable is the fact that today, thirteen centuries later, the traditions, culture, language and religion of Songtsen Gampo have survived practically unchanged throughout what were his vast domains.

Songtsen's political empire did not split up until the tenth century. It was divided first into three parts, then shattered into hundreds of small Tibetan feudal states and principalities. After this it becomes difficult to follow the battles and intrigues which have alternately divided and united these many principalities, all speaking the same language and possessing the same faith. These feuds and struggles to recapture the lost political unity of greater Tibet have not ceased even yet.

For centuries Tibetan lords have tried in vain to reunite the immense realm of 'The Three Religious Kings', the mighty Tibetan Empire of Songtsen Gampo and his descendants. The best attempts were those of great religious leaders, powerful abbots who exploited the common religion of all Tibetans as a means to control the arrogant and aggressive Tibetan princes. Although these monks were never entirely successful, the Dalai Lamas, first with the help of the descendants of Ghengiz Khan and later with the assistance of the Chinese Manchu emperors (both converted by them to Tibetan Buddhism), were able at times to unite a large part of the Tibetan world – particularly the central kingdoms of U and Tsang and the three kingdoms of Ngari (western Tibet) which constituted what we normally consider as modern Tibet, the Dalai Lama's realm.

But alongside the Dalai Lamas' territories, there still survived the independent Tibetan kingdoms of Laddak, Spiti, Kulu, Kangra, Mustang, Sikku, Bhutan and Dergue, as well as the large principalities of Amdo and the warring kingdoms of Kham.

In modern times, from 1850 onwards, some of these Tibetan kingdoms were annexed to British India (Laddak, Spiti, Kulu, Kangra), others, such as Kandze and the principalities of Amdo, fell under the chaotic rule of semi-independent Chinese warlords, while the kingdoms of Mustang, Sikkim, Bhutan and Dergue have remained independent until today. On the other hand in Northern Burma in the twentieth century they still speak Tibetan, as they do over great areas of northern and western China. Tibetan is also spoken in half of Kashmir, in a third of Nepal, as well as in parts of Sinkiang and most of Baltistan; while in Mongolia, although they speak another language, they still retain the religion of Tibet.

By 1949 most of the world at large had forgotten the common bond uniting these lands, and only the reduced kingdom of the Dalai Lamas was considered, wrongly, as Tibet. This was because neither the Chinese, the British nor the Indians were keen for Tibet to reunite and control the strategic heart of Asia once more.

Yet in 1949 the memory of Songtsen Gampo and his realm still shone brightly in the minds of seven million Tibetans, because, while the political and military power of greater Tibet had been weakened through internal divisions, nothing over the centuries had opposed the development of the great culture and religion of the Tibetan world.

Physically isolated and well protected, unlike all other lands of Asia, greater Tibet had not known the destructive intrusion of colonialism. The Tibetans had pursued their way of life uninterrupted since the seventh century, building new monasteries, erecting new forts and perfecting their sophisticated culture.

Such in 1949 was the sleeping giant of Songtsen Gampo's realm, a huge territory politically divided yet united by strong cultural and religious ties, an empire forgotten yet very much alive and of which the Khambas were the most arrogant subjects.

That same year (1949) east of Tibet there came to power in the low lands of China another great leader, a man nourished on western thought but motivated by a traditional passion for his motherland. Mao Tse-tung dreamed of creating a new world, one that should embody the myths and legends of his nation's long and ancient past. He dreamed of seeing the celestial empire, China, the oldest civilization of the globe, dominate and control Asia.

Many people will claim that the man is a saint. Beyond doubt, Mao is a genius, one of the greatest strategists the world has produced, a soldier without equal, a poet of merit, a man imbued with a mission, set upon a task so fantastic that no one ever believed it could be done. A monk at heart, he was a man of religion, one that offered all to the motherland, to China, to an image of China as great as it had only been in the minds of those scholars who for thousands of years had patiently written upon silk the Confucian philosophy of Chinese history.

Slowly, with courage and determination, Mao moved the resigned hearts of the underfed peasants, of the bitter scholars and of the enfeebled nobles. Province by province, he had rallied his followers while being hunted by the government of his land. Pursued, he had crossed his country like a fleeing fox, silently but carefully leaving in his wake thousands of souls stirred by his words and conquered by his ideals.

So strong was this man's love for his country that he swallowed his pride and united with his enemy Chiang Kai-shek to drive out the Japanese invaders. Having succeeded, in a matter of a few years the whole land lay opened to welcome the new prophet. Acceding to power in 1949, Mao refused honours, and discarded the brocade robes of his predecessors. He stood up, a simple man in grey cloth, to preach in Peking the greatness of China, its mission in the world, its heritage and its future.

Looking back at his country's heritage, Mao knew better than most that although for three thousand years China had produced the greatest scholars, artists and philosophers in the world, her wisdom had never been a match for the cunning and strength of the conquering hordes of central Asia.

Indeed, for as long as men could remember (which in China is longer than anywhere else), the story had been the same: sweeping into China from the desert voids of the west had come wave after wave of fierce, warring conquerors, who, for all their barbarism, had overcome the theories of scholars, the spells of sorcerers, the powers of philosophy, to dominate the great motherland and to put fear into the hearts of the Chinese. Chinese philosophy, religion, technology, magic, even the Great Wall, had never stopped the vital force of these men bred in the wilds of the windy steppes and the vast plains of Tibet, Sinkiang, and Mongolia. It was as if a force stronger than that of the mind flowed in the blood of these 'ignorant barbarians', 'savages and grease-eaters'.

Songtsen Gampo had been followed by Kublai Khan who eventually was succeeded by the northern Manchus. When the names of the Chinese emperors were known and respected around the world, when the throne of the celestial empire ruled most of Asia, the men who sat upon that throne were not Chinese, but sons of the steppes, men of a different race, men born in tents and fed on raw meat and the milk of yaks, mares and camels: men who looked on Lhasa as the spiritual centre of the world.

So, when he came to power in Peking on 20 October 1949, Mao vowed from the dais built by Mongolian kings before the Forbidden City of the Manchu emperors that the time had come when the Chinese would rule their own land. More, they would rise and rule the East. To achieve this it was, Mao knew, imperative for China to control at last the strategic heart of Asia. For this reason, in his first speech Mao solemnly declared that the primary and most urgent goal of the new Chinese People's Republic was to 'liberate Tibet'.

Mao expected this to be an easy task. Technology, so he believed, had killed the power of the barbarians once and for all. He was confident that China, with its fertile soil, its five hundred million souls and its well-armed peasants, could laugh at the two million Mongolians, the nine hundred thousand Uigurs of Moslem Sinkiang and the seven million Tibetans.

These last might be the most numerous, but Mao was well aware that, for over two hundred years, progress had by-passed the divided kingdoms of greater Tibet. Even the darkest corner of Africa or the remotest island of Melanesia possessed more machines, techniques and modern tools than did Tibet in 1949 : Tibet, a land where people still went about in the saddle or on foot, spinning their only machines, the prayer wheels of their simple faith, that 'opium of the people', which over the years had done a great deal to lessen the former aggressiveness of most Tibetans.

But, as Mao prepared to send his men out on to the high plains of Tibet to preach the doctrine of enlightened materialism and Han superiority, in the minds of the new Chinese leaders there lingered, occasionally, a faint fear, the atavistic terror of those born in the lowlands of China, springing from centuries, from millennia of sleepless nights, in fear of the great empty spaces from which, time and again, had arisen a race of kings, great warriors, men reared on nameless pastures, yet whose very names had made all China tremble.

2

A Race of Kings

Little did the Chinese appreciate how this fear was justified. 'The Khambas are a race of Kings.' This sentence was one of the first the young nobles and monks of Kham were still taught as they learned to read and write the intricate Tibetan language. The arrogant claim was well founded, for never in its long history had Kham ever been successfully invaded. Even Ghengiz Khan, whose warriors had conquered all China, India, Persia and much of Europe, had been unable to defeat the Khambas – with whom he had eventually to come to terms.

Through the centuries nothing had succeeded in weakening the aggressive spirit of the Khambas, not even the countless monks who since the days of Songsten Gampo had preached throughout the land a docile doctrine of non-violence. If Kham was studded with monasteries, many amongst the finest in Tibet, in Kham even these monasteries were known to wage war.

The entire history of Kham is one long series of wars and feuds, pitting the lands, lords and tribes against each other in bloody forays. But when, as occasionally happened, a foreigner was foolish enough to challenge the Khambas, they would unite, their quarrels momentarily forgotten. When this occurred there was no one to oppose the 'Race of Kings', not even the Chinese.

The Chinese had experienced this on many occasions even recently. One was in 1918, when, exasperated by a Chinese warlord named Peng, the Khambas had risen in force to drive him out of Tibet. In doing so, they had invested the border town of Kanting whence the fearless Khamba army threatened to invade the Chinese plains of Szechwan. Hastily the Chinese had swallowed their pride and called upon the British to use their power and influence to prevent a further advance of the Khambas into China.

The British stopped the war by curtailing the supply of arms and ammunition filtering into Tibet by way of Kalimpong. They then delegated Mr Eric Teichman, the British consul in

Chengtu, to negotiate with the Khambas. Single-handed, with what has been termed 'the greatest show of courage and diplomatic ability in colonial history', Teichman struck out alone, across the high, unexplored mountain ranges of Kham, to get the warriors to agree to an armistice. A ceasefire was ratified (for the Khambas had no ammunition left), and a kind of demilitarized zone established between the east bank of the upper Yangtse and the trading town of Kanting.

From then on, the upper Yangtse divided Kham in two, the area of Kham west of the river falling under the administration of Lhasa, whose representative lived in Chamdo, while the demilitarized region east of the Yangtse remained independent under nominal Chinese administration.

Such a solution was hardly likely to please the Khambas, so when in 1928 two monasteries rose in arms against each other it was war once more. A Chinese warlord named Liu took the opportunity of sending troops into the demilitarized zone to support one of the warring abbots. As soon as Liu's troops were involved, the Khambas again rose up against the Chinese intruders. After five months of bitter fighting Liu's men were thrown back beyond Kanting into Szechwan.

Thus for the second time in ten years the Khambas menaced China. This time Chiang Kai-shek blamed the British who, of course, could do nothing beyond urging Chiang to reach some kind of solution with the 13th Dalai Lama, the only authority who might have some influence on the Khamba warriors. After long parleys, a new armistice was signed early in 1923, and the Khamba armies disbanded.

A few months after the armistice, in April 1932, Liu invaded Kham again, taking the Tibetans by surprise. This attack greatly embarrassed the central Chinese government which was forced to admit that it could no more control the Szechwan warlords than the Dalai Lama could in fact control the Khambas. Indeed, in the following year, on the death of the powerful and much respected 13th Dalai Lama, the Khambas rose against both Lhasa and China!

Led by Rapgya and Topgyay Pangda Tsang, sons of a rich merchant, the Khambas tried to throw the Lhaseans out of Chamdo and drive all Chinese out of Kham. The Pangda brothers nearly succeeded in their wild bid for power by which they had hoped to únite under their own rule not only Kham, but the entire ancient Tibetan world of Songtsen Gampo. For two years, the Pangda Tsangs fought with desperate courage. Alone, they fought not only the Lhaseans and then the Nationalist Chinese, but even the retreating armies of the Chinese communists, the soldiers of Mao who in those early days of the 'Long March', had entered eastern Kham seeking refuge.

The Pangda Tsangs might have been defeated but they were not to be forgotten. Their ambitious bid for power became legendary; all over Kham their praises were sung: how they had dared to challenge Lhasa and had bravely fought the Chinese, although outnumbered ten to one.

The effect of all this turmoil was to revive again, in Chiang Kai-shek, China's age-old ambition to take over Kham.

Already as early as the beginning of the century, with what has been described as 'China's infinite capacity for mis-representation', maps had been produced showing great extents of Kham as part of China. Chiang Kai-shek now created (on paper) two new provinces, the first Chinghai, encompassing all the Tibetan region of Amdo, the second Sikang (not to be confused with Sinkiang), with Kanting as its capital covering a great extent of Kham. Because neither the Khambas nor the Lhaseans published any maps or had any representatives abroad to refute these ridiculous claims, maps all over the world showed these provinces, while, in fact, after the defeat of the Pangda brothers Kham remained divided as in 1918. A Lhasean governor still ruled in Chamdo levying taxes by force throughout the area west of the Yangtse, while east of the river the Khamba lords continued to rule their feudal estates up to the outskirts of Kanting, now the residence of the so-called 'governor' of Sikang, whose power hardly extended beyond this town.

In the years between 1933 and 1949 the large towns of Kham, with the exception of Chamdo (under Lhasa) and Kanting (under Chinese control) continued to assert their autonomy in a turmoil of medieval intrigues involving the local princes of Dergue, the rulers of Batang, the great abbots of Litang and, all these in turn, with their unruly vassals, the nomad princes, heads of the country's numerous tribes.

Such was Kham, that land of 'gentlemen robbers', when Mao rose to power in 1949 and such were the origins of some of the disputes and hatreds that still burned over the vast territory of the kings of ancient Tibet: a land of warrior tribes, divided among themselves and divided in their affection for their God King, then a child only fifteen years old.

Meanwhile that same year in Peking Mao Tse-tung with his most trusted generals was laying down the strategy which he hoped would give him control of the heart of Asia. By 1950, two worlds were about to clash, one old, divided, backward, and superstitious, and the other new, united and versed in the latest theories of social revolution and familiar with the most efficient strategy of modern warfare.

No evil omens were observed in Chamdo (the capital of western Kham) during the three-week festival that ushered in the fateful Iron Tiger year, 1950. In Lhasa, four hundred miles away, a dragon gargoyle was seen to drip water from its mouth, although it had not rained, yet such a sinister occurrence was hastily dispelled by an appropriate religious ceremony. That year the Tibetan state oracle had little to say, while the oracles of Kham simply reiterated, in veiled phrases, the secret desire of all: 'Away with the Lhaseans.'

Robert Ford was the only inhabitant of Kham possessing a radio, so he alone in Chamdo heard the New Year's speech from Peking in 1950 which proclaimed that 'the Chinese People's Liberation Army must liberate Tibet from the British and American Imperialists.' At the time he, Reginald Fox and Hugh Richardson were the only British nationals actually living in Tibet, and as they knew that there was not one American there they were disturbed to hear of Peking's crusade. They themselves were not very plausible agents of western imperialism: Ford and Fox were employees of the Tibetan government (Fox being married to a Tibetan), while Richardson was head of the Indian mission in Lhasa.

But apart from the young British radio operator, nobody in the Chamdo area was apparently very worried by the Chinese threat. Kham was a huge isolated territory and in 1950 it still took more than a month to travel from Chamdo to the distant Chinese border at Kanting. The Khambas' feeling of security was bolstered by the slow, perilous and infrequent communications with the outside world.

Among those who felt no alarm was my own friend Tsering. He was at that time master of Ulag Dzong, a small fortified manor located fifteen miles along the trail leading from Chamdo to Dergue. Tall and handsome, Tsering, like many Khambas, bore in his features no trace of Mongolian blood. He fitted the general description given of Khambas as being 'taller and stronger than most Tibetans'. Anthropologists have called the Khambas the tallest race in Asia, men with a quite European cast of features, although with their long aquiline noses and weatherbeaten complexions many Khambas have the keen, arrogant look of 'Hollywood' Red Indians.

I first met Tsering in Kalimpong, shortly after my meeting with Betty-la, after the Tibetan invasion began. He was then a flamboyant and arrogant commander in the Khamba guerrilla forces. Wearing spotless black boots and a vast, flowing, dark blue gown slung over a white raw-silk shirt, his six-foot-three figure towered impressively head and shoulders over the emaciated Indians, squat Lepchas and short Nepalese who crowded Kalimpong's bazaar.

I was later to meet Tsering on many occasions after 1959, and, although he had then shaved his head, when we first met he still wore his hair in long braids wound around his head. This typical Tibetan hairstyle gave him a wild, masculine appearance, in no way lessened by the long gold-and-turquoise earring he wore as a sign of his rank. Tsering's height and lean, aristocratic profile, combined with the leopardskin lining of his vast, flowing gown, gave him the rare elegance of a true warrior. At that time he was still a man to be reckoned with, an impressive figure not yet ravaged by the tragedies that were eventually to lead him to despair.

It was at Ulag Dzong in 1950 that Tsering first heard from passing travellers that 'New Chinese' troops had entered eastern Kham near Kanting and that detachments had been sent to Kandze. But he did not feel that there was anything alarming in this since for many years Chinese troops, the troops of warlords and those of the Chinese Nationalists, had circulated freely on Kham's eastern borders. No one in Chamdo had therefore any reason to believe that the new soldiers meant any harm. 'Indeed, they are an army of Bhuddas,' reported travellers coming from China; for the Tibetan merchants from Kanting, like the Chinese peasants, had been amazed at the good behaviour of Mao's army. The new Chinese forces, far from living off the land, respected the local inhabitants. They paid for everything in silver, and they paid well, in sharp contrast to the conduct of the troops of Chiang Kai-shek in Kanting in the last days of his decline.

Anyway, if the Chinese came to Chamdo, they would be Lhasa's problem. 'Let the "sweet mouths of Lhasa" fight, and we'll watch while they and the Chinese army destroy each other. Just wait and then our time will come to fight.' So spoke most Khambas who hated above all the Lhasean administrators of western Kham.

To wait was, for other reasons, the reaction of most Lhaseans to China's menace of invasion. Tibet, they all knew, had in the past succesfully withstood the threat of colonialism, and had always succeeded in opposing China. In Lhasa, as in Kham, no one was unduly worried, except for Tsarong (Betty-la's father) and Shakopa (the minister of finance) who were among the few Tibetans conscious that beyond the great peaks, below the endless plains, there existed a world which, if no happier than Tibet, lived by the clock of a technological and social revolution. They knew also that Tibet could not remain forever aloof and isolated as it always had in the past.

These top members of the Tibetan cabinet and a few members of the aristocracy, contrary to the general belief, were fully aware of the world around them. It had been by choice, to avoid being colonized, that Tibet had adopted its 'closed door' policy, and had become for Europeans a secret land. But if this policy cut off Tibet from most modern technology it did not imply that all Tibetans were ignorant of what technical marvels the world possessed or of what went on in the world at large.

The old Tsarong, Betty-la's father, had been the first to advocate the introduction of technology in Tibet. He had participated in sending Tibetans to school in Europe, and had even built a modern steel bridge and brought the first wireless sets to Lhasa. Indeed his house was filled with modern gadgets, and was a home for the few foreigners who managed to enter Tibet's forbidden holy city.

Tsarong had even sent his children, including Betty-la, to English schools in Kalimpong and given them English names.

He, more than anyone, was aware of the foreign policies of nations, of the meaning of communism, of democracy and of the fate of monarchies and feudal societies.

But few in Lhasa heeded his advice, for now, at sixty-three, he was an old man. It was a shame, he thought, to see that so many young men in Tibet were more conservative than he. The world's change of pace was proving much too fast for Tibet. Even if there were six radio transmitting and receiving sets in Tibet in 1950, Lhasa was hopelessly isolated and its administration slow. Every secular official, every district administrator, every minister and governor had his religious counterpart. Administrative decisions were lengthy affairs and the execution of orders slower still. There were, Tsarong knew, 'six centuries of dust to be moved', and any change required years of negotiation. Against this situation Tsarong had reacted in vain all his life. He had wanted Tibetan embassies set up abroad, international relations established and Tibet to begin assuming a new role. But what could one do with the regents and monks who were all-powerful while the Dalai Lama was still only a child? Yet the news emanating from Tsarong's radio set was clear. The speaker on the radio had said: 'It is the duty of the Chinese Republic to liberate Tibet.'

'Liberate.' The term was ridiculous, so strikingly stupid, indeed, that China's ultimate goals were more obvious than ever. The Communists, Tsarong knew, were following the dreams of Chiang Kai-shek and of all those Chinese emperors, who, when they had been powerful, had planned to extend their dominions westward into a country that had for so long eluded their grip. Despite various attempts at conquest, Tibet had never been Chinese. At most, China (after 1720) had considered Tibet her vassal; but had not China at one time or another considered all of her neighbours vassals[1]? At worst, the status of vassal had only involved Tibet in a small annual tribute symbolizing a certain religious relationship between the Lamaist Manchu Emperors and the Dalai Lamas, their spiritual leaders.

China had never in fact ruled Tibet in the past. Only, from 1720 on, China had sent occasional 'advisers' to Lhasa, the

[1] It should be remembered that the Manchu Emperors even listed Great Britain among the vassal states of the Celestial Empire on receiving gifts from Macartney, King George III's ambassador.

Ambams, ambassadors whose advice was rarely heeded and none of whom had in any case been allowed to set foot in Lhasa since 1912. From the days of Songtsen Gampo, central Tibet had always had its own government, which issued its own passports, signed its own treaties and possessed all the attributes of a truly independent nation, issuing its own postage stamps and printing its own currency.[1] Yet now the Chinese were claiming, through all their embassies abroad and with the power of their great propaganda machine, that Tibet was an 'integral part of China'.

Tsarong knew very well that Tibet was in no way related to China, either linguistically or ethnically. Tibetan is quite unrelated to Chinese or Mongolian or the Indo-European languages, but is the cornerstone of a separate linguistic group, Tibeto-Burmese. Ethnically, scholars had shown that the Tibetans, both the small Lhaseans and the tall Khambas, were non-Sinetic. The Khambas' true ethnic origins remain a mystery; they have even been classified by some scholars as Proto-Nordics; that is, men of the tall, nordic type. But, Tsarong thought sadly, were not most Asiatics stupidly believed to be Chinese by most of the distant inhabitants of Europe?

Historically, Tibet and China were traditional opponents. Had the Communists forgotten Songtsen Gampo and the days when it was Tibet who placed an emperor on the throne of the Celestial Empire? Tsarong knew very well that the Chinese, with their passion for history, had not forgotten. Their present claims, he thought, could only hide a treacherous policy of expansion. But who abroad would oppose the Chinese claims? Who could read the Tibetan documents or the stone steles erected in Peking and Lhasa recalling the ancient treaties stipulating the boundaries of Tibet and its true limits on the other side of Kham on the shores of Lake Kokonor?

The only hope for Tibet in the face of China, thought old Tsarong, was now to be found abroad in the United Nations, in Great Britain and America. There was reason for hope, or was it already too late? . . . On 1 May 1950 the Chinese again repeated their intention of liberating Tibet. On the same day Betty-la told her father she was expecting her first child.

[1] In 1959 it was proved by the International Commission of Jurists that according to all canons of international law Tibet was *de facto* an independent country.

3

Evil Omens

Ex-R.A.F. pilot Robert Ford, now a member of the fifth degree of the administration of his holiness the Dalai Lama, had been sent in 1949 as radio operator to Chamdo. The only European in Kham, Ford had spent more months speaking only Tibetan than he cared to remember. He was now living what he would later recall as the most exciting years of his life. Little did he suspect that this would prove to be his last year of freedom for a long time to come.

From Chamdo, on the orders of Lahu, the Tibetan governor, Ford had despatched two operators and a radio set to the remote border village of Denko a hundred and twenty miles north-west of Chamdo on the west bank of the upper reaches of the Yangtse.

On 10 May Robert Ford was sitting before his set in his cold quarters on the outskirts of Chamdo. Automatically he had been recording the coded signals coming in from Denko – numbers to a code that only the governor and higher Lhasean officials could decipher.

Loud and clear came the signals in short bursts that flew over the isolated camps of the nomads across the high passes and barren plains from Denko. Then suddenly, as Ford recalled later, the radio crackled, there was a pause ... then, haltingly, the voice of the Denko operator came on the air with one quick phrase: 'The Chinese are here....' Then radio Denko went silent.

'The Chinese are here!' Ford rushed to the governor's residence. On his return, he relayed the news to Lhasa. *The Chinese have arrived.* The news flew across the assembly halls, up the notched tree-trunk ladders, into the remote chapels, through the antechambers of the abbots, into the cells of hermits, down through the bazaars, into the shops where wool was stacked high against harness; it swept around the corrals, it went from tent to tent, from valley to valley. The Chinese had crossed the Yangtse, 'They' were now in Lhasean territory.

The following morning, in the storerooms of his home, Tsering was busy supervising the measures of corn to be given to the labourers working on the irrigation canals of the village. The barley was scooped from a large wooden chest with a round measure and placed in a bag. At each scoop, Tsering made a note, counting: forty-five, forty-six ... Through the thick wall of the storeroom, he heard dogs barking, then the clatter of horses' hooves. The dry thump of boots coming down the corridor!

'Kusho Tsering! Kusho Tsering!' Temba, Tsering's cousin was calling. 'The Chinese have entered Denko!' From Ulag Dzong the news was carried out into the plains by the muleteers gathered before Tsering's house.

'The Chinese have entered Denko.' Tsering's immediate question was the same as that of most Khambas: what would the Lhaseans do?

'What will the Khambas do?' the Tibetan cabinet asked in turn when its members had convened urgently in Lhasa. Lungkhangwa, the prime minister, explained his point of view: Tibet must resist. Troops should be sent out at once from Chamdo to oppose the Chinese. A long message to that effect was prepared, to be radioed to Lahu, the governor of Chamdo. It was already being coded by a fat monk sitting in a corner of the assembly hall beneath the silk banners that dangled from the red-and-gold roof beams.

Luckily, thought Lungkhangwa, there was a detachment of troops already on the way from Lhasa to Kham. They should arrive in a few days. Shakopa, who had been present at the meeting, was deputed to set out immediately to Kalimpong on a peace mission to seek aid from India, Nepal, Great Britain, and the United States. The ministers elaborated the text of the cables to be sent in advance to all these countries. It was a humiliating task to beg for assistance so it was decided to make no mention of the Denko incident in the cables. These were translated into English and sent out via India. This urgent business had been handled with unusual speed, but no one had answered the key question, 'What will the Khambas do?'

Everyone in Lhasa knew that no battle could be fought in

Kham unless the Khambas backed the Tibetans. But would they fight for Lhasa?

Meanwhile, in Chamdo, Lahu, the Lhasean governor, had made up his mind. 'We must fight back,' he told Ford, 'even if it is only to keep the Khambas' respect. We cannot hope to have them stand by us if we do not react firmly.' The cable from Lhasa confirmed his opinion. It was up to him to judge the feelings of the Khambas and prepare for war.

Immediately, Lahu gave orders for two scouts to be sent out to Denko to size-up the enemy, and a third courier was dispatched in great haste to advise Muha Dedpon, one of the most valiant of Lhasa's soldiers, who with four hundred men was encamped along the Chinghai (Amdo) border of Kham, north of Chamdo.

Five minutes after the order had been given, Ford recalls, three of the governor's finest ponies clattered out of the yard, passed below the monastery and set off north.

Four days later the scouts returned from Denko, having covered two hundred miles at full tilt. Their report was reassuring: 'The Chinese were no more than five or six hundred; seven hundred at the most. There had been no fighting and they had remained in Denko.'

Two days later, Muha arrived in Chamdo with his four hundred well-trained Tibetan regulars. To these men were added two hundred Khamba recruits, looking anything but a disciplined army in their ill-assorted garments with their heavy silver and gold charm boxes slung over their backs, and their wild-looking fur hats.

All that week following the news of the fall of Denko, religious ceremonies were held in the monasteries of Chamdo, to chase away ill luck and to bless the holy relics. Secret charms were distributed to the Khamba soldiers, charms which everyone believed would ward off Chinese bullets, and make the wearers invincible.

A rider was dispatched to Ulag Dzong, requesting Tsering for two hundred of the district's best ponies for the troops. Because of the importance of such a demand, Tsering decided to set out himself to speak to the heads of the nomads under his jurisdiction. All day he galloped over the rocky trails that led down gullies and across the high plateaux to the little spring where from far off he saw the tents of the Chengtu Drokpas, the largest of the four clans of his district. Great black dogs prowled round while young men were capturing the burly yaks and roping them to the ground.

All stopped to watch as Tsering approached. Dogs barked and the disturbed cattle shuffled. Tsering halted before the largest tent, its base surrounded by a low stone wall. Outside children stared in surprise. A woman stuck out her tongue respectfully, then shouted to someone inside the tent. The tribe's old 'Gap' (headman) came out, rifle in hand. Placing his sleeve before his face, he bowed and beckoned Tsering to enter. Inside the tent, Tsering relayed the new order of the Chamdo governor. One hundred of the animals, he explained, were to be taken from the herd belonging to the monastery, the other hundred were to come from the nomads' own stock. Tsering was only half surprised to meet with a firm refusal from the old headman who argued: 'Drink the village water, carry the village law. We nomads are tired of drinking at the spring of Lhasa's government. The Chinese have attacked Lhasa, it is Lhasa's affair, not ours. Who will pay for the horses if the central Tibetans are defeated?'

Tsering was too embarrassed to protest. As lord of Ulag Dzong he owed allegiance to Lhasa, yet like most Khambas he also disliked the Lhaseans. The Khambas' traditional dislike of Lhasa often bordered on hatred; it was a perpetual topic around every fire, in every tent and home in western Kham among all those who envied the towns of Batang, Dergue and Litang (in eastern Kham) where Lhasa's authority did not extend. But since the unsuccessful revolt of the Pangda Tsang brothers in 1933, the western Khambas had been unable to agree on who should lead them in a new struggle against Lhasa.

Tsering, like all the more rugged inhabitants of eastern Tibet, might look respectfully on Lhasa as the historical heart of greater Tibet, the holy epicentre of the universe, but this did not prevent him thinking of the inhabitants of the 'Land of the Gods' (*Lha-sa*) with quite irreligious sentiments. Like most Khambas and many other Tibetans, he did not consider the Dalai Lama as the rightful heir to the throne of Songtsen Gampo, and indeed the Dalai Lamas were not the legitimate kings of the Tibetan world. Similarly, although the spiritual authority of the Dalai Lamas extended beyond the limits of their political territory, they were not the only religious leaders of

Tibet. As head of the 'reformed "Yellow hat" ' sect of Tibetan Buddhism, the Dalai Lamas' spiritual overlordship extended only over 60 per cent of the total population of the lamaist world. A great number of Tibetans belonged to other sects, each with their own great abbots, most of whom belonged to the ancient 'Red hat', unreformed sects, which were particularly powerful in nearly all the border areas and especially in the principalities of Kham.

Further, although the prestige of the Dalai Lama as a holy incarnation was considerable, the great respect shown to him by all had to be differentiated from the attitude of most Tibetans towards his government, the ruling clique which wound and unwound its intrigues in Lhasa, a city of priests but which was also governed by a handful of rich and often corrupt lords.

In the opinion of the Khambas, these were a despicable breed of courtiers who, because the Dalai Lamas were selected as children and incapable of ruling until their majority, ruled the land for long periods on their own. Tibet was frequently administered by ruthless, unscrupulous regents who over the past two hundred years had more than once murdered young Dalai Lamas before they came of age. Such had been the fate (or so some claim) of the 9th, 10th, 11th and 12th Dalai Lamas who all died mysterious deaths before attaining their majority.

Many Khambas, and in particular the nomads of Tsering's domain, felt that they should have no part in the impending war. Had not Lhasa since 1918 beseiged Kham with taxes and requisitions for which the Khambas had received little or nothing in return? How could the governor now expect to receive help from the people to maintain this tyranny? Yet the Chinese were foreigners and more despised than Lhaseans. Tsering was at a loss at what to do. The old village headman, in spite of long arguments, refused to change his mind. The next day Tsering returned to Ulag Dzong with only a hundred horses. The Khambas had begun their first silent boycott.

Lahu's prestige and his reputation as a 'just' governor did much in the summer of 1950 to prevent most of the Khambas from rebelling against his administration. His firm decision to oppose the Chinese at any cost and to defend Chamdo were appreciated by many Khambas who, unlike the nomads of Ulag Dzong, guessed that the Chinese might bring more evil than had already been experienced under Lhasa's rule.

It should be said that Lhasa's decision (along with Lahu's determination) to oppose the Chinese was beyond doubt one of the most courageous any country could have made. For, at that time, the Tibetan army had only 8,500 men equipped with aged rifles and some fifty Bren guns. Never in the history of the world had so few determined to fight so many.

It was no secret to the Tibetans that the Chinese army was the largest in the world; an army remarkably well-trained in guerrilla warfare according to the textbooks written by Mao himself, books which, twenty years later, are still considered the world's best treatises on modern guerrilla warfare. There is no doubt that after victoriously fighting the Japanese and defeating the American-equipped forces of Chiang Kai chek, Mao's troops in 1950 were in excellent condition and hardened to war.

Tsering, along with the entire population of Chamdo, turned out to see Muha march northwards to Denko with six hundred men, two hundred of whom were Khamba recruits, noisily shouting and whistling as they cantered their ponies, showing off to the girls and firing shots in the air. When they were out of sight, an uneasy calm settled on Chamdo. Without any means of communication with the troops, the officials could only turn to the monastery and offer more butter lamps. Who could tell what might befall the men who had marched off with such cocky assurance? Would they return, or would the next dust cloud to appear on the northern horizon be the Chinese army? There was no way of telling.

Messengers on horseback were the Tibetan troops' only means of communicating with headquarters in Chamdo. So, for a week, every approaching rider brought the townspeople out to their doorsteps. 'Had he come from Denko? And if so, what was the news?'

In Chamdo itself, defences were quickly set up. Stone barricades were erected on the hilltop monastery and by the bridges over the two rivers that met below the town.

In the meantime in Lhasa the replies to the cables sent abroad began arriving. The British explained in polite terms that owing to the remoteness of Tibet, and since India was now independent, they could do nothing to assist Lhasa. In turn India, which had been the first nation in the world to recognize Communist China, in spite of the treaties binding her to Tibet and the traditional link with Tibet inherited from British rule,

simply urged Tibet to settle her differences with China peacefully: the Indian reply expressed confidence that a 'peaceful
solution could be reached'. Tibet, the Indian message added,
could not in any case rely upon shipments of arms across
Indian territory as she had done in the past. This last information came as a terrible blow. To make matters worse, and to add
to Lhasa's disappointment, the United States flatly refused to
receive the Tibetan peace mission. As for Nepal, bound by
treaty with Tibet to send men in case of an attack, its government declined to give Lhasa any support.

More than ever before, Tibet stood alone. In those cables
Tsarong saw all his hopes shattered. The United Nations
remained as the one last recourse. But there matters seemed
hopeless too: no one wanted to take up the Tibetan question.
Indeed, it was not until a few months later that the small
republic of San Salvador, of all countries in the world, had the
courage to raise the cause of Tibet before the assembly of
nations. But by then it was already too late and anyway the
delegates of the United Nations refused by a vote to put the
Tibetan question on its agenda. The only other alternative for
Tibet was now that Shakopa and his peace mission might be
able to settle matters directly by negotiation with the Chinese
communists' representatives in Hong Kong. But even this plan
was opposed by, of all people, the British who refused to allow
the peace mission to fly to Hong Kong as they believed a meeting between the communists and Tibetans in the crown colony
could be detrimental to their colonial policy. The Tibetan
mission was therefore detained in Calcutta.

While this was going on, after arduous forced marches
Muha's Tibetan and Khamba troops came to a crest from
which they looked down on to the little town of Denko. This was
in fact a large village set on the western banks of the Yangtse,
whose turbulent waters ran behind the Chinese lines. From his
high vantage point the Tibetan commander could see the grey
and khaki uniforms of the Chinese, just visible against the
earthen buildings and the green willow trees surrounding the
larger houses and the small monastery of Denko. At midday
Muha gave the order for the Tibetan regulars to attack, keeping the Khamba recruits in reserve.

With his four hundred men, Muha set upon the already well-
entrenched enemy troops. For three hours the battle raged.

From the rooftops the Chinese machine guns mowed down the Tibetans as they ran from cover to cover, towards Denko, slowly approaching, hidden by rocks then slipping behind the stone walls that encircled the first fields and the corrals of the outlying houses. Running behind prayer walls, masked by holy *chortens,* they came ever nearer to the monastery as the dry air of the valley rang loud with gunfire. Being both better armed and solidly established, the Chinese held off the attack. For an hour Muha contemplated defeat. His casualties were high, bodies littered the narrow paths between the fields; yet his men fought on. Some scrambled ever closer to the heart of the village. Towards evening it seemed a stalemate when, an hour before sunset, Muha signalled the Khamba recruits to make contact.

Howling like a pack of wolves, the men on horseback charged down, their braided hair swinging as their mounts rushed on, cutting the corners of the little lanes, trampling some of the Tibetan soldiers who lay crouched behind the walls. The reckless speed of the Khambas allowed them to penetrate right into the village, forcing the Chinese snipers on the rooftops to stand up in order to shoot at them. Then the Khambas jumped from their ponies and rushed for the doors of the houses, leaving the horses to gallop wildly around, clogging Denko's narrow streets.

Unflinchingly the Khambas entered the houses. Panic spread among the Chinese and they began jumping down from the roofs. Slowly the patter of machine guns became less insistent. Dying shrieks now mingled with the war cries of the Khambas, still slashing frenziedly at the Chinese with the deadly blades of their swords. The sounds of battle rang from the surrounding cliffs until dark, as one by one the Chinese were cornered and killed.

Muha himself was horrified by the massacre. The Khambas took no prisoners, left not one Chinese soldier alive. In vain Muha and his men searched for even a solitary survivor, if only to get information on the position of other Chinese troops in the district. But the Khambas had not spared a single soul. Close on five hundred Chinese bodies were thrown into the river the following day. With sinister efficiency, in a few hours two hundred Khambas hastily recruited seven days previously had exterminated an entire garrison of three times as many well-trained veterans of Mao's army.

At first the victory of the Tibetan troops in Denko was received with great joy in Chamdo, but as the summer dragged on this joy was replaced by anxiety. The Chinese, everybody knew, would retaliate. When, and how, was the question in everyone's mind.

Oracles were consulted. Monks looked for signs. But a month passed by and nothing happened.

Abroad, the attention of the world was turned towards Korea, where war broke out on 25 June. At Lake Success, Long Island, a tempestuous meeting of the Security Council had everyone fearing a third world war. The news of the fall of Denko and its reconquest was never spread abroad. Diplomats had other problems to worry about than Tibet, that never-never land above the clouds.

As the weeks dragged by, every caravan entering Chamdo told of the build-up of more Chinese troops in eastern Kham. Then, one morning, up the Mekong river came news that a large detachment of soldiers had actually entered Batang.

In Chamdo conflicting rumours began circulating about an imminent uprising of the eastern Khambas under the leadership of the famed Pangda Tsang brothers of Po Dzong, who had fought both Lhasa and China in 1933. Indeed since their defeat these merchants had succeeded in rebuilding their vast commercial empire, and once again their warehouses were the largest in Lhasa, Kalimpong and Kanting, their business extending even to Peking and Calcutta. Some rumours claimed that the Pangda Tsangs were now planning a new revolt against Lhasa, while others said they were secretly negotiating with the Chinese communists for support to create an autonomous Kham. Nobody in Chamdo understood clearly what they were up to or why they had so far allowed the Chinese to enter their territories unopposed.

One of the very few people to know what exactly was going on in eastern Tibet was a missionary by the name of George Patterson. While living in Kanting he had made the acquaintance of the Pangda Tsang brothers, Topgyay and Rapgya, who had taken a liking to him, and had invited him and another missionary, Geoffrey Bull, to go with them to their headquarters at Po. From George Patterson's book *Tragic Destiny* we know how on the eve of the fall of Chiang Kai-shek's régime the Pangda Tsangs were secretly planning, in contact with the Amdo leaders Lobsang Tsewan and the monk Geshe Sherab Gyaltso, to levy an army and throw the Chinese out of their so-called provinces of Chinghai and Sikang. When they had reunited all the eastern portion of Greater Tibet, they meant to force the Lhasean government formally to recognize eastern Tibet as an integral part of a new, larger, independent Tibet, encompassing the territories the Chinese had succeeded in separating from ancient Tibet. A new Tibet, thus enlarged, would then stand a chance of opposing China in the future. If Lhasa refused to cooperate it was the Pangda Tsangs' intention, according to Patterson, 'to march on Lhasa calling on Khambas and Amdowans in the Lhasa government army and monasteries to desert and fight with their own leaders, and so take over the government of the country by force'.

By early 1950 the Pangda Tsangs had good reason to believe that the Lhaseans would not go along with their proposal for a united Tibet and consequently they were preparing to implement their projected attack on Lhasa when a courier galloped into their headquarters with a message from the Chinese communists.

The message informed the Pangda Tsangs that the communists had come to hear of their intention to conquer central Tibet, and that the Chinese were prepared to support the Khambas with arms, ammunition and funds, on condition that their attack was transformed into a communist-type 'people's revolution'. The message further explained that this 'people's revolution' to unite Greater Tibet would be part of the vast plan by which the Chinese intended to 'liberate' not only Tibet but Nepal, Bhutan, Sikkim and eventually in a few years India!

Reading this startling news, the Pangda Tsangs understood clearly that they could no longer proceed with their original plan, because if they attacked Lhasa now they would be playing China's game. On the other hand the unexpected revelation that the Chinese were preparing a massive drive into central Asia, not only to overrun Tibet but all the Himalayan states and eventually India, indicated that at all costs Tibet must be united to face an invasion force which the Khambas could never oppose alone. More than ever the Pangda Tsangs felt that Lhasa must be warned immediately of the scale of the impending invasion and convinced of the necessity of joining hands with Amdo and Kham.

With this object Rapgya prepared to set out to Chamdo to negotiate with Lhasa again via the radio and through the Tibetan governor. At the same time the two brothers dispatched George Patterson to India over the difficult route that led from Kham to Assam via Sadyia, with the delicate mission of advising the western nations of China's intention (revealed for the first time) to invade the Himalayan states. Patterson was also asked to try to persuade Lhasean officials in Kalimpong to forget past quarrels with the Khambas and to unite with them against China.

In India Patterson contacted the American ambassador, Lou Henderson, and the British High Commissioner, both of whom now learned for the first time of the Khambas' existence as a true political power. But to no avail. Meanwhile, the Chinese were already advancing into Kham and Amdo, further undermining Tibetan unity by winning over to their cause Sherab Gyaltso, the Pangda Tsangs' supposed ally in Amdo whom the Chinese now named deputy governor of Amdo Chinghai. At the same time, also in Amdo, the Chinese approached Thubten Norbu, the Dalai Lama's eldest brother, then abbot of Khumbum monastery near Lake Kokonor, promising to make him governor-general of Tibet if he could persuade the Dalai Lama and his government to 'welcome' the Chinese army. It was hinted that, if necessary, Thubten Norbu should not hesitate to use force or even to murder his own brother! Pretending to agree with the Chinese, the Dalai Lama's brother left Amdo for Lhasa intending to warn the central Tibetan government of China's plans and then flee to India. Such were the tactics the Chinese employed all over eastern Tibet to divide and weaken the Tibetans, which explains why they were able to infiltrate the area unopposed. The lack of rapid communications made the whole situation highly confusing for western Khambas under Lhasean rule, like Tsering in Chamdo.

As a consequence, by August tension in Chamdo was higher than ever. Strange rumours began to spread terror in the minds of the simple peasants, and it is true that there were certain omens of a most alarming nature. In Lhasa the stone capital of a pillar which had stood for hundreds of years suddenly toppled and fell. Then a mysterious unknown bird was found, a sure sign of ill luck. People began recalling the fearful prophecies of the 13th Dalai Lama, who had written in his testament in 1932: 'The present is the time of the Five Kinds of Degeneration in all countries. In the worst class is the manner of working among the Red people.' This clear warning was followed by a prediction, too horrible to believe, describing the destruction of Tibet.

By mid-summer the victory at Denko had become a sour recollection. Then, from the north, came the tragic news that the Chinese had sacked the Amdo monasteries of Serten and Shatsong. 'Surely', everybody thought, 'the anger of the gods will be terrible.' Nervously, fearing the worst, Robert Ford pored over his inaccurate map of Tibet, searching for an eventual escape route out of Kham to India.

At that time a great lama arrived in Chamdo from the east escorted by three pretty women. This unorthodox reincarnation stopped at Ulag Dzong, where he confided to Tsering that the new Chinese were virtuous men who had come to end the abuses and sufferings of the Khambas. 'The Chinese', the lama explained, 'seek to bring education to the Tibetans, with all the progress that is denied to them because of the white men's evil influence on the Lhasean nobles.' It was known that this lama, whose name was Geda, had a Chinese communist proposal for peace and was seeking permission to proceed to Lhasa.

To his surprise, Tsering heard a few days later that the lama, Geda, had suddenly died in Chamdo. His body contrary to tradition was burned immediately after his death and the people in the bazaar were now saying: 'The disposal of the body was too hasty.' Rumour had it that the Chinese envoy had been assassinated. As a result more signs of ill luck were seen by all in the sky; the evil eye was now upon Kham, the eye of the fearful demons.

Special assemblies of monks were hastily convened and Tsering was continuously being taxed for additional butter to fill the holy silver lamps set at the foot of the twenty-foot statue of 'The Buddha-who-is-to-come' that dominated with its austere smile the great assembly hall of the monastery of Chamdo.

Then, in the stillness of a warm night, dogs suddenly began to bark in the suburbs. They howled as they tugged at their chains before the doors of the monasteries and were heard screaming beside the tents of the nomads on the plains. The end of the world was surely at hand. Houses began to rock, beams fell through the roofs, the holy *chorten* of Ulag Dzong split down the middle, other monuments collapsed, bridges plunged into the depths of the rivers which themselves burst their banks.

On 6 August a strong earthquake rocked the foundations of Chamdo, Kandze, Litang, Dergue and Batang, destroying thousands of houses and hundreds of monasteries. Divine wrath had struck. The omen was clear: hard times had come again.

The terrible earthquake of August 1950, the worst in central Asia for over fifty years, had many side-effects besides shattering the morale of the Tibetans. Robert Ford suspected it might have blocked his planned escape route which ran south from Chamdo to the bend of the Brahmaputra and into Assam. His fears were confirmed when he heard on the radio that the mighty Brahmaputra had changed its course where part of a mountain had slid down into its waters; in Assam thousands lost their lives in the floods that followed. The earthquake had also blocked the secret supply line of the powerful Pangda brothers, one of whom was then in Chamdo using the radio in a last attempt to negotiate with the Tibetan government through his brother in Lhasa. The Pangda brothers proposed that their private army be used to support the Tibetans against the Chinese, promising that all eastern Kham would stand by them to fight. All they asked in return was some guarantee from Lhasa of future Khamba autonomy under their jurisdiction. This proposal was received with apprehension and the traditional mistrust in Lhasa, especially as the governor of Chamdo had just informed the Tibetan cabinet that the Pangdas were also in contact with the Chinese communists.

After the earthquake, the last days of the Tibetan summer passed. The harvest was gathered and Chamdo echoed with song as the women and the men came in from the fields. The wrecked houses were hastily patched for winter. For part of the time everything seemed normal, too normal; but no one forgot, and Lahu more than any felt the web slowly closing in on Chamdo. From all quarters came information pointing to the communists' imminent arrival. In Chinghai to the north their grip was nearly complete, while in Moslem Sinkiang the rugged Uigurs were being forced one by one to capitulate to the Chinese.

With September, the first cold winds began to buffet the high monastery of Chamdo. Hurriedly, on the flat rooftops, the grain was dried in the sun. Loads of wood were carried into the houses for the coming winter.

There was nothing to do but wait and hope, and wait again. Tsering was kept busy. The government's demands were ever-increasing as more Tibetan troops arrived in Chamdo. And then there was the fine, the affair of the horses. In the anxiety of the battle of Denko, the stewards had temporarily overlooked the refusal of Tsering's nomads to give their horses. The victory had proved Tsering wrong and the governors reacted to his insubordination by sending a detachment of ten soldiers to Ulag Dzong. With the detachment came the secretary to the governor's chief steward, a man detested by the Khambas because he was himself a Khamba, a 'traitor', working for Lhasa in an unpopular function. His greed and craftiness were legendary. Everyone knew how many men he had ruined, the bribes he had extorted, the beatings he had served out to all who opposed his covetous ways.

This man's rank in the Lhasean hierarchy obliged Tsering to address him in the high honorific language of Lhasa. This angered Tsering all the more as it was considered an insult to have to use the court speech of the Lhaseans.

Tsering offered him tea which the man sipped with a look of disgust. Ceremoniously, in a high unnatural voice, the secretary announced that by decision of the governor's council Ulag Dzong was to pay a fine of six thousand silver Chinese dollars, for traitorous, shameful insubordination. And so that it should be known 'whose hand reins the horse' and that 'No mule can carry two saddles', a letter with the governor's seal was given to Tsering requesting him to report to the governor in Chamdo.

Insubordination in time of war is no light offence and Tsering greatly feared the reaction of the governor, who could break him and seize every coin he possessed. Such was the rigid law of Lhasa.

A few days later Tsering stood before Lahu, the governor of Chamdo, a member of the first degree of Lhasean nobility, a descendant of the 8th and 10th Dalai Lamas, once a member of the cabinet of the regency and one of the richest and most respected of the nobles of Lhasa, a man admired and feared even by the Khambas. Lahu was a man with few or no friends in Kham, since any intimate contact with such a noble person was forbidden by court protocol. His robes of bright yellow silk, his splendid turquoise earring, a jade thumb ring and the gold coils on the four fingers of his hand gave him a regal appearance. To be a great noble and a governor of Tibet's most turbulent province required qualities which we in the West would never expect of our most important officials.

Although the same age as Tsering, the resplendent governor looked older than the lord of Ulag Dzong. The two men sized each other up at a glance. They had met often before in the course of Lahu's three years' duty in Chamdo, although they had never confronted one another directly as they did on that day. The governor ordered his people to leave him alone with Tsering.

Tsering, who had feared the worst, was surprised when the governor did not refer to the matter of the horses at all. 'You must know', he told Tsering, 'that I am leaving Chamdo. I have been replaced by Nawang Ngabo. The new governor will arrive in two weeks. His party left Lhasa nearly a month ago.'

'I shall leave Kham with regret,' Lahu went on. 'In time of danger it is not opportune to leave but such is the wish of the cabinet. You must tell your men that only the Chinese will gain by their obstruction, only you will lose by tolerating insubordination. We must fight together for the faith and for Tibet. If the soldiers of Lhasa are prepared to fight for Kham, if our soldiers have died at Denko, it was on your soil that they spilled their blood. Will you be so foolish as not to realize that the Chinese today are not what they used to be? Their government has no religion, they are here to extend their own faith, a faith in which our temples have no place. Tell the nomads that we will fight to the end and if they choose to obstruct then they are not worthy of the name of Kham.'

'Yes, it is so,' was all Tsering was allowed to answer, but indeed, he felt that there was nothing more to say.

The fine was upheld but Tsering was released and, as he rode back, accompanied by his cousin Temba, he determined to fight the Chinese. So it would be war, war against China, and Lhasa would stand up to defend Kham.

Tsering's cousin was less convinced. Were not the Lhaseans only 'beautiful mouths'? Why were there no more than a thousand soldiers in the whole Lhasean region of Kham? One thousand men, if you could call the Lhasean troops men. And now a new governor. Who could trust him? Why had Lahu been called back? This sounded like a political manoeuvre.

'The future of Kham depends on the Pangda family,' said Temba, as he galloped towards Ulag Dzong along the banks of the swift Mekong, now full to the brim with the muddy waters of the last melting snows before winter. Even so, Tsering felt that Lahu was right. The Khambas should stay with Lhasa to fight for their faith and for their common blood.

Nawang Ngabo, the new governor, was a little older than Lahu, who had set out to greet him. He arrived surrounded by all the ceremony due to his rank. Ngabo's entrance into Chamdo, as recorded by Robert Ford, was marked by a caval-cade in the finest tradition. Heralded by trumpets, blessed by monks and followed by a large crowd, the tall Ngabo cut a fine figure, riding on his white horse, its gold-inlaid saddle smothered beneath the finest rugs, the turquoise of the harness glowing purest green on the silver bridles.

Thus came Ngabo, a favourite of the young Dalai Lama, a man respected for his intelligence and for his very name since he was a member of the oldest family in Lhasa, claiming direct descent from the great Songtsen Gampo himself. Some said he was the most progressive of Tibetan officials; others that he was a weak, confused person. Everyone in Kham approached him with awe, for the tongue of a governor, they all knew, could kill as his smile could shower wealth. In appearance Ngabo was stern, uncommunicative, even more aloof than his rank required. Nobody in Chamdo was able to grasp what exactly went on in this man's mind.

To be an aristocrat in Tibet was a lonely task, one in which individuals were left on their own, to condemn and to praise, at every moment having to bear the entire weight of each and every one of their actions. In Lhasa, Ngabo might find counsel among his equals. In Chamdo he was completely isolated. For Ngabo this meant facing a population he knew disliked Lhasa, a land of brigands as ruthless as they were handsome, and at times as cruel as they were carefree. It also meant facing the Chinese, and Ngabo, better than anybody, knew of what metal the new Chinese were made. He had followed step by step the history of the Long March, the victory of the communists over the Japanese, the crumbling of Chiang Kai-shek's régime, the fall of Sinkiang and of Chinghai, and the advances of the Chinese troops in eastern Kham. He was also informed of the fruitless negotiations being held in New Delhi between the Tibetan peace mission and the newly arrived Chinese ambassador to India.

Ngabo also knew how the British, the Nepalese and the Americans had abandoned Tibet and that the Pangda brothers were unreliable. Ngabo knew that Lhasa and the kingdom of his ancestors stood even more alone in the world than he himself, over eight hundred miles from the capital in the most distant district of Tibet, on the eve of war. 'War against China': a war, Ngabo knew, or thought he knew, that Tibet could never win, not even if the Khambas united, not even if America sent arms and men, because five hundred million people, drunk with success, imbued as the Chinese were with their fanatical nationalism, could never be opposed. Ngabo had followed the news of the Korean War, the setbacks suffered by the combined armies of so many nations who were unable to dent the Chinese positions in spite of their napalm and fantastic American equipment.

Perhaps, all told, Ngabo knew too much, and this was the cause of his weakness, the reason why he would soon be remembered as a traitor. Arriving in Chamdo, Ngabo assured Robert Ford that he would 'resist' the Chinese and that 'there would be no surrender'. Yet twelve years later Ngabo assured a British journalist that 'after arriving in Chamdo, I had not the slightest wish to pursue a war aimed at separating Tibet from the Chinese motherland'.[1]

Beyond doubt, Ngabo hoped to spare Tibet the inevitable crisis that was drawing nearer every day. Indeed, to achieve this, he was ready to go further than anybody, further even than his government had requested; and so, in the not-too-distant future, he was to earn the abuse now showered upon his illustrious name. 'Lhasa would defend Kham', was what Lahu had declared to the Khambas. This Ngabo now confirmed but, as the Khambas say, 'the Lhaseans have beautiful mouths . . .'

And so came the month of October 1950 . . .

On 6 October a bright sun shone hard through a clear sky

[1] Interview with Stuart Gelder recorded in *The Timely Rain*.

upon Chamdo, that small town set at the confluence of the Upper Mekong and the Dze Chu. It shone on the square houses lining its wide dirt streets, their walls of pounded earth still showing the cracks of the fateful earthquake of August. It shone too upon the monastery on the hill dominating the town. The walls of the monastery, along with the cracks from the earthquake, also still bore traces of its plunder thirty-two years before by the ruthless followers of Peng, the Szechwan warlord. The same sun brightened the courtyard of the great assembly hall where a white cotton awning with a blue patterned border had been strung up to shade an assembled crowd.

On a high pulpit sat one of the most venerated reincarnated lamas of Kham. In a monotonous voice he was repeating the endless prayer: 'May the jewel of the Lotus grant you fruitful reincarnations and a long life.' One by one, men, women and children approached and deposited white scarves (*katas*, a ceremonial token of respect) on a table before him. The faithful bowed to have their heads touched by the sacred silver vase in ritual blessing, as the monk continued to recite the sacred formula: '. . . a long life'; Tsering quickly thought of the meaning of his name – 'Tse' meaning life, and 'ring' meaning long. Dressed in his leopard-lined *chuba*, Tsering sat among the Khamba dignitaries on carpets placed a little below those of Ngabo, the new governor. Fifty monks in four rows sat holding round drums, silver bells, and human bone flutes.

It was a beautiful ceremony and Tsering prayed more intently than usual. His second child, the little girl, was ill. When his turn came to advance and receive the benediction, he presented a fine silk scarf in which he had placed ten silver coins; he also extended a little red cap belonging to his child for the lama to bless with 'fruitful reincarnation and a long life'.

The monastery was packed to the highest galleries, and even outside by the gate there was a crowd turning prayer wheels beside the ponies of the lords. The governor's horses were held by retainers and stood beside those of the stewards and secretaries and those of all the officials of the third and fourth rank. Khamba merchants and lords had also come in large numbers to Chamdo because this was the month of the great market.

The ceremony over, everyone set out for the market-place, already thronged with a noisy crowd. Above the din rose the wails of lost children, the whinnying of nervous horses and the lowing of yaks. Everything seemed normal except that the name of the Chinese, the 'Gya-mi', cropped up unusually often in the talk. Some of the merchants whose caravans had arrived from beyond the Yangtse were more loquacious than usual. Mingling with the crowd were also small groups of men, heavily armed *Chalpas* (brigands) come down to buy bullets or swords or to sell some of their loot: turquoise necklaces ripped from frightened women, silver holy boxes stolen from the backs of terrified travellers, horses and cattle of dubious origin – all for sale. They rode round proudly, prodding their stolen cattle with the long bayonets made of antelope horn lashed to the ends of their muzzle-loading rifles.

Tsering joined the crowd and ran into the *gap* of the Chengtu nomads. The great burly headman who had caused him so much trouble was standing, draped in his rough cloak, beside a large flock of sheep. It would have been hard for anyone to guess that the old nomad was a chief of wealth and power, the leader of a thousand men, the owner of vast herds, a man far richer than his overlord Tsering. The old headman offered to pay Tsering's fine. Tsering accepted but was worried when later, as they parted, the rough old *gap* smiled and quoted the Tibetan proverb: 'To throw a man in the river, you must lean over the bank.'

What had the old nomad meant? Tsering wondered as he left Chamdo in the peaceful afternoon sun, unaware that, that very day, a hundred and twenty thousand Chinese troops stationed to the north, to the east, to the west and to the south of Chamdo had received orders to invade Tibet.

4

The Chinese Invasion

On that same day, 6 October 1950, in his temporary head-quarters near the town of Dergue in eastern Kham, General Wang, commander of the Occidental forces of the Chinese People's Liberation Army, had received orders from Peking to attack.

It was revealed later that Lin Piao, the most trusted of Mao's commanders, the Minister of Defence, had himself planned the strategy for the invasion of Tibet. The date had been fixed by General Chu, the commander-in-chief of the Chinese army, after he had received confirmation from agents in Kalimpong that neither Nepal, India or any Western power would come to Tibet's rescue.

The same Chinese agents in Kalimpong had also confirmed that the entire Tibetan army numbered a mere 8,500 men. Even so, the Chinese were taking no risks. Not only had their best military brains gone over the plans, but the prime units of Peking's political cadres had been sent along with the troops. Nothing was left to chance. Even cameramen were standing by to make a film of the Tibetans welcoming the Chinese soldiers.

No fewer than 120,000 troops had been put on alert on 6 May: 50,000 at the headquarters of Yaan, a town in Szechwan near Kanting on the border of Kham; another 40,000 in the province of Chinghai, which had been seized a few months earlier from its warlord Ma, who had fled by plane to Hong Kong taking with him the accumulated loot of years of tyranny.

All these troops were now poised ready to seize Kham, aiming for Chamdo, the capital of eastern Tibet. Yet 90,000 men were not considered enough. Two thousand miles away, in the Moslem province of Sinkiang, another 30,000 men were also standing by to attack Tibet. The Chinese troops in Sinkiang had been given the dangerous task of crossing the Aksai Chin desert, the terrible 'frozen sea' of Marco Polo. If they succeeded they would take by surprise the unguarded far western borders of Tibet. No one in Lhasa had thought of this possibility – not only because the desert was considered impassable to a modern army, but also because since 1850 the 'frozen sea' had been mapped as Indian territory, a part of Kashmir. Neither Lhasa nor New Delhi, or indeed any nation of the world, believed that the Chinese would dare violate the territory of their greatest ally in Asia.

From his tent General Wang relayed by radio the order to attack to the advanced battalions lying ready along the eastern banks of the Yangtse. These units were to cross the mighty river simultaneously at three points and enter Tibet.

It was pitch dark on the night of the sixth when Muha, the commander who had seized Denko from the Chinese three months earlier, was awakened suddenly by the explosions of heavy artillery fire. Fumbling in the dark, the four hundred men in Denko under his command rushed for their arms. With twelve Bren guns, the only 'artillery' he possessed, Muha had his men fire back across the river at the invisible enemy.

Meanwhile, sixty miles to the south, in the dead silence of night, hundreds of Chinese soldiers in their grey uniforms slipped across the Yangtse on rafts and yak-skin coracles.

Creeping down the eastern bank of the Yangtse, these men fell upon the fifty Tibetan soldiers guarding the ferry crossing of Markham Druga. In twenty minutes Markham Druga had fallen. Not one soldier or villager escaped to warn the large Tibetan garrison at Rangsum, twenty-five miles inland. Using the ferry crossing, the Chinese quickly carried thousands of fresh troops over into Kham.

According to the pre-arranged Chinese plan, two thousand more Chinese soldiers crossed the Yangtse a hundred and thirty miles farther south. This force then split into two and headed north for Chamdo. The left branch attacked the southernmost Tibetan garrison at Markham Gartok. The two hundred and fifty Tibetan soldiers there returned the Chinese fire for a while; then, seeing that they would inevitably be overwhelmed, the Tibetan commander ordered his troops to withdraw, whereupon the Khamba levies attached to the garrison trained their rifles on the Lhaseans, calling them cowards obliging them to fight on to the death. Inevitably the communist troops quickly wiped out what had been the Tibetans' only strong post south of Chamdo.

On 7 October heavy fighting continued in the north at Denko where Muha had prevented the Chinese from crossing the river. Farther south, from the ferry crossing, a large Chinese force had already set upon the garrison of Rangsum, taking its commander and three hundred men by surprise. The Rangsum garrison retreated to the first high pass on the road to Chamdo. There, at 14,000 feet, with the rugged terrain in their favour, the Tibetans prepared to block the Chinese advance. On the 8th, the Chinese came up towards the pass. Wave after wave of men were shot down by the Tibetans like dolls at a fair, but immediately another wave arrived, each wave getting closer and closer to the summit. By then the Tibetans were beginning to suffer heavy casualties as field artillery blasted the rocks behind which they crouched. Eventually, as night fell, the Tibetan commander of Rangsum told his men to disband. The main road to Chamdo lay open.

While Muha struggled desperately to keep the Chinese at bay and Rangsum and Markham Gartok fell, life in Chamdo went on as usual; people were unaware that the invasion had begun. With no means of communicating with the remote border garrisons of Kham, the governor continued to attend religious functions and administer the affairs of his district, ignorant of the impending disaster, while from the south and east the Chinese troops converged on Chamdo.

It was not until the night of the 10th that, according to Ford, 'at 11 o'clock a solitary soldier galloped through the empty streets towards the governor's residence'.

The following morning, Chamdo awoke to the terrible news that Rangsum, Markham Gartok and Markham Druga had fallen. The Chinese were coming. Nothing was known of the fate of Muha, who was in fact successfully continuing his lonely struggle.

At the news, panic spread through Chamdo as hundreds rushed to the monastery to pray or seek asylum in the sanctuary of their gods. The Chinese were said to be only two days away. Some of the townspeople fled to distant villages. By midday, when the first impact of the news had had its effect, a crowd of determined men marched to the governor's residence; Khambas bristling with swords and knives, shouldering flintlock rifles of every description, ready to place themselves under the command of Ngabo, men ready to fight for their homes and their land. Along with this crowd went some famous brigands attracted by the smell of war and prospect of loot. Among them could be seen the robbers who had plagued the market a few days before, but beside the brigands stood the local lords, Tsering among them, resolute and prepared to forget the grievances of the past, willing to die for Kham under Lhasean commanders.

The older men recalled how in 1918 and then again in 1928 the Khambas had successfully thrown out the Chinese soldiers of Peng and Liu. Once again the warrior blood of the Khambas came to the surface. It was a resolute crowd that Ngabo heard milling outside his residence, demanding to be supplied with arms and ammunition from the government arsenal. But only reluctantly did Ngabo agree to incorporate a few more Khambas into the ranks of the three hundred Tibetans guarding Chamdo. He refused, however, to the discontent of the crowd, to open up the arsenal and distribute the arms and ammunition which were needed. Was he afraid of the Khambas? Did he not understand that now he had at his disposal the entire population of Kham, the most arrogant and fearless race of central Asia? Ngabo apparently lacked the courage of his predecessor Lahu and was unworthy of his own great ancestors, for even as he reassured the crowd that he would stand up and fight, Ngabo was secretly dispatching a message to Lhasa asking the government for permission to capitulate. This he did before a single Chinese soldier had appeared on the horizon.

The Tibetan government refused, reiterating its instructions to resist the Chinese. Nevertheless Ngabo remained idle, apart from dispatching the town's small garrison, in three sections, to cover the possible Chinese approach routes. What went on in Ngabo's mind no one will ever know. He must have known that the only way the Chinese could be halted was by the Khambas. All these men were born warriors whose reputation had spread to the four corners of the Tibetan world. Indeed, the very name of Kham obliged caravans to group together to make their way along the lonely trails. Certainly, Ngabo knew that every house in Kham was a little fortress, accessible only by a ladder which could be pulled up during raids by brigands. Surely it would have been possible to make the Chinese fight for every inch of land they claimed? Or was Ngabo too intelligent to believe that Tibet could ever face the masses of China?

The Khambas sensed his weakness and their displeasure turned to anger. A day later, without warning, in spite of all their promises, Ngabo and his associates were seen fleeing from Chamdo, heading west. The Khambas' anger flared up into violent rage. The governor was leaving Chamdo undefended, abandoning them to the Chinese. Silently, dressed in the miserable, common clothes of a third-class official, Ngabo fled, leaving behind the town he had entered only a few months earlier as an arrogant lord dressed in flamboyant brocades.

Tsering's heart swelled with the ancient hatred of all Khambas for the 'beautiful-mouthed Lhaseans'. In the face of danger, Ngabo was running like an old woman ... Ngabo the liar, the coward and the traitor.

Hardly had he disappeared over the first ridge before the brigands began looting the residences of the now fleeing officials. Gunfire was already echoing in the town, even before it was rocked by two great explosions. These were followed by muffled concussions and then everybody knew that the last Tibetans to leave had blown up the arsenal. Ngabo had deprived Chamdo of its ultimate means of defence.

When the people saw the smoke rising from the governor's compound and heard the bullets bursting in the fire, the Khambas' rage reached the limits of helpless frustration. Anarchy set in. The brigands intensified their looting. Tsering hurried back to Ulag Dzong to protect his family. There he found the villagers, along with a group of nomads, armed to the teeth, avid to fight, awaiting orders. All Tsering could tell them was that the governor had fled: Lhasa had betrayed them after all.

During this time, Muha continued, alone, to stall the Chinese at Denko. In his sudden mad decision to flee and abandon Chamdo, Ngabo had neglected to inform his soldiers and most of the Tibetan officials of his decision. Even Robert Ford the radio operator was left without transport to arrange for his own speedy departure. But worst of all, Ngabo had forgotten about Muha, or at least had underestimated the strength and resolution of that excellent soldier.

After six days of incessant harassment by the Chinese,

Muha[1] had continued fighting until Denko was assailed by Chinese soldiers crossing the Yangtse from a point twenty miles upstream. Finding himself attacked from the mainland, Muha ordered his men to retreat calmly down to Chamdo, where they arrived the day after Ngabo's departure. Muha immediately put an end to the looting then, leaving a few soldiers in the town, he set off to find the governor and persuade him that efficient resistance could still halt the Chinese.

That same night, Muha with his four hundred men in relatively good condition found Ngabo cowering in a lonely monastery surrounded by the disheartened Tibetan soldiers of Chamdo and the trembling Lhasean officials. A day's march out of Chamdo, Ngabo had been told that a Chinese army coming from Chinghai had attacked the Tibetan outpost of Riwoche and cut the route to Lhasa. In the face of this news, he had stopped in the small monastery.

Muha assured Ngabo that with his men and those of the governor as well as a further detachment from Lhasa (encountered by Ngabo just out of Chamdo) it would be easy to break through the Chinese lines. But Ngabo declined to resist, informing Muha that he would stay put and wait for the Chinese in order to surrender.

The next day, 17 October, a small detachment of Chinese soldiers came upon the monastery quite by accident, and without any exchange of fire received the submission of the Governor General of Chamdo, captured seven hundred of his well-armed troops and Robert Ford. Tibetan resistance had lasted for ten days.

Ironically on the same 17 October the three-month-old rumours about Muha's attack and victory in Denko reached Kalimpong. The world's press retailed the now old story of the Denko incident and announced that there was 'fighting in eastern Tibet'. Although, since the Denko incident, Tibet had been invaded and was now on the point of capitulating, India and the Dalai Lama's peace mission still denied that there was any fighting in Kham! For some strange reason the Tibetan government delayed announcing that there had been fighting in Tibet, while Nehru jubilantly repeated that 'any differences that might arise between China and Tibet would certainly be settled by peaceful means'.

[1] according to Robert Ford.

It was China, strangely enough, that announced to the world on 26 October that war had indeed broken out in Tibet.

When the Dalai Lama, who had been installed as full ruler at the age of sixteen during the fighting learned the news of the defeat, he fled to the borders of India and there, with some of his ministers, he awaited developments, ready to abandon his country. It is hardly surprising that in these circumstances and given such leadership fighting had almost completely ceased in Kham by the end of October.

Tsering, like most Khambas, was disgusted. Lhasa had betrayed his trust and to add to this blow he learned that contrary to all expectations the warriors of the Pangda brothers, the great merchants of Po, had not taken arms against the Chinese east of the Yangtse.

Tsering did not know that the Pangda Tsangs had had no choice. Having seen the collapse of their plan to unite Kham and Amdo, they had further found out from conversations between Topgyay and Ngabo that there was no hope of Lhasa assisting the eastern Khambas. They had been obliged therefore to negotiate with the Chinese in the hope of salvaging their dream of Khamba and eventually of Tibetan unity.

Because of Tibetan retreats, betrayals and internal dissension, the new Chinese had apparently conquered the 'race of kings' at last. In fact, the war in Kham had only just begun.

What followed immediately after the fall of Chamdo and the capitulation of Tibet was felt by all the inhabitants of Kham to be the most extraordinary thing in the world. Men like Tsering were preparing to be thrown into jail, enslaved or killed by the Chinese. Instead there arrived in Ulag Dzong a pleasant group of smiling young men. The Khambas had hidden their swords and muskets but the Chinese did not ask for these. Indeed, they did nothing but praise the Khambas – they said in fact what everyone was thinking: 'The Lhaseans are beautiful mouths, ensnared by the evil influences of foreigners.' They added that they had come to reassert the autonomy of Kham, to build up again the unity of the great plains of eastern Tibet under the leadership of Khambas, not of Lhaseans.

The Chinese, they said, would help build schools and hospitals and would introduce new agricultural techniques. No one would be harmed, neither the lords nor the priests. The lords would keep their positions, since they were the rightful administrators of Kham. China had no ill-feeling towards the Khambas, none whatsoever, assured the political officers.

The Khambas had taken these speeches for 'beautiful words' but they soon had to agree – as Tsering later told me – that the Chinese 'did in fact speak truthfully'. The captured Khamba levies were returned to their homes with their rifles, and not only that, but with their pockets full of fat silver dollars.[1] The Chinese pillaged no granary nor did they touch a hair of a single Tibetan girl. People remembered what they had heard a few months ago from travellers coming from Kanting: 'They are an army of Buddhas.'

Never in the memory of any Khamba had a victor behaved in this way. They even paid for the transport they used and paid well. Tradition allowed them to take everything, for they were victorious, yet they took nothing, not even a needle and thread. Indeed the Chinese did nothing they were 'supposed' to do. They did not kill the monks or burn the holy books, and 'they even paid for butter lamps in the monastery chapels' when they were invited to visit the holy shrines.[2]

Talking was what they did most. They made a lot of speeches and had a Khamba from Kanting translate their meaning. They talked about progress, about a road, and many other good things.

They also said a good deal about Kham. They seemed quite familiar with all that had worried the people over the past years and they were in complete agreement with even the most difficult to please. They announced their intention of helping to set up an autonomous government of Khambas in the Chamdo region which would unite Chamdo, Dergue, Batang, Kandze and Litang. This had been part of the agreement the Pangda Tsangs had been obliged to make with the Chinese after Lhasa's refusal to stand by eastern Tibet: the creation of an autonomous Khamba district under Chinese tutelage with

[1] Again according to Robert Ford; films of these surprised Khambas being set free were made to prove that the Khambas had welcomed the Chinese.

[2] Robert Ford was, as it turned out, the person who suffered most, since he was taken as a prisoner into China and jailed for five years, accused of being a British spy and of having assassinated the pro-Chinese monk Geda.

Topgyay Pangda Tsang as vice-president of a proposed 'Chamdo Liberation Committee'.

Most of the peasants and herdsmen, of course, understood little or nothing of the more complicated things the Chinese had to say. But then, despite their general mistrust of the Chinese, they felt they would have nothing to fear out on their pastures because they knew the Chinese were poor horsemen and seemed to know nothing about cattle, which was evident from the way they looked at yaks and refused to eat butter or drink the good salty Tibetan tea.

Tsering of course understood most of what the Chinese said and being an intelligent man he was among the first to leave Kham in the following year, enchanted at the prospect of acquiring in Peking the administrative knowledge and skills which would allow him, so he hoped, to become one of the many administrators who in the future would build up a new Kham, a Kham more prosperous than it had ever been, a Kham ruled by the Khamba (with the assistance of the Chinese 'motherland'), a Kham which would be introduced to all the advantages of science which it had been denied by the 'clique' of Lhasa misled by the foreign governments of the 'long-nosed' Europeans.

With these illusions Tsering went to spend eighteen months in Peking. While there, two sons were born to him in a clinic where his wife benefited from the miracle of anaesthesia.

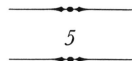

5

'An Army of Buddhas'

It had taken five days for Ngabo the governor of Chamdo to learn that the Chinese invasion had begun and weeks for Lhasa to hear, through Peking, that their province of Kham had fallen. It was a further six months before a treaty was signed between the Dalai Lama (represented by Ngabo) and China, and a year and a half before the first 'liberators' in Chinese uniform marched into Lhasa. It is not surprising, therefore, that it was three full years before all the isolated nomads of Tibet understood what had actually happened in the autumn of 1950. Even among the nobles of the towns, men like Tsering, no one grasped at first the true intentions and motives of the new Chinese, because sophisticated social theories, international politics, along with the ideals of Marx and Lenin, were totally alien to the Khambas' way of thinking.

There were thousands of years of political evolution to bridge between the cunning ideological motives of the Chinese political officers who came to Chamdo and the feudal concepts of men like Tsering. For Tsering, fear and force had been the only known tools of administration. The sword, he felt, was the only foundation of man's right to rule. So when the Chinese invading Tibet apparently declined at first to exploit their victory, most of the lords of Kham were misled into believing that the Chinese were indeed an army of Buddhas come to help right the evils of Lhasa and sincerely help Kham 'upon the road of autonomy and technical evolution'.

After much contact with the Chinese, Tsering became more than ever aware of the inadequacies and shortcomings of his past way of life. A lord himself, he well knew that the rule he had helped Lhasa to extend over Kham had been merely a legalized form of banditry. He now agreed that the nobles had often abused their strength to rob the poor and the weak. They had never given anything in return for the taxes they levied. No public services whatsoever had existed in Kham. There was taxation without compensation, a taxation enforced by fear. Schooled by the Chinese, Tsering rapidly perceived that Tibet was long overdue for a radical change, and it was for this reason he had agreed to go to Peking.

Such complex reasoning as that which took Tsering to Peking was quite beyond the grasp of the nomads who lived outside the towns, free of the rule of the lords, with whom they had little or no contact. Between these men and the Chinese lay an abyss that no logic could ever bridge – not because the nomads were unintelligent but because in the vast open spaces of Tibet the herdsmen lived according to laws as ancient and as wise as they were unsophisticated, laws that were dictated by nature, and by man's struggle for survival and which followed a pattern drawn from his deepest instincts. The rough plainsmen believed that every individual was embarked upon a personal struggle for survival and the right to the pleasures and joys of existence. They lived in a world made for 'men' and not for 'the people', a world where such abstractions were unknown. They lived according to no written code or preconceived political theories; their only laws were instinctive.

It was not long before the Chinese understood that although they might have temporary control of the major garrisons and towns of Kham they could not as easily control the elusive tribes of the great plains, the nomadic herdsmen who made up the greater part of the population of Tibet. Nobody knew exactly the names or the numbers of these clans and sub-clans of rugged nomads scattered over the most inaccessible valleys and plains. These men lived, not in sturdy Mongolian-type *yourts* or the vast camel-hair tents of the Arabs, but in small, beetle-like domed tents of rough, brown yak wool, low and dark, little elusive dots that could be seen from afar, clustered in circles or scattered untidily in ever-changing patterns.

It was only occasionally, reaching a pass or surmounting a ridge, that the Chinese saw these tents which formed the only home of the strange 'Drokpa' tribes. Nobody knew the origins of these people whom even the Lhaseans called savages. There were countless jokes about their stupidity and ignorance – tales that were outdone by others describing their ferocity. Fabulous stories were told, especially about the tribes of Kham and Chinghai, the fiercest of them all. Their chiefs were said to be richer than any men alive and legend had it that the Goloks of the Amne Machin were ruled by a queen with seventeen husbands. Some of their herds consisted of hundreds of thousands of animals, representing a huge fortune even by Wall Street standards, while the smallest of their flocks was worth 200,000 *trankas* or 60,000 Chinese silver dollars in the market of Chamdo.

Because of the nomads no one in Kham had ever been safe outside the immediate vicinity of a fort, not even the Tibetan or Khamba lords – and how much less the Chinese! After 1950 the distant tribes continued to live as before in constant turmoil and on the alert. Each tribe was a menace to the others, jealousy guarding their grazing rights or attempting to extend them in their endless struggle for survival. It was hardly surprising that, as the Dalai Lama has written, these men's most precious possessions were their guns.

Jolted on horseback from the day they were born, only the strongest survived, to live in the flimsy shelter of their small tents, struggling against the cold and the howling winds, fighting the wolves, snow leopards and bears that shared with them the coarse grasslands running down to isolated lakes fed by glacial waters.

To the nomads a gun meant hope and survival; and guns and ammunition could only be acquired by looting. Theirs was a lonely life, populated mainly by the ghostly presence of the spirits who, on every pass, in every crag, beneath every rock and lake, menaced them with fates crueller than death from a bullet in an attack.

Every facet of life on the great plains was marked by cruelty – nature teaching man through its beasts and through a constant battle against cold, against drought, and against hail, the terrible hailstorms that could kill entire herds of gazelles, wipe out whole flocks and bring death to any man caught in the open. It is hardly surprising that the 'Hail Men', the mysterious priests of the ancient pre-Buddhist Bon religion had more sway over the nomads than the sophisticated monks who lived in the superb monasteries of the valleys. The farmers clinging to the riverbeds in their squat fortress-like homes might be well protected by agricultural barons and lords like Tsering, but most of the herdsmen knew no overlords; their only political ties were those of blood, or rather of 'bone' – as they called the sign of kinship that related some of the tribes to each other.

Twenty young nomads could attack a caravan of two hundred rifles, and even the most daring soldier of fortune, accompanying the boldest of merchants, or the most arrogant of lords, would tremble when he had to pass a narrow gorge and temporarily break up the defensive order of his march: caravans had always travelled through Kham and most of Tibet like armies – preceded by scouts, flanked by armed patrols that combed the surrounding hills and peered down the gullies before giving the signal to advance to the lowing yaks and pack-ponies that made a slow fifteen miles a day from camp to camp across Tibet.

Cat-calls marked the progress of these caravans, spied on by the nomadic brigands who, according to need or to their mood, would attack anyone who dared intrude into their grazing lands. They attacked in order to replenish their ammunition or to acquire new guns and occasional saddles, tents, pots and pans, all the artefacts they knew no other way of acquiring.

It was to protect the great caravans that the princes and lords had erected the many forts that dotted the trade routes in key places. The garrisons of these fortresses would lock themselves in at night, leaving their strongholds only in force to protect a passing lord or lama and rarely attempting retaliation against the attacking tribes that could vanish into nameless swamps and unknown gulches.

Osher came of such a tribe. Born a nomad and a brigand, he had never seen a wooden roof until he was nine. For him the world extended only a little way beyond the grey, rounded peaks covered with snow that formed the limits of his clan's grazing grounds. To Osher, born in the so-called 'Chinese half' of Kham east of the Yangtse and south of Chamdo, near Batang, the names Tibet and China were only words to describe the origin of the caravans his clansmen attacked as they crossed the grazing lands of his tribe in autumn. While very young, he had seen human heads dangling from their bloody pigtails beside the trade route, reminders of the price of sin. Indeed no punishment was too severe for brigands caught in the act. Osher had often seen the stumbling figure of a beggar whose eyes had been gouged from their sockets for stealing only a single sheep.

'The rich think of religion, the poor of crime,' is a popular saying in Kham but in fact the brigands were not poor. The herdsmen were sometimes incredibly wealthy, especially the heads of the clans who owned one tenth of all the animals in the tribe. But looting was part of their lives and, as Osher knew, it was also essential to a clan's survival, since the herdsmen's only weapon in their struggle for existence was fear. You can fence in a field and fortify the walls of a house but you cannot guard hundreds of square miles of pasture without a reputation of ferocity.

For thousands of years, since well before Ghengiz Khan and Songtsen Gampo, the tribes of Central Asia had quarrelled over water-holes and space on the unfenced grasslands. Slowly, through the generations, driven by territorial instinct and conflicting seasonal migrations, these tribes had bred the fiercest warriors of Asia. From the tents of these nomads had come the men who had conquered the world and made the Chinese tremble.

This was the blood that flowed in the veins of my friend Osher. Such were the origins of the force that from 1950 on was slowly, against all probability, gathering strength to oppose China. It was this force which would soon lead to what has been called the Kanting rebellion, which broke out in 1953 when the Chinese road surveyors began entering the grasslands of Kham with their talk of reforms.

Everyone agreed that it had all begun with the road, the 'machine trail' which the Chinese had begun pushing hurriedly across the nomads' territories. The fact that most of China's available planes had been needed to supply Mao's troops while advancing on Chamdo in 1950 brought home to the Chinese that no true conquest of Tibet could be attempted without the construction of strategic motor roads.

For this reason, and to gain time after the fall of Chamdo, Peking had allowed Ngabo to sign the 'seventeen-point agreement'[1] (which was later approved by the Dalai Lama). This agreement called for a ceasefire in Tibet and, by promises of continuing Tibetan autonomy, allowed the Chinese to enter

[1] Officially called 'Agreement on Measures for the Peaceful Liberation of Tibet'.

Lhasa and consolidate their foothold in central Tibet while officially sanctioning once and for all the loss of Amdo (the Dalai Lama's birthplace) and of Kham to China.

Under cover of economic development, two highways were immediately begun. One ran from Lake Kokonor to Lhasa across Amdo; the other was an ambitious road 1,400 miles long cutting right across Kham from Kanting to Lhasa. This second road, running at an amazing mean altitude of 13,000 feet, crossing fourteen ranges and seven large rivers, was completed by the end of 1953.

At first, Tsering had been a great advocate of the roads and the benefits they would bring to Kham. On his return to Chamdo from Peking in 1953 he was an enthusiast for progress and the introduction of modern techniques. He now spoke Chinese and had amassed a great deal of information in the Chinese capital, although he was still a little confused by the visions of a 'new world' and by the slogans he had learned. Tsering was nevertheless proud to have been nominated to the projected People's Liberation Committee of Chamdo, the assembly that was to govern Kham as an autonomous region of the Chinese People's Republic. This partially satisfied the Khambas' ancient dream of independence; but in fact, as the years went by, eastern Kham was never entirely united to the Chamdo region, as the Chinese secretly planned to keep the Khambas divided while at the same time separating the Chamdo area from central Tibet.

When he reached Ulag Dzong on his return from Peking, Tsering was surprised to find in his cousin Temba, and many others there, a slowly mounting resentment against the Chinese. 'I did all I could at first to help the Chinese,' Tsering later confessed to me, 'but already by 1953 it had become plain that the Chinese were also just "beautiful mouths".' The good treatment of the first months of occupation had given way to many antagonizing encroachments into the customs and traditions of Kham. The presence of so many Chinese had made prices soar and hundreds of complaints were voiced against the communists. Tsering did not believe these at first, not until, after a few months, he began to hear what was happening in far eastern Kham and in Amdo.

There the communists had started carrying out what they called 'democratic reforms'. These reforms were geared not so much to introducing communism and socialism as to dividing the Tibetans amongst themselves and so giving the Chinese a stronger grip over these areas. While Peking lulled the Khambas of Chamdo, Batang, and Dergue into co-operation and promised the Lhasean government 'autonomy and respect for its traditions and institutions', the Chinese in the border districts were seeking to destroy the very foundations of Tibetan culture. In every village, public meetings were held and the population formally divided into five 'classes': capitalists, landowners, middle-class, smaller peasants and lastly agricultural labourers and servants. The lowest class were asked to denounce and abuse their masters, who were labelled 'reactionary serf owners', but the first of these 'struggle meetings' soon proved to be failures. To their surprise the Chinese discovered that in spite of the 'feudal' appearance of Tibetan society, no such 'class hatred' as in China existed there. Tibet, it seemed, lacked a discontented proletariat and peasantry, the two cornerstones on which communism usually flourishes.

To awaken the 'class consciousness of the masses', the Chinese soon adopted new tactics. Beggars were bribed to accuse the rich and told (as was later testified to the International Commission of Jurists) that if they refused they would be considered reactionaries and shot. The penniless and the beggars were told that 'this was the only chance of the poor and that they should accuse the rich', whose wealth they were promised. But even such methods were without success.

It takes an intimate knowledge of the basic Tibetan character and the laws of the land to understand that Tibet, however feudal it may have appeared, was not a country operating on a system of oppression.

If there were in Tibet many inequalities between various individuals, these did not fall as in most countries of Asia and medieval Europe within a set social pattern. There existed in Tibet no caste system or social prejudice commanding an attitude of scorn towards the poor and the less fortunate. If the poor in Tibet undoubtedly had a harder time than the rich and although criminals were punished by ancient methods such as flogging, the placing of hand and neck in wooden stocks and on rare occasions by physical mutilation, nevertheless there was in Tibet a great respect for all individuals regardless of their social position. After all, in Tibet even to harm an animal was considered a sin.

Tibet was also a land without a monetary economy and because of this there was very little difference in point of wealth between the poor and the rich, except for the great lords and abbots, a very small minority who ruled as it were by 'divine right', a right which was never questioned or considered unjust since Tibet was the most religious of all lands. In fact the only people who ever questioned the moral basis of the power and wealth of the aristocrats of Lhasa were the lords themselves, not the peasants but people like Tsering and the Pangda Tsangs.

But even lords in Tibet were far from having the power of their medieval European or Asian counterparts, for they ruled and managed estates and not people. The relationship of individuals to the lords was strictly economic, the lords having no rights over individuals or over how they lived and what they did.

Tibetans in every walk of life were famous for their outspokenness, their humour and their friendliness, devoid of all servility, characteristics which set them apart from most Asians. 'He who carries the bag eats the barley' is not a Chinese slogan but an ancient and popular Tibetan saying. Tibetan history also records how 'three times the descendants of Songtsen Gampo equalized the rich and the poor'.[1] In Tibet, 50 per cent of the agricultural population owned land which was theirs 'until the crow turns white, until rivers flow uphill'. This was a far higher proportion than in any other Asian country. It was only this privileged majority (whose holdings were all approximately the same size) who paid taxes to the state. Now because taxes in Tibet were linked to landholdings, and because these taxes were paid in services rather than in money, the Chinese claimed that all Tibetan peasants were 'serfs'. This erroneous belief was widely publicized by China and readily accepted in the West because of ignorance of the Tibetan system and because many 'feudal' aspects of Tibet made Europeans believe that Tibet must have a peasantry similar to that of Europe in the Middle Ages. This was not the case. The peasant in Tibet was free to do as he pleased with his land, with his money and his person. His only obligation was to

[1] This was achieved by equalizing the land holdings of the peasants.

pay his land-taxes or services. On the other hand, those who did not own land paid no taxes or services to the state, except for any that they might have agreed to pay as rent for land belonging to other peasants or to lords.

It was in fact only a small minority (10 per cent of the population according to Chinese statistics), classified as beggars or household servants, who could rightly be branded as 'serfs' (i.e. unable to dispose either of property or of their own persons).

Any comparison between the Tibetan peasant and his feudal European counterpart was therefore only superficial. No more than those of medieval Europe were the Tibetan farmers prepared for a marxist revolution; nor did they want one, much less one imposed by the Chinese, the traditional enemies of their country.

Infuriated by Tibetan resistance to change and the failure of their 'revolutionary doctrines', the Chinese soon abandoned all pretence of legality in imposing their will on the people of Amdo and of the border areas of Kham, the districts of Liangsham, Apha and Kandze, which were not included in the Chamdo autonomous region of Tibet. Chinese soldiers began publicly abusing the landowners, riding them like horses, in an effort to humiliate them in front of their fellow villagers. When such childish measures also failed, the Chinese simply rounded up all landowners and members of the three 'upper classes' and shot those who opposed reform. In Doi, a township of Amdo, out of five hundred so-called 'serf owners' three hundred were shot in the back of the head in 1953 before a horrified crowd, which was then told that such would be its own fate if it opposed socialism.

This was the beginning of the acts of barbarism by the Chinese, a pale foretaste of the incredible atrocities to come, the mass murders, child deportations and public tortures that were eventually to be China's policy and answer to Tibetan opposition, tortures of the refined sadism for which the Chinese are unhappily famous.

When refugees escaping from Amdo and the areas around Kandze arrived in Chamdo with accounts of what they had suffered and witnessed, Tsering began to understand the true nature of the 'democratic reforms' he was helping the Chinese to introduce. Already he had discovered that the 'Chamdo Liberation Committee' and the 'Preparatory Committee for the

Autonomous Region of Chamdo' of which he was a member were mere fictions to lull the Khambas into co-operation while the Chinese built strategic roads and extended their foothold in Kham. The real leaders of the committee, Tsering now saw, were the Chinese officers of the newly founded 'Political Department of the Tibetan Military District'; while by conscripting Khambas into the Chinese army, and through the monopoly of business by the 'Chinese State Trading Agency', Peking was tightening its grip on Kham.

The year 1953 was a difficult period in Tsering's life, a time beset by doubts and frustrations as he saw the dreams he had had on setting out for Peking three years earlier crumble before his eyes. Equally painful was the situation of the famous Pangda brothers of Po, the living yet legendary heroes of so many Khambas.

In 1950 these brothers had seen their hopes of unifying Tibet shattered for the second time since 1933. Yet, much as the Pangda brothers despised the Chinese, they had one special reason for hoping that an eventual agreement could be reached with the 'new Chinese'. This was because Rapgya Pangda Tsang was not completely opposed to communism. In 1940 this amazingly well-read and highly educated Khamba had been expelled from Lhasa for founding a 'Progressive Tibetan Party'. Rapgya Pangda Tsang had even translated extracts from Karl Marx and Sun Yat-sen's *Three Principles of the People* into Tibetan, works for which he had been hastily branded a communist. Although this was untrue, Rapgya Pangda Tsang did hold leftist views, views remarkable, to say the least, in a Khamba warrior. The Pangda brothers had always hoped one day to introduce liberal-social policies into Tibet when the Lhasean lords could be replaced by a unified Tibetan government.

By 1953 the Pangda brothers, like Tsering, knew of the events in extreme eastern Kham and understood how they had been fooled by the Chinese promises. The long-awaited benefits of the road were suddenly transformed into an influx of more Chinese troops and, more frightening still, of thousands of Chinese peasants sent to 'colonize' the now accessible regions of eastern Tibet.

This flood of human 'locusts' into Kham corresponded to a similar one in Amdo. When, early in 1954, the Chinese began to establish co-operatives in the Kandze and Litang areas, confiscating land and taking cattle counts, they encountered open rebellion at last. Osher's tribe, with countless others, marched out into the hills ready to fight.

At first the Pangda brothers tried to dissuade the rebels, but this proved an impossible task as blatant Chinese chauvinism brought about the inevitable crisis. Once again the Pangdas talked of war. Once again, despite the clouded past, the Khamba leaders looked towards Lhasa, the heart of the Tibetan world, for support. Secretly, Rapgya Pangda Tsang, who resigned as governor of the Markham district in 1953, set out for Lhasa on pretence of a trading mission to make one more attempt to secure Lhasean backing for a 'massive Tibetan uprising against China'.

But in the Tibetan capital all was quiet. Life there continued practically unchanged. Ngabo the traitor had been made a minister and the young and guileless Dalai Lama was to all appearances on good terms with Peking. An advocate of nonviolence, the pious god-king seemed to lack the energy, courage and ability to react to the slow encroachment of China. Advised by Ngabo, he accepted, one by one, the requests of the Chinese military commander of Tibet. At the request of the Chinese he even deposed his trusted prime minister, Lungkhangwa. This wise, greying old man eventually fled to Kalimpong, there to become, in 1954, the first Lhasean to think seriously of war against China.

In the same year (1954), despite the protest of many Lhaseans, the Dalai Lama agreed to go to China. By so doing, he was playing into Chinese hands: inevitably they would use him for propaganda purposes. The Khambas realized this immediately and when it became known that the Dalai Lama would cross Kham on his way to Peking a number of them planned to kidnap him. Foreseeing this, the Chinese on 8 July 1954 massed troops along the Lhasa-Chamdo-Kanting highway to protect their naïve hostage from his own people!

On 20 August 1954, a week before the Dalai Lama reached Yaan (in Szechuan), rebellion broke out in southern Kham.

6

'Lean Over the Bank'

Few persons in the West took any notice when the news came from Formosa of the beginning of what was to prove, to everyone's surprise, one of the longest and most arduous struggles in Asia's recent history. Fewer still, in the summer heat of New York, were those who read the short article in the *New York Times* on 28 August 1954 which reported:

> Formosa says that 40,000 farmers took part in an uprising in East Tibet. Most of the rebels were killed, the announcement said. Many were killed by communist regular troops sent to the area to suppress the revolt.

'Most of the rebels were killed.' Formosa's statement was a distortion of the facts, as was shown five days later by another report published in the *Guardian* stating that the Chinese 18th Army had been rushed to suppress the revolt in Kham, the Tibetan Resistance Movement had put out a manifesto and that armed clashes were becoming everyday events. In fact the situation in Kham was such that it became known a few days later that the Soviet army had sent reinforcements to help the Chinese.

As these reports filtered through to the West, the same newspapers published widely the unexpected and contradictory news that 'the Dalai Lama in Peking proclaims his fidelity to Mao Tse-tung'. If every one had heard of the Dalai Lama and knew who he was, no one had the faintest idea who the Khambas were. To outsiders all the news about Tibet now seemed confusing and incomprehensible, especially when, on 19 September, three days after the announcement that the Dalai Lama proclaimed his fidelity to Mao Tse-tung, the *New York Times* went back on its previous report that 'most of the rebels were killed' and printed under the small headline, 'Tibetan Rising', that 'fatal clashes between East Tibetan tribesmen have been reported by travellers', and that frequent 'free for all' fights had broken out.

Three days later, on 21 September, Associated Press attempted an explanation in a dispatch titled 'Tibetan Rebellion' and subtitled 'Tribal uprising of no real significance':

> ... Informed sources say the warlike Khambas who live in a small remote mountain area have always opposed any control from the outside. They speculate that the tribe is not giving the communists any more trouble than they gave the Tibetan government before the occupation. These sources (no doubt Lhasean) said the Khambas are a relatively small tribe without means of obtaining large quantities of arms.

Two days later, on 23 September, the New China News Agency made public the Dalai Lama's speech in Peking, a speech that spread further doubts about the authenticity of the reported uprising of that 'small tribe'. In his widely distributed speech, the Dalai Lama said that 'close unity is growing daily among fraternal nationalities, in particular between the Han and Tibetan people; a new and peaceful and friendly atmosphere now prevails in Tibet.'

Just how peaceful and friendly became known two days later, on 25 September, when the London *News Chronicle* announced: 'Tibetan monks flee Reds.'

Nobody had any very clear idea of what was going on, so that it came as a total surprise when, on 21 October 1954, the *New York Times* revealed the startling news that the 'Chinese communists had withdrawn from Eastern Tibet' adding that 'the Reds have been forced to turn over the administration of the region to the powerful abbot of Litang'. With the withdrawal of the 18th Chinese Army and its Russian advisors and the turning over of the administration of Litang to its abbot that 'relatively small tribe', the Khambas (consisting in fact of 30 per cent of Tibet's total population) had seriously shaken the Chinese. The communists had been obliged to withdraw temporarily from eastern Kham in order to prepare for an inevitable head-on collision.

On 10 November 1954 General Chang Ching-wu, a strategist of great repute, was given absolute authority as military governor of Tibet. The stage was now set for a long and bloody war.

The revolt of the autumn of 1954 had in fact only affected the regions east of the Yangtse. In Chamdo the Khambas had not yet taken up arms; Khamba unity was yet to be achieved. In the meantime there was a momentary lull in the fighting because of the Chinese retreat and because the Dalai Lama was still in China. For although most Khambas disliked Lhasa, many feared that if the rebellion spread the Dalai Lama could become the victim of Chinese reprisals. In all the monasteries of Tibet, including those of Kham, great concern was shown by the monks for the safety of the holy Lama. Three thousand monks sent a petition to Nehru (via Kalimpong) asking him to press China for the swift return of the Dalai Lama, whose visit had unexpectedly dragged on for nearly a full year.

At long last, in April 1955, the Dalai Lama returned. On his way back to Lhasa he stopped in Chamdo. There, as a docile tool of the Chinese, he 'urged' moderation on the Khambas who dared to voice their discontent against China, saying that they should accept 'whatever was good in Chinese methods'. But moderation was no longer possible. News had already reached Chamdo of the fighting in Litang and the success of the 'rebels', and now the Chamdo Liberation Committee was being pressed to introduce in western Kham the same reforms that were causing so much strife the other side of the Yangtse.

As in Lhasa, the Chinese army in Chamdo had so far had strict orders to treat the monks relatively well. But now they began discouraging the peasants from visiting monasteries and began openly to attack the church.

There are two things Tibetans and especially Khambas will never tolerate. One is any interference with their religion and the other is attempts to relieve them of their most precious possessions: their weapons. All over eastern Tibet the Chinese now planned to do both.

In October 1955 large detachments of the Chinese People's Liberation Army entered Batang, Kandze, Litang and Dergue with orders to disarm all Khambas. Their instructions read that they were to relieve the nomads, the lords and the monasteries of any weapons they might have. Simultaneously it was declared that 'religion was a poison', that 'monasteries and lamas must be eliminated', and that 'God and gods are the instrument of exploitation'.

All over eastern Kham the reaction was instantaneous: war! The male population of large villages and towns took to the hills to join the nomads, while the monks in their monasteries also prepared to fight. These, with the nomads and brigands, began harassing the Chinese. As if from nowhere, horsemen swept down on three points along the two roads leading to Kanting, temporarily cutting the supply lines to all Chinese garrisons.

In Litang armed Khambas attacked the Chinese garrison and invaded the great monastery, ready to stand and fight beside the holy abbot to whom the Chinese had turned over the administration of the district since 1954.

From Batang all able bodied men retired south to the stronghold of the Pangda family. Po Dzong, inaccessible to vehicles, now became the headquarters of the eastern Khamba military leaders.

On hearing in Lhasa of the new outbreak of hostilities, and confronted with Lhasean indifference, Rapgya Pangda Tsang secretly left Tibet for India. There he tried in vain to elicit support from the exiled Lhaseans living in Kalimpong. From Kalimpong Rapgya Pangda Tsang also got in touch with American officials who relayed to Washington the news of the rising rebellion in Kham. According to George Patterson, on learning of the unrest in eastern Tibet 'an official from Washington, in the guise of a tourist, was flown to India for secret personal talks with Rapgya'. Alas, nothing concrete was to come at first from these discussions so that Rapgya was obliged like Gompo Sham (an Amdo rebel leader who had also fled to Kalimpong), to negotiate with Taiwan agents for Chinese Nationalist support. This was granted on the basis that the Chinese Nationalists still claimed Tibet to be theirs and also because it was known that in Amdo there were still in hiding some twelve thousand Chinese Nationalist troops who had fled there after 1949. Such were the strange circumstances that led to the unexpected involvement of the United States in the so-called war of Kanting. It was a half-hearted involvement on both sides. The Khambas reluctantly having to seek support from their ancient enemies . the Chinese Nationalists, the United States catering not so much to Tibetan interests as to those of Taiwan, and their own national fear of communism.

Meanwhile in Chamdo the Chinese gathered together two hundred of the local leaders and members of the Chamdo Liberation Committee, Tsering among them, and asked them 'whether the reforms in Chamdo should be put into effect immediately or be deferred'. These reforms were to be similar to those being applied by force in eastern Kham, i.e. redistribution of land, common ownership of herds by co-operatives, abolition of large land holdings, including those of the monks (who would then be obliged to leave the monasteries), the disarming of the population and the settlement of Chinese squatters.

The Chinese officials were naively surprised when this assembly, by an overwhelming majority, flatly declared itself absolutely opposed to all reforms!

For Tsering, the magic and the marvels of Peking had by now completely worn off. Betrayed once by Lhasa, he now saw how he had been misled by the Chinese and betrayed by slogans and political theories, vast intellectual structures, airy logic built on nothing because without foundations or roots, lacking any relation to man and his true aspirations, his inner need for dignity, respect and independence.

Tsering remembered now what the old nomad headman had told him five years before when he had been wavering about what action to take. 'To throw a man in the river, you must lean over the bank.' He now saw clearly that he had been a 'mid-way man' and had lacked the courage to go all the way, to lean over the bank and stand firm against both the Chinese and the Lhaseans. Since 1950 he had been merely a silent witness of the slow erosion of words, the discreet undermining of ideals through talk. And now he saw himself sitting on a puppet committee whose only goal was to destroy all the values which had been his and those of his people, men whose only constraints, just a few years ago, had been those of the limitless plains. For too long he had lain under the influence of the communist drug. Now, thought Tsering, it was time to 'lean over the bank'.

This was why Tsering, along with the majority of the Chamdo Liberation Committee, stood up and openly opposed the reforms of the Chinese government, deriding the very basis of China's new ideology.

Shocked, the Chinese general in command of Chamdo stood up before the assembled Khamba leaders. For him it was a matter of losing face; to be ridiculed or caught off guard is the nightmare of every respectable Chinese. The general thanked the assembly with a charming but forced smile and gave every member a present: pens, ink, and (insult) soap!

Tsering returned immediately to Ulag Dzong, his home, which he now shared with a detachment of Chinese soldiers. Things had changed a great deal over the past years. In Ulag Dzong the old transport tax had been abolished now that large Russian trucks and jeeps rumbled past the holy *chorten* which stood before Tsering's home. But the trucks never so much as stopped at Ulag Dzong, where all caravans had once gathered. There were no more merchants either to bring the news and stories which, in the flickering light of the butter lamps and the smoky red glow of the fire, had filled the evenings in the past.

Instead, every night, Chinese strangers spied on Tsering's family life in the large main hall where his wife and four children slept on the red and blue carpets spread around the monumental clay stove.

Transport duty had been replaced by 'volunteer' labour gangs to build the road, then to build the school and hospital of Chamdo. To be obliged to work for little or no pay was resented perhaps just as much as the old Tibetan taxes, because the Tibetans had never got used to the grind of regimented work. Work itself they did not fear. It was the loss of freedom they resented, being herded like animals into trucks, and working to the blast of a whistle, bullied by the Chinese who despised them because of their clumsy boots and long hair, their 'green brains', and their ignorance of all things mechanical.

At first, attracted by the prospect of silver coins, the nomads of Ulag Dzong had complied with the order to work on the road. Then they had stopped sending men and Tsering had been unable to persuade them to come. The Chinese had raised a great fuss but none dared to go out into the plains to enforce their orders. Now the Chinese were without illusions. The nomads were beyond their control, even 'tamer' nomads like Tsering's. As for the 'brigand' tribes, they were left alone, pending the reforms that would allow the Chinese to seize their guns and cattle and organize them into co-operatives, breaking up their clans. Tsering vowed that he would never let those reforms happen.

A few days later, after the meeting at which Tsering had opposed the reforms, a truck stopped at Ulag Dzong with a message that an urgent meeting of the officials of the Chamdo region was to be held in Jomdho Dzong on matters of 'vital importance'. Reluctantly, against the advice of his wife, Tsering decided to attend the meeting.

The following day he joined friends in Chamdo and drove off in a Russian jeep to the great fortress of Jomdho forty miles away. With him in the jeep were some of the men who had sat with Tsering in the monastery before the invasion, when Chamdo had been the centre of so many great festivals; young men who, like Tsering, had been to Peking, where most had become ardent communists. A few had cut their hair and now sported Chinese clothes: jackets with buttons and zips, and 'sweat shirts' under their voluminous Tibetan gowns. Tsering did not approve of these foreign clothes and wore, as usual, his fine cloak with the two pleats in characteristic Khamba fashion, such as the one in which I first saw him at Kalimpong.

As soon as all the delegates and representatives had reached Jomdho Dzong a thousand Chinese armed guards suddenly surrounded the fort. The meeting was a trap.

The decision of the Chinese military commander to imprison most of the top men of the Chamdo Liberation Committee was a fatal mistake. When it was clear that the Khambas were prisoners, the general entered the assembly hall. He announced that 'democratic reforms' were to begin immediately in Chamdo and required all those present to ratify this decision.

Even the few truly convinced Khamba communists now understood Peking's true intentions. Many of the prisoners had knives and no doubt some considered committing suicide. Other members present had pistols. These they discretely hid, for strangely enough, no one had been searched on entering the fort.[1]

It soon became apparent to the Chamdo leaders that the Chinese general was more stupid than they had ever imagined. He next attempted to persuade his Khamba prisoners to 'confess' and to sanction the proposed reforms. Such a strange attitude can only be explained by the Peking régime's hypo-

[1] According to H.H. the Dalai Lama in his memoirs.

critical fondness for 'apparent legality', a form of ancient Chinese historical tradition that wanted legal formality always to be preserved even if the facts had to be distorted to suit the case.

The outspoken Khambas, Tsering among them, faced now with the near certainty of inevitable massacre in Jomdho Dzong, openly denounced the fallacies of the proposed reforms and the mistakes of the entire Chinese Tibetan policy to the general's face. One by one the delegates stood up and spoke their minds, warning the Chinese general that the reforms, like their imprisonment, would inevitably lead to a rebellion of all the peasants and nomads of western Kham, as indeed was happening at that very moment east of the Yangtse.

Even when the prisoners had spoken their minds, the Chinese still attempted to indoctrinate them. Ten days dragged by, until at last the Khambas began to think of escape. In small groups, they discussed various plans; but their chances were slim as there was only one door out of the fort and this was heavily guarded, while a large detachment of Chinese soldiers was billeted all around.

Playing their last card, the men agreed on a desperate ruse. Slowly, one by one, the delegates began to 'confess', pretending to be swayed by the Chinese arguments. By the fifteenth day, they had unanimously approved the introduction of the 'beneficent reforms'.

The Chinese general, although somewhat surprised, beamed. The Khambas smiled back, eagerly confessing their past short-sightedness and their 'political errors'. Delighted, the Chinese general began a long sermon littered with the usual clichés, and concluded that to help the delegates back on to the road of 'right thought', the following day, the sixteenth of the Khambas' imprisonment, they would begin a course of 'fresh' political instruction.

That night, as a consequence of the general 'confession', the guards were apparently fewer and more relaxed. This was what the prisoners had hoped for. Knives in hand, armed also with a few pistols, the Khambas jumped and killed the sentries and then, in a desperate, mad rush, they broke out into the night.

Outside, guns fired wildly at the escaping men. The toll was never established but one thing was certain, the Kanting rebellion had gained more than a hundred and fifty resolute members in the Chamdo area, local leaders, the men best fitted to lead the Khambas of Chamdo to battle, and who now set off across the mountains to join their clans. On that historic night all Kham stood united once again.

Under cover of darkness, running for his life, Tsering escaped from Jomdho Dzong. Stumbling in the night with a dozen other men, he made his way to the chapel of a small hamlet. There, in the pale flicker of the butter lamps, he waited while a young monk set off to secure horses from a near-by farm. Eager faces soon crowded the doorway of the chapel to look at the fugitives, while outside could be heard the rattle of harness hastily secured to nervous, disturbed animals.

Fearing the worst for his wife and children, Tsering's first thought was to return to Ulag Dzong but, on weighing the risks, he determined to set out immediately in search of the Chengtu nomads of his own domains.

With two other men he headed hurriedly south, keeping to the small trails along which the Chinese never ventured. All night the men rode, swaying to the rolling gait of their ponies, broken only by the sudden jerk of an occasional stumble.

Hours later, a bitter wind greeted the cold glare of dawn, while great whirlwinds of dust blotted the horizon of lonely hills around the exhausted men. When the sun came up, the horses' flanks were cloaked with foam mingled with grit that, driven by the hard wind, now hissed in mad scurries through the scrub.

The cry of wild geese echoed mournfully over the desolate landscape as, in the frigid light, the three men sighted the dark waters of the Lha Tso. Beyond the lake Tsering parted from his companions and each made off to their own districts and the shelter of the isolated monasteries where they knew they could find refuge.

Coming on a group of tents, Tsering stopped to inquire the present whereabouts of the Chengtu nomads. Late that night he reached the plain where the clan of the old *gap*, the headman whose advice had bothered Tsering for all these years, was encamped.

It was with pride that the lord of Ulag Dzong entered the *gap*'s tent to bring the news that the time had come to oppose the Chinese.

All night, around the fire, the three men talked of the future,

A Khamba guerrilla and his mount.

In 1950 the Tibetan Army counted 8,500 men equipped with antiquated machine guns and a few field guns. The uniform of its officers was inspired by the British Indian Army. This is the force that set out to oppose the Chinese People's Liberation Army.

(Atlas Photo)

The Dalai Lama (*right*) and the Panchen Lama with Mao in Peking in 1954. While they smiled the Khambas were fighting.

(*U.P.I.*)

of war. From the four nomad districts of Ulag Dzong it was calculated that a thousand horsemen could be armed. At dawn messengers set out to warn the other tribes and gather these men.

A hasty plan was agreed whereby Tsering, at the head of this small army, was to set out for the motor road, ambush any passing convoy and then push on to Ulag Dzong. There he would rout the small detachment of Chinese billeted in the fort. Later, in Ulag Dzong, the inevitable battle against the large garrison of Chamdo could be prepared in detail.

Tsering knew that soon all those who had escaped Jomdho Dzong would, like himself, be raising bands of armed men. During their two weeks' confinement the leaders of Chamdo had discussed at some length the tactics they might use, the arms at their disposal and the places that could serve as bastions for attack or refuge in case of temporary setbacks.

It had also been agreed that the men of Chamdo should immediately contact the lords of Po Dzong, the Pangda brothers, and attempt to unify operations on both sides of the Yangtse in eastern and western Kham.

As Tsering rode off at the head of his men, he knew that all over eastern Tibet, along the loneliest trails, other riders were spurring their mounts on their way to spread news of the rebellion. And, indeed, forgetting their blood feuds and old disputes, all the tribes of Kham rose united against the Chinese: the ten clans of Nangchen, those of Nakchu and Rakshi Gumpa, the Horpas of Kandze, the Chengtreng herders of the south and the dozen tribes of Markham. Even beyond Kham, in Chinghai to the north the twenty thousand horsemen of the much-feared Goloks of Khangsar, Tsangkor, Khangring and Butsang, rose up in arms.

The hour of revenge had struck on the timeless wheel of life. These men felt that the gods rode with them as they set out against the faithless 'Gyami'. The Khambas' banners were the flags of prayer that fluttered on every knoll and above every pass to the glory of the gods of war, the sacred horse of the winds, the bastion of the faith, the symbol of courage.

All knew that the struggle would be terrible, for by 1956 the Chinese were well entrenched in Kham. Every twenty miles along the two branches of the highway across Kham stood an armed military depot, supposedly for 'road surveillance' and local 'pacification'. Kandze, Dergue, Batang and Litang were heavily garrisoned, as were all the key towns of the Chamdo region. It has been estimated that there were over forty thousand soldiers in Kham, along with twenty thousand trained militia from the Chinese-operated communes. Chinese soldiers were further stationed in every one of the hundreds of small forts of the land.

All these men were well armed with Russian and Chinese rifles, while thousands of heavy-duty trucks provided them with the mobility that the Tibetans lacked. With Szechwan only two days away now that the roads had been built, the Chinese could now call, in addition, on the millions of the Chinese army.

On the eve of the 'great leap forward' in 1956 China was possibly at the peak of her unity, more powerful than she had ever been and, it may be argued, more powerful than she has been since, in view of the eventual fiasco of the 'great leap' and the subsequent troubles leading to the turmoil of the cultural revolution.

The Korean War was over; and Russia had not yet curtailed her aid to China. She was selling and giving the best of her planes, MIG 15s and Ilyushin 28 bombers, along with armed cars, tanks, and all the trucks that China could ask for.

What happened in Tibet in the following months can only be explained in the light of the skill, and incredible courage of the Khambas.

Riding in from nowhere, or so it seemed, with swords waving and gleaming rifles sighted along the necks of their ponies, the brigands and nomads stormed the long columns of Chinese trucks and rapidly closed down most of the roads of Kham. The fall of Litang, from which the garrison had fled, was followed by the assault on Batang and its conquest by the Khambas. Then Dergue, Chamdo, Kandze, and all other major garrisons were attacked. Minor garrisons were also stormed, and the throats of their defenders cut with a pious oath. Chinese squatters were herded together and sent back east, many to die of cold on the way, some more mercifully allowed to flee with provisions. The rebellion soon developed into a full-scale war centred around Dergue, Chamdo, Kandze, and Litang.

The reputation of the Khambas as crack shots had been established centuries before. They combined the skill of the hunter with that of the soldier. Stalking gazelles and attacking caravans had taught them the greatest mastery of their rifles, however antiquated or battered.

Thousands of years of struggle for survival, a survival of the fittest in the most rugged conditions, had fashioned the young men who, like Tsering and Osher, set out to fight for their homes, for their faith and for their very race.

Familiar with every crag, with every trail, with every rock, nook, creek and gully, moulded to their saddles and accustomed to living by plunder, the so-called wild cavaliers, powered by desperation, united by blood and bone, represented a force worthy of their great ancestors. Songtsen Gampo and Ghengiz Khan rode among them.

Alongside the nomads and brigands, the monks also joined in the rebellion. Many of these red-robed priests had been among the first to unearth their arms, weapons put away from the times of bloody Chao and General Lin, or kept since the not-too-distant days when the monasteries had fought among themselves. In those sanctuaries without weapons it was to the sacred chapels that the monks went to take the long swords and pointed daggers from the hands of masked divinities, unhooking also from the walls of these sanctuaries the muskets and other old weapons which had been deposited there through the centuries by repentant bandits, lords and peasants.

The entire history of the gunsmith's art through the ages could have been read on the battlefields of Kham. Their weapons ranged from flintlocks and muzzleloaders to the finest sporting rifles purchased by lords in Kalimpong to shoot gazelles, sophisticated guns from Calcutta's best *shikari* outfitters.

Taken along with the arms were sacred reliquaries whose charms and small copper divinities could guarantee to everyone the long life and holy immunity of the just.

Apart from the better-organized troops of Po Dzong and those who rallied around the Prince of Dergue and the lords and leaders of Chamdo, each tribe constituted an independent force with its own obscure leaders.

Leaving their cattle, wives and children in the care of the old men, fifty thousand nomads set out across the scrubby plains, heading for the roads where they knew they could find the enemy.

Their numbers grew as they advanced. Pouring down the slopes where they had been waiting in ambush, still more men appeared, men from distant tribes come to join the main forces. In their thousands, they fell upon the Chinese garrisons, charging the barracks of the maintenance units at a gallop, more cautiously besieging the isolated forts perched on rocky crags. These ancient structures, now Chinese controlled, overlooked the narrow passage where once the thin line of the trade routes had passed and through which now swooped the massive curves of the 'National Defence Highway', a road according to Alan Winnington[1] 'built' to take heavy traffic and wide enough at every point for two trucks to pass with ease'.

While Osher headed for Litang, attracted by the name of the famous town which was the seat of eastern Kham's largest monastery, Tsering was marching at the head of twelve hundred horsemen toward Chamdo.

After his flight from Jomdho Dzong Tsering reached Ulag Dzong without firing a shot, to find that the few Chinese soldiers had fled, making for the large garrison of Chamdo, a series of temporary buildings set inside a barbed-wire enclosure which had once been the market-place.

This camp the Chinese had turned into a stronghold, with trenches and stone barricades. There too were parked the trucks, along with a few armoured cars whose purpose had seemed obscure to most Tibetans when the clumsy vehicles had first arrived along the roads. These armoured cars now became the most deadly, vital weapon of the Chinese.

From Chamdo and beleagured Batang the Chinese sent desperate radio messages to their military headquarters in Yaan, the largest Chinese garrison of Szechwan, a few miles from Kanting. From all corners of eastern Tibet Yaan was receiving similar cables reporting the build-up of 'barbarian' forces, telling of breaks in the road or querying the fate of small garrisons from which nothing had been heard over the past weeks. There were also desperate appeals from isolated Chinese units fighting off wave after wave of frightening cavaliers who galloped down upon the Chinese, howling, fearless of the machine guns, waiting until the last moment to fire at close range.

In Peking, Lin Piao with his chiefs of staff pored anxiously over the new maps of China, maps on which the old contours

[1] British journalist who visited Tibet.

of the great motherland had been extended to include vast territories, larger than China itself: Kham, Tibet, Sinkiang and inner Mongolia. There, beyond the crenellated line of the ancient Great Wall, stretched the new territories of the so-called 'national minorities', the Mongolians and Tibetans. The extended borders of China were shown reaching northwards around Manchuria, above inner Mongolia, then encompassing the tribes of Moslem Sinkiang, swelling to enclose the great Tibetan Chang Thang, sweeping south to Afghanistan then on to the Himalayas. There the new frontiers came within two hundred and fifty miles of New Delhi, turning east along the northern limits of Nepal, splitting Mount Everest in two before following the watershed of Sikkim, Bhutan and the North East Frontier Agency (N.E.F.A.) of Assam. Then came the borders of southern Kham, across northern Burma to the bulge of Yunan. From there China's Frontier swept south along Burma's eastern flank to within seventy miles of Thailand, before climbing up Laos and eventually reaching the sea by North Vietnam. This was the immense territory, a continent, which the Chinese leaders proudly claimed as their own. Yet everyone present that day in Peking sensed that these claims might only be the shaky over-extensions of wild visions of past Chinese conquests. If all until then had believed in the power and magic of Mao, their great leader, the man they had followed on the rugged trail of the long march, there was now around the table reason for doubt: cables from the North reported general unrest in Chinghai, signalling incidents near Khumbum; others, more surprisingly reported rebel movements in the Kansu province, right inside China, as well as the more frightening messages from Yaan, announcing the general rebellion of the Khambas.

From Yaan headquarters the news was terrible. The situation there was completely out of control. The reasons officially given by the Chinese were that 'the barbarians, led by reactionary elements of the bourgeois serf-owners in collusion with the running dogs of Western imperialists, were obstructing the introduction of beneficent reforms'. 'Cattle owners'[1] opposed to change had risen, in some areas reinforcements were urgently needed, the road was closed, Litang and Batang had fallen, Chamdo was threatened.

Additional cables from Chinghai gave notice of the Amdo

---

[1] The name given by the Chinese to the nomads who opposed the régime.

and Golok rebellion. The situation in Golok country was particularly critical. These tribes, known as the most dangerous of all Tibet, had captured a large detachment of Chinese troops. Having rounded up their prisoners, the Goloks set about cutting off the men's noses. More than two thousand maimed and bleeding Chinese soldiers were then driven off into the frozen deserts. Most died, although a fair number, disfigured for life, returned to tell of their humiliating defeat. The cables also told how in reprisal the Chinese had hurriedly dispatched to the area three regiments of their best troops who in turn were ambushed by the Goloks and annihilated. Between seven and eight thousand Chinese were reported killed.

The cables also told how, because of the uprisings all over Chinghai, China's alternative route to Lhasa from Sinning across the barren north-eastern plains had also been closed. On the map this left as the only access to Tibet the new Sinkiang Road, which had been pushed across the Aksai Chin desert from Khotan and was now in the process of being extended westwards to Lhasa. This road, the most secret and strategic of all China's projects, was being built right across Indian territory. Such gross infringement of Indian territory was a gamble that, so far, the Chinese seemed to have won. Nobody in the world at large, nobody in India even, had noticed the encroachment onto Indian soil. New maps were being prepared in Peking to show the road as lying within China, or rather claiming the 'frozen sea' as an integral part of Chinese Tibet on the basis that it had been annexed by 'unequal treaties' by imperialist England.

This long, circuitous route was now China's last safe supply line to Tibet. The situation was critical. Never before had Peking confronted opposition on such a scale. Unless immediate action were taken, China risked losing control of her new territories in central Asia.

7

The Kanting Rebellion

To the Chinese leaders in Peking the situation in early 1956 must have appeared as dramatic as it was for the most part unexpected. The only bright note in the matter of Tibet was the fact that in Lhasa all was quiet. A poem celebrating the glory of Mao written by the Dalai Lama himself testifies to the young god-king's docile attitude. This poem now hung in the Temple of Broad Charity in Peking for all to see that the great spiritual leader of central Asia, the figurehead and respected divinity of thousands of Buddhists, thought highly of the person and policies of Chairman Mao. Only a poem, it nevertheless had its propaganda value and seemed to reassure the men in Peking as to the support of the most influential individual in the new, troubled half of China:

> O Chairman Mao! Your brilliance and deeds are like
>   like those of Brahama and Mahasammata, creators
>   of the world.
> Only from an infinite number of good deeds can such a
>   leader be born, who is like the sun shining on the world.
> Your writings are precious as pearls, abundant and
>   powerful as the high tide of the ocean reaching the
>   edges of the sky.
> O, most honourable Chairman Mao, may you live long.
> All people look to you as a kind of protecting mother,
>   they paint your picture with hearts full of emotion.
> May you live in the world forever and point out to us the
>   peaceful road.
> Our vast land was burdened with pain, shackles and
>   darkness. You liberate all with brilliance. People now
>   are happy, full of blessings. . . .

There followed twelve more lines which, to use Osher's favourite expression, would make him vomit.

'A long life to Chairman Mao': this was the biggest joke in

Kham. 'Tse-ring' in Tibetan means long life. 'Tung', however, means short, and Mao Tse-tung, as everyone knew, meant Short-Life Mao: a name to be uttered with smiles in a land where a long life had so much significance, and where thousands were called Tsering, but none suffered the indignity of being named Tse-tung. (Eventually it was forbidden in Tibet to refer to Mao as anything but Mao Tsochi – Chairman Mao.)

Because all was quiet in Lhasa, little or no news appeared in the West about the development of the first small Khamba uprisings of 1954 into a full-scale war by the end of 1955. In fact one could read most newspapers in the West and never find a line about the first years of the war which the Chinese came to call the Kanting Rebellion, and which marked the united uprising of eastern Tibetans against China.

Yet a war it was, with all the horrors of our age: the dive bombers, the glaring flash of incendiary charges, the billowing clouds of smoke from muffled explosions and the deep thuds of heavy artillery interspersed with the rattle of machine gun fire. Modern war, with the whine of planes drawing closer to their targets, the shattering of planks, the thunderous rending of collapsing walls and smashing timbers, the sliding avalanche of crumbling partitions and, in the sparse silence of stunned shock, the lonely bark of muskets aimed at the steel birds, the 'sky boats', that came in from the east, one after the other, to bomb the monasteries of Kham and the towns of Batang and Litang in the fateful years that followed the first uprisings.

The war of Kanting. . . . Some will argue that it never happened. No one has ever written the truth, either because it has never been known or because the few who did know could not write or did not care. To our shame, only in China can one find official reference to this war; I quote from Anna L. Strong's book *When Serfs Stood Up*, published in Peking:[1]

> The Kanting rebellion broke out in the winter of 1955–1956 and took the form of murdering Central Government officials and Han [Chinese] citizens, there being no P.L.A. [People's Liberation Army] in the area. As soon as the P.L.A. arrived, they easily put down the rebels, but these fled into deeper

[1] Mrs Strong, who lives in China, is the most celebrated of Communist China's European aides and author of various books extolling China's achievements, all published in Peking.

hills and eventually into Chamdo. Arms were easy to get, for at least fifty thousand muskets and rifles had been left in that area from the warlords' battles between Tibetan and Szechwan warlords. The few air drops from Chiang Kai Chek of American weapons and radio transmitters were hardly needed except for the sense of 'foreign support' they gave the rebels. The Szechwan-Chamdo rebellion was 'basically suppressed' by the end of 1956, though isolated groups would remain as bandits as long as any monastery fed them or until 'local peoples control' was organized. The bulk of the defeated rebels moved into Tibet. They were the Khambas, Sikang troops, cavalry, wild and undisciplined, accustomed to living by loot.

'The Kanting Rebellion.' It sounds like the title of an opera. Yet even in these words of Anna Louise Strong, written and published in Peking by this notorious Chinese collaborator and sympathizer, it rings tragically, loaded with double meanings. 'The P.L.A. easily put down the rebels but they fled to become bandits as long as they were fed'! 'Arms were easy to get', everyone seems to have had an 'easy' time! It is unfortunate that Mrs Strong forgets to mention the planes bombing from the air the 'cavalry' with its antiquated, 'easy-to-get' muskets. It is unfortunate that she omits to mention that sixteen years later, in 1970, the rebellion was not yet over, as is witnessed by numerous Chinese communist reports. Press releases prove that even today the Kanting Rebellion is still going on, with its 'wild cavaliers' who have refused to be suppressed even 'basically'.

As for the United States' eventual involvement in this war, it is now no secret. For a long time the C.I.A. had a Tibetan file, its name a joke to those with access to the classified material lying on the shelves in Washington. In 1954 the American file was neither large nor glorious. It contained the reports of two O.S.S. agents, Colonel Ilya Tolstoy and Major Dolan, on crossing Tibet in 1944 'seeking an alternative route to China after the closing of the Burma road'. ... 'Two of my country-men who hope to visit your pontificate,' as Franklin D. Roosevelt had described them, with his tongue in his cheek, no doubt, in his letter of introduction addressed to the young Dalai Lama, then eight years old.

There was also a report by Leonard Clark, once also of the

O.S.S. who in 1949 became the first foreigner to penetrate deep into the territory of the feared Tibetan Golok tribes, trying to determine how Tibet could become 'a bastion against Chinese communism'.

All these cases are based on ways the 'pontificate' could prove useful to United States interests.

The Tibetan file in London, on the other hand, was much larger but was slammed shut in November 1950 after the fall of Chamdo when, to quote Hugh Richardson, 'it must be recorded with shame that the United Kingdom delegate [at the United Nations], pleading ignorance of the exact course of events, and uncertain about the legal position of Tibet, proposed that the matter be deferred'. As a consequence Tibet's appeal to the United Nations in 1950 was rejected. 'The conduct of the Indian and British governments', adds Richardson, 'amounted to an evasion of their moral duty to make plain what they alone had special reason to know, that there was no legal justification for the Chinese invasion of Tibet.'

From then on the name of Tibet was not mentioned at the United Nations for fully nine years. As for evidence of the breaking out of war in Tibet in 1955, this was quietly suppressed or ignored by an indifferent world. It was truly alone that the Khambas took it upon themselves to avenge the humiliation of Lhasa's capitulation and attempt to regain their lost independence.

Only when the Khambas had made the Chinese suffer their first defeats did the Chinese Nationalist (Taiwan) and the United States become interested in the advantages to be gained from the struggle.

The scale of the conflict became evident abroad only when in January 1956 Peking published an order stating that 'every possible means should be put into action to weed out the Tibetan reactionaries and exterminate the rebels'. This wish of Mao's was now literally carried out. Exterminating the rebels meant exterminating all the Khambas, for, despite Peking's claims, it had not been the lords who had instigated the revolt but the dispossessed peasants and the simple nomads who had seen their flocks and lands taken away to be given to Chinese squatters, and, worst of all, who had seen their faith derided. As for the reactionary bourgeois lords, men like Tsering who had been trained in Peking, the Chinese themselves had thrown them into the rebellion. 'Political power comes out of the barrel of a gun.' So Mao had said in 1937 and he remembered it now.

'Your work for peace is a white jewelled umbrella, giving shade over heaven and earth and mankind,' the Dalai Lama had written in one of the verses of his ode to Mao in the Temple of Broad Charity in Peking. The 'white jewelled umbrella' was now about to turn into a shower of bombs raining from heaven as scores of Ilyushin 28 bombers converged on Yaan airport and the new airport of Jeykundo (reputedly the largest in Asia) ready to send down the 'timely rain' of Mao upon the rebels.

'With a little meat in the hand you can catch the mighty eagles up in the sky,' runs the Khamba proverb. But there were no words in the Tibetan language to describe bombers and no way known to the Khambas of intercepting the sky boats that now flew out to hunt the mounted troops of the nomads.

The situation of the Chinese in Kham was critical enough to justify a full Chinese military operation. Batang had fallen to the Khambas, who after days of fighting had seized the garrison there and sacked the military post. All the Chinese strongholds except Chamdo had fallen. There Tsering's horsemen had been held at bay by artillery fire, grenades and machine guns. For four months, the long siege of Chamdo had been broken only by occasional sorties of the armoured cars, for which no means of destruction had yet been devised.

From all the evidence I have listened to from Khambas in ten years, it would still be impossible to reconstruct all the battles that were now fought or to record the victories and defeats. Tsering, Osher, Urgyen, Amdo Kesang from Litang, Gompo Sham from Amdo and countless others could tell only a fraction of what happened. No one will ever know or understand fully how far these warriors, armed with muskets, riding horses, sporting fur hats and vast flowing gowns 'leaned over the bank', to use the Tibetan proverb. Today most of them are dead, and those who survive have still not ceased to fight, adding to the list of campaigns, all destined to remain unrecorded.

In 1956 fourteen Chinese battalions (according to the Indian intelligence service, eighteen according to other reports) prepared to move in on Kham and wipe out the guerrillas.

While the hastily organized bands rose in arms in the Chamdo region to join the disorderly hordes of nomad brigands, the Pangda brothers, aided by Nyma Tsering, one of their most trusted officers, prepared in a more military fashion to face the inevitable onslaught by seeking aid abroad.

They began dispatching mysterious caravans along the rugged trails running southwards across the Brahmaputra to Assam and India. Thousands of mules laden with Chinese silver dollars were sent by this route to collect sealed cargoes of rifles and ammunition purchased in great secrecy under the very noses of the Indian officials. For the men of Po arms-smuggling was an old game, one they had played with great success and for high profits towards the end of World War II. Although central Tibet had been neutral in that war, when the Burma road was closed the Pangda brothers had made a small fortune conveying arms and equipment to the isolated Chinese Nationalists, despite Lhasa's refusal to allow Tibet to be crossed by arms destined for the relief of Chungking.

Once again the Pangda brothers had reopened the mysterious trails that led from Mela Bazaar (in Assam) via Bhutan to Kham, and those which crossed the Himalayas from Towang and east from Sadiya, then over the great bend of the Brahmaputra before entering their domains.

Yampel, the eldest of the three Pangda brothers, with the help of Rapgya, who had evaded Chinese surveillance to flee to India in March 1955, directed this traffic from Kalimpong, an easy task for the greatest merchants of the Tibetan world. Although Lhasa declined to support the Khambas they were to find unsuspected allies in the Dalai Lama's two elder brothers. Unlike the Dalai Lama, the elder, Thubten Norbu, the ex-Abbot of Khumbum, the largest monastery of Amdo, had been among the first to realize when the Chinese entered Amdo-Chinghai that co-operation could lead only to enslavement of Tibet. When he fled to Lhasa he had become friendly with Yampel, whose ideas for a united Tibet he shared. On leaving for India in 1950 Thubten Norbu had secured from the Dalai Lama orders to seek help abroad for Tibet.

The American Society for Free Asia was only too pleased to procure an American visa for the Dalai Lama's eldest brother and to be his host in the United States. This politically-orientated organization was among the first in America to become sincerely interested in Tibet, or at least to understand how the 'Holy Pontificate' could be used once again to serve the national obsession with halting communism in Asia. At the height of Senator Joseph McCarthy's influence it was not very difficult, with a hint from the American Society for Free Asia (in which the C.I.A. took a great interest), to make Washington reopen its Tibetan file. Thus, after refusing to support Tibet at the United Nations and turning back its desperate peace mission, America came in 1956 to reconsider its Tibetan policy. How the United States could help Tibet was a question no expert in Washington could answer until the appeal came from Rapgya Pangda Tsang.

From Kalimpong Rapgya and Yampel Pangda Tsang urgently pressed the Dalai Lama's elder brother, who was on a visit to India, for help. Then suddenly the solution was found through Gyalo Thondup, the second of the Dalai Lama's brothers. He too had fled from Tibet, but to Taiwan, where he had married the daughter of one of Chiang Kai-shek's most trusted advisers.

Taiwan could not but be interested in what was happening in Kham, where the 'barbarians' in successfully resisting Mao Tse-tung were now doing what Chiang had failed to do. With American approval the Chinese in Taiwan suddenly saw how Kham could be used to serve their own interests and also those of Washington. The irony of the fact that the only support the Khambas could secure was from their traditional enemy, the Chinese, was later to have tragic results. But in 1956, as Mao's troops massed on the borders of Kham, the Pangdas had no choice but to accept United States aid by way of Taiwan.

Kham lay 1,600 miles away from the island of Taiwan, and it took all the cunning of the C.I.A. and the agents of Chiang Kai-sheck to set up one of the most incredible clandestine operations in Asia's recent history.

While still in Kham, Topgyay Pangda Tsang began dispatching small groups of hand-picked soldiers from Po, along with the mules setting off to pick up arms in Assam. Slowly, these men made their way southwards on the first leg of a fantastic journey. It took most of them a month to slip into India and converge on the small railroad station of Gohati in Assam. From there they crossed the sweltering plains of the Brahmaputra by train to Siliguri. Thence they were driven by jeep up to

Kalimpong, where they joined other Khamba recruits in the large offices and warehouses of the Pangda family. To begin with, everyone received a haircut. Shorn of their pigtails, they were handed train tickets to Calcutta and given the address of a contact there.

From the capital of West Bengal the men were then carted by night in trucks to Dum Dum Airport, and from there smuggled unseen out of India in chartered planes. Most of them had never seen a plane before. Now from Calcutta they were flown east to Bangkok, where all blinds were drawn while the planes refuelled. There was another stop, equally anonymous, in Hong Kong, before they flew over the China Sea to Taiwan.

'There we were put up in tents on the edge of a huge lake,' I was told later by Tobrang, one of the survivors of this operation. This man had never seen or heard of the large 'lakes' which we call oceans before he landed in Taiwan. There, on the shores of the 'lake', the Khambas were put through a strange course of instruction.

Some were taught how to jump from sky boats, with sky cloth attached to their backs. Others were introduced to the intricacies of modern weapons, the use of bazookas, mortars, hand grenades and light anti-tank rockets. Others were briefed in setting flares for parachute drops. Still others were initiated into the operation of the field radio sets so badly needed to unify the scattered operations of the men in Kham.

From the files of World War II in Washington, maps and aerial photographs were dug up showing the geographical features of Kham. These photographs were numerous because it had been over Kham that thousands of missions had been flown by the American Volunteer Group, the Flying Tigers, and the young pilots of the 10 U.S.A.F. on their way to Chungking at the end of the war, flights over the 'hump' to China: the 'hump' being none other than the Himalayas of southern Kham.

The Khambas in Taiwan identified the rivers and named the ranges that showed their jagged peaks on the photographs. They pinpointed the location of villages and selected sites for airdrops. Codes and dates were agreed upon and other vital details arranged.

The soldiers were then divided into three groups. The

majority were flown back to Calcutta, in the greatest secrecy, so as not to arouse Indian suspicion. From there, by the same route, they made their way laboriously back to Kham, where most of them became leaders of guerrilla outfits.

Others remained in Taiwan, a few selected for what were to prove suicidal parachute missions. I met one of these men in Nepal. He explained to me how, before leaving to be parachuted into Chinese-held portions of Kham, he and his companions had been given suicide capsules of poison that were attached to their wrists by bracelets, poison they were instructed to use in the event of capture.

Another, smaller, group was flown secretly out of Formosa for further training, in a country not yet identified. For a day and a half they flew across the sea; then they were led from the planes 'under covered passages' to trucks and taken to a camp on a large barren plateau. All these men could tell for certain about their clandestine destination was that they were instructed by Americans and that all signs were written not in Chinese as in Taiwan but in English.

Before Taiwan could send its first contingent of arms to the rebels, the Chinese communists began their major offensive. The Ilyushins were refuelled to begin their first air raids on the Khamba positions in February 1956, ready also to support the eighteen divisions sent into eastern Tibet.

At that time Osher was in Litang. February, the first month of the Tibetan year, is looked forward to by all Tibetans with great anticipation. With it begins the three weeks general celebration of the New Year, three weeks in which all rivalries are forgotten and people flock to the towns and camp around the monasteries to pray, to barter and to make merry.

The population of Litang had seen the crowds, drawn from all the adjoining districts, flock as usual to the bazaar and more especially to the monastery. To the four thousand monks who inhabited the great sprawling monastery (a town in itself) had been added two thousand monks from the surrounding area, monks registered in Litang but living in the dependent monasteries. As for the secular population of the town, a bare two thousand merchants and shopkeepers, they were now outnumbered three to one by men come to celebrate the New Year, the first New Year since the outbreak of the war in a Litang that the rebels had just seized.

On the third day of the New Year ceremonies the monastery enclosure was packed. Everyone had flocked there to attend one of the many religious festivals. This was the day the Chinese chose to begin their offensive. Taking everyone by surprise in a sweeping move, their soldiers surrounded the monastery.

A Chinese ultimatum was handed to the Abbot, Khangsar. It said that there were only two ways, 'socialism and the feudal system'. The monks were called on to 'surrender all their property' and told that if they refused the monastery would be destroyed. Khangsar, who was already famous for his opposition to the Chinese in 1954, curtly refused.

The Chinese emissary had hardly gone before news of the ultimatum had spread through the crowd. Osher had no time to understand what was happening before a few Tibetans who had heard of the message began to leave the monastery in panic. Immediately the Chinese opened fire. The siege of Litang had begun.

This siege was to last for sixty-four days, sixty-four days better remembered as one long nightmare, for close to eight thousand people were trapped within the monastery. Like all large Tibetan monasteries, that of Litang was a town in itself. Some thirty chapels and assembly halls surrounded the massive sixty-foot-high 'cathedral', a huge pillared hall adjoining an immense chapel in which rose a forty-foot statue of the smiling figure of Maitreya. All the lesser chapels and assembly halls were surrounded in turn by village-like clusters of buildings: the medical college, the libraries, the hostels for travelling monks, the halls dedicated to the printing of books and to the making of Tibetan bark paper. Then there were the numerous communal kitchens, the storerooms and the granaries holding the hundreds of tons of barley and wheat, dried meat, tea, butter and lard necessary to feed such a large community. To all these public buildings were added the many residences of the great abbots and those of the monks, buildings ranging from vast private houses to little cells dotted around the large 'residential' colleges, the dormitories where most of the four thousand monks lived.

This incredible world was linked by narrow alleys passing beneath prayer arches and burrowing under the larger buildings to join the numerous stone-flagged courtyards crowded, on the fateful first day of the siege, with, in addition to the four thousand monks, nearly three thousand pilgrims, merchants, nomads and beggars: men and women and countless children, babies carried by their mothers, little boys and little girls all dressed in their best holiday finery.

The whitewashed buildings and the bright red assembly halls rising in the shape of a low pyramid high above the vast, flat plain from which Litang took its name made a clearly visible target. The great walls and the solid bastion of the outer houses now turned the monastery into a gigantic trap, from which came cries and wails of panic as the incessant machine gun fire spattered the buildings.

Rushing in by the road, the Chinese had caught everyone off guard. Now trucks poured more than three thousand soldiers into the surrounding countryside. The troops wasted no time in setting up mortars and machine guns in the small houses of the bazaar and inside the ruins of what before the 1950 earthquake had been the 'old town', a short distance from the monastery.

Inside the monastery there was general panic for nearly an hour. Women and children screamed, monks scurried around aimlessly while others, overcome with fear, increased the din by banging their sacred drums and blowing their horns as if to wake the gods.

With great difficulty the Abbot restored order. The women and children were hustled into the dark underground store-rooms from which the few firearms and silver swords of the monastery's arsenal had already been taken. These were hastily distributed to the monks who joined the other men on the roofs of the taller buildings or beside the gates.

It was fortunate that according to custom, most of the men caught inside the monastery carried rifles or muskets in addition to the Khambas' inseparable sword-like knives. With Osher in the monastery were gathered four hundred more hardened guerrillas, men who over the past months had been harassing the Chinese and were now prepared and determined to fight to the last.

At the end of a week the Chinese at Litang had succeeded in building fortifications and digging trenches all around the monastery. From these they now showered the holy enclosure not only with bullets but with mortar shells, their roar deafening in the assembly halls. Fortunately these, like most Tibetan buildings, were built of 'chan', Tibetan cement, with thick walls of packed and stamped clay which, to quote Captain B. Pemberton, 'is so hard that even at a short range a bullet penetrates less than an inch.'

As the weeks dragged by, the Chinese made various attempts to rush the monastery's most vulnerable points of access. But these attacks failed, although the Chinese managed occasionally to break into the monastery enclosure and throw in hand grenades. Inside the monastery the Chinese soon found out what was to become one of the unfailing rules of the long war in Kham: that nobody could ever hope to match the Khambas in hand-to-hand fighting. In the narrow alleys of Litang the Chinese assault parties were inevitably repulsed or cut down and massacred.

A month passed and still the Chinese had made no progress. Their troops were considerably strengthened but they soon ran into trouble when the Khamba guerrillas, learning of the siege, came out from Po to raid all their supply columns until eventually the highway was closed once again and the Chinese isolated.

Inside the monastery the days and the nights 'dragged on in fear', in the words of the prophecy of the 13th Dalai Lama. Disease now joined the enemy bullets to weaken the besieged Khambas. Sanitary conditions were at their worst, for although there was plenty of food and water there was not enough fuel to burn the bodies of the hundreds who lost their lives.

Again and again the Chinese rushed the monastery. Again and again they were thrown back. By night there was the incessant pounding of the mortars, the bark of field artillery, the clatter of machine guns. But Litang's monks held strong, all those within were determined to resist and if necessary to die, with the courage associated with the name of the 'race of kings'.

Nothing, it seemed, could dent the Khambas' positions. Every day the Chinese could hear above the gunshots the wail of trumpets, the clash of cymbals, the throb of the great drums that to the eternal rhythm of prayer answered the Chinese oaths with the melody of the Khambas' faith.

The Chinese must never be allowed to take Litang. So thought Osher and all those with him when, on the sixty-third day of the siege, in the stillness of dawn there came faintly in the distance an unfamiliar whine, a muffled screech that rose, rose slowly over the plain of Li, to fill the quiet morning and crowd the limitless sky, reaching an inexorable crescendo, a thunderous roar, growing ever louder, rumbling like a thousand horses, a thousand bells, a thousand laments of despair. The Ilyushins appeared suddenly, flashing across the sky, their throttles wide open. The sky boats, the deadly sky boats had arrived!

No one had been prepared for this. To the Khambas it was as if the end of the world had arrived. Bomb after bomb hit the clearly visible target, showering death on the men, women and children packed into the monastery. The bombs shattered the assembly halls and blasted the buildings where once monks had prayed in peace.

Surrounded by the enemy, who now resumed their shelling of the monastery while it was still being bombed from the air, the Khambas suffered a terrible defeat. In one desperate attempt a thousand monks and some six hundred men broke out and faced the Chinese in the open, overrunning their trenches, and in a mad rush made off to the distant hills, leaving behind the smoking sanctuary which, the following day, fell to the Chinese, though not before the monks armed with swords had attempted vainly to resist the final assault.

What happened to those who remained behind in Litang is best told in the words of one of the prisoners, a survivor who testified in 1959 to the International Commission of Jurists.

Sokru Khantul, a very learned and respected lama [of Litang] was attacked by the Chinese because he had not prevented the monks from fighting them. He was arrested and taken into a field where his legs were tied to two pegs and his arms were stretched across a plank. Then he was shot in the chest. The lama Khangsar, the Abbot of Litang, was accused of leading the attack. His feet were chained together and a pole was placed across his chest and arms. Then his arms were bound with wire. He was suspended by a heavy chain around his neck and hanged, although the people asked for his release. The unze [second in charge of the monastery] was arrested, stripped naked and burned on the thighs, chest and armpits with a red hot iron about two fingers thick. This was done for three days, with applications of ointment daily between sessions.

This was the treatment reserved by the Chinese for those courageous monks who had fought for their faith and for Kham, who for sixty-four days had faced modern weapons with swords, and had been defeated only by the crushing superiority of arms they had never known existed.

Of the other monks, five hundred were made prisoners; a seventy-year-old former abbot by the name of Ga Ngori was shot through the eye while meditating; fifteen hundred of the besieged were imprisoned. According to another eye witness:

That night [after the bombing] about two thousand escaped and two thousand were made prisoners. Those captured were gathered together. Holy pictures were stamped upon and thrown away. The captives were taken to the Chinese headquarters where they were told that they would be executed within an hour.

Although this threat was not carried out they were kept prisoners for nearly a month, only the women being freed after a week.

This was the fate of the old and the weak who could not escape into the hills beyond the reach of the Chinese where the Khambas were now united and preparing to retaliate.

As Litang fell, so too the monastery of Batang was bombed[1], as were those of Changtreng and Geling and hundreds more. Simultaneously aerial patrols set out to destroy every likely place where the rebels could hide: forts, monasteries and villages where, rightly or wrongly, Khamba guerrillas were believed to be stationed.

No precise records exist of the extent of the damage done by Chinese bombing in Kham. The same International Commission of Jurists that in 1959 was to gather statistical data on the war reported that two hundred and fifty monasteries were destroyed.

Now the Khambas were menaced constantly from the air, while on land the Chinese also began their greatest offensive. The roads were closed but the Chinese Liberation Army poured in over the wide-open plains. Slowly, one by one, they re-

[1] Fifteen separate bombing raids were necessary to destroy the monastery of Batang.

conquered the towns and villages lying closest to the Chinese border.

Yet the Khambas were not disheartened. Quite the reverse. South of Batang the first planes began arriving from Taiwan, flying over Burma by night, making their way to the pre-arranged dropping sites in Kham. There in the dark, lighted only by the flares signalling to the planes, the Khambas waited as the camouflaged parachutes descended slowly with their precious cargo of weapons and much-needed ammunition. The air drops also brought hope, the short-lived illusion that out there beyond the great peaks somebody really cared for Kham, for the ideals and holy doctrine of its rough people.

If the first Chinese air raids had momentarily disconcerted the Khambas, they were far from being defeated. Every day their forces were growing as Khambas of all ranks took to arms, even the most timid of peasants and the youngest monks. Harassment of Chinese positions was renewed, the roads kept under such constant attack as to remain, in fact, out of operation for two entire years.

In the few towns and villages reconquered by the Chinese the communists now began to torture the monks and openly to hold their religion up to ridicule. Abbots were lashed to the tails of horses and dragged before crowds of terrified old men, women and children, all those who were unable to join the soldiers in the hills.

Mass executions took place and terrible tortures were inflicted, tortures of the most sinister kind, many recorded in the reports of the International Commission of Jurists. Children were forced to shoot their parents, monks were wrapped in wool, covered with kerosene and set on fire, while the Chinese mocked the living torches and told them to have Lord Buddha intervene for them. Between 1956 and 1957 over four thousand five hundred people were massacred in the Kandze area alone as part of the Chinese reprisals.

The plight of those who fell into Chinese hands was horrible. A massive migration began of weak survivors making their way slowly west, cluttering the minor trails, heading for Lhasa, the centre of the Tibetan universe, the place to which the most desperate now pinned their last hopes.

Tsering too dispatched his wife and four children to the comparative safety of the capital. Along with them, hundreds of women and children took the road to exile, refugees often penniless, begging and dragging their limbs not for one hundred, two hundred, but for a thousand miles. These refugees were animated by their faith. The road to exile became a pilgrimage. Many, in these tragic circumstances, were seeing the unexpected realization of an almost impossible dream of seeing the holy city.

Those who were able to flee to the fragile sanctuary of inner Tibet were lucky, for those who remained behind were marked for extinction. In Kham the war raged on more violently than ever, and as it developed, the Chinese became ever more aggressive and arrogant towards all Tibetans they could lay their hands on, not in Kham alone but in the Tibetan regions of Chinghai and Kansu. Such measures, far from suppressing the rebellion, as the Chinese had planned, helped to spread it with alarming rapidity.

The news of the atrocities had reached the most remote corners of central Asia, where it triggered off more open revolt. Suddenly China felt her grip upon the entire world of the high plains slipping. After the Goloks, the Amdo of Chinghai now rose in battle along with the Amdo Sherpas of Kansu. The Mongols themselves became restless and when in late 1956 eight thousand Chinese troops in Sinkiang defected and fled into Russia, the Moslem Kasbecks and Uigurs of Sinkiang rose up again against China.

Once again the old spectre of the lords of central Asia began to haunt the Chinese. By August it looked as if the whole Chinese dragon might crumble. Even inside China Mao detected signs of growing unrest.

Strangely, no one in the West seemed aware of all these events. Indian security measures along the Himalayan border, and the interest of the United States in keeping silence, allowed the Khamba struggle to continue unknown to the world.

When George Patterson (then a resident of Kalimpong), the close friend of the Pangda Tsangs, began to write a series of articles for the British press about the Khamba uprising, he was called by the Indians a liar and a troublemaker.

Later, when Prince Peter of Greece, also a resident of long standing in Kalimpong and an anthropologist of international repute, confirmed Patterson's statements, he found himself threatened with expulsion from Kalimpong, a threat carried out two years later. Such behaviour by India towards a person of such international standing could only be a sign either of blind stupidity or, what was more likely, of a shameful collusion with the Chinese in the extinction of Tibet. And, indeed, since 1950, India, through its attitude and diplomatic policy, had been the first to 'hand over Tibet to China', facilitating China's ambitions in Tibet in every way.

Mao had now good reason to fear the worst as reports came in of uprisings in many parts of central Asia, and even inside China. Everywhere, except in Lhasa, China's great offensive had proved a failure.

The Hungarian revolt in Europe further spelled out to Mao the risks that he was running. Reports from the front in Kham seemed to prove that nothing, not even the air raids, could weaken Khamba resistance. When a village was seized, the Chinese found it full only of old people and infants, all the able-bodied men having preferred to abandon their kin and fight in the hills rather than surrender. Even the most trusted of Peking-trained Tibetans, believed to be communist collabora-tors, now opposed the Chinese, among them Lobsang Tsewan. A few great abbots who in the past had been induced to back the Chinese régime also turned against the communists. The Chinese were not safe anywhere in Kham or Chinghai and their planes and armoured cars were proving useless against the rebels, who were perfectly at home in the hills and able to fight at altitudes where most Chinese had trouble in breathing. The terrain of Kham is so rugged that the Chinese rightly feared they were engaged in a guerrilla war of indefinite duration.

Faced with these facts, the leaders of Communist China had to admit for the first time that the situation was out of hand. In Lhasa the Chinese openly admitted at a public meeting the existence of the rebellion of Kham. This severe loss of face was further underlined by their request to the Dalai Lama to intervene.

Never in his career had Mao received such a blow or gone so far in publicly admitting failure.

Chou En-lai officially declared that 'mistakes had been made' as he considered negotiating for peace.

Naïvely the Khambas felt that victory was now within their grasp, that with the gods in their favour, and through their determination, they would soon triumph and set free the great united Tibet of their ancestors.

Again the Khambas looked to Lhasa, crying out with the very blood of Tibet to the capital, to the holy city, to the Dalai Lama, to the very epicentre of the world and of the values for which they fought, asking central Tibet to join in their crusade. But once more they encountered only obstruction and indifference.

Although he refused actually to send Tibetans to fight the Khambas the Dalai Lama officially condemned the rebels. In the name of religion he called for peace in the middle of the bloodbath, in the middle of Kham's supreme effort, the Dalai Lama urged the Khambas to surrender their arms.

A word from the Dalai Lama, one single proclamation, and all Tibet would undoubtedly have stood up and faced the Chinese. The Dalai Lama's failure to understand this, his failure to act, to speak and to lead his people to war, is perhaps the greatest tragedy of Tibet's long history.

It is hard to blame a man, but harder still to blame a god and a king, yet to a certain extent the Dalai Lama is to blame for failing to back the Khambas. Not only did he not support them, but he continued to preach against their crusade, officially calling on all Tibetans to stop fighting. The Dalai Lama's own words give, better than anything, the tragic reasons for his strange attitude, and allow one to measure his incapacity to grasp the true issues at stake in Kham. He says:

Slowly, from reports of refugees, we began to receive a clearer impression of the terrible things that were happening in the East [Kham] and the North East [Amdo], though the exact history of them is not known to this day [1962] and possibly never will be. There, in the districts which had been entirely under Chinese rule since the invasion began, the number of Khambas who had taken to the mountains as guerrillas had grown from hundreds to tens of thousands. They had already fought some considerable battles with the Chinese Army. The Chinese were using artillery and bomber aircraft, not only against the guerrillas, when they could find them, but also against the villages and monasteries whose people they suspected, rightly or wrongly, of having helped them. Thus villages and monasteries were being totally destroyed. Lamas, and the lay leaders of the people, were being humiliated, imprisoned, killed and even tortured.

There follow two pages in the Dalai Lama's memoirs confirming that he was fully aware of the situation and its implications, that he 'protested very strongly to the Chinese general in Lhasa against these shocking tactics. When I did so, for example, against the bombing of villages and monasteries, he always promised to put a stop to it at once, but it continued exactly the same.'

Before such evidence and the desperate nature of the situation, some reaction might be expected; but we read on the following page of his memoirs a disheartening admission of the Dalai Lama's lack of personal strength and resolution. Fully aware of all the implications of the war, of its extent, and of the terrible fate of his people and race, the Dalai Lama writes:

Part of me greatly admired the guerrilla fighters. They were brave people, men and women, and they were putting their lives and their children's lives at stake to try to save our religion and country in the only way that they could see. When one heard of the terrible deeds of the Chinese in the East, it was naturally human to seek revenge. And, moreover, I knew they regarded themselves as fighting in loyalty to me as Dalai Lama: the Dalai Lama was the core of what they were trying to defend.

In spite of this declaration, the Dalai Lama, standing by his pacifist principles, concludes: 'However great the violence used against us, it could never be right to use violence in reply.'

In the name of such a principle the Dalai Lama condemned those fighting for his religion and everything he represented. Truly, the Khambas were right: the Dalai Lama was not a legitimate or a worthy heir to the throne of Songtsen Gampo. The Dalai Lama claimed to be God and King of Tibet. He had now failed them in his role as king.

It can also be argued that he failed as a divinity, or so at least Tsering, Osher and countless others believed, seeing their people exterminated, their children waste away and die while the great 'compassionate one' stood by.

Surely it would have been just and moral for the god king to stand up and support the guerrillas? Unfortunately such considerations did not seem to occur to the Dalai Lama as he prepared quietly in the midst of the heaviest of fighting to leave for India to attend the festivals that were to be held in October 1956 to mark the two thousand five hundredth anniversary of the birth of Buddha. Secretly the Dalai Lama intended never to return back to Tibet.

Regardless of the Dalai Lama's apparent indifference the situation in Kham and much of central Asia remained critical for the Chinese who, in July 1956, decided to send Marshal Chen Yi, their vice-premier, in person to eastern Tibet to investigate what should be done to stop the ever-spreading revolt.

What he saw and what happened to him confirmed China's worst apprehensions. Not only did Marshal Chen Yi see a situation that seemed without issue but the vice-premier's own party was ambushed and attacked by Khambas[1]. Marshal Chen Yi barely escaped with his life after losing three hundred men. This sobering welcome decided the Chinese government to swallow its pride and make peace overtures to the Khambas. Accordingly they arranged for Ngabo to be sent to Kham as leader of a Tibetan 'peace delegation' to try and stop the fighting.

The choice of Ngabo was a stupid mistake and on hearing of it the outraged Khambas informed the Chinese that if Ngabo arrived for peace talks he would be the first to be shot. The Khambas then let it be known that they would only accept as negotiator Topgyay Pangda Tsang, their leader. With no alternative, the Chinese sent back Ngabo and began negotiating directly with the rebels. For the Khambas it was a great moment and towards the end of September the fighting abated rapidly while Topgyay sat down to negotiate on equal terms with the Chinese.

With arrogant pride the Khamba commander began drafting an agreement demanding that all 'reforms' in Tibet should be postponed for at least six years, that the Chinese should withdraw their troops entirely and respect Tibetan autonomy in future.

This agreement, it was understood, would extend to the entire ancient realm of Songtsen Gampo, and in return the fighting in Kham would cease. In point of fact the Chinese agreed to these terms, and publicly confirmed them in the

[1] according to Lois Lang-Sims

Chinese press. Mao Tse-tung himself declared publicly that reforms in Tibet had been 'hasty and would be postponed until 1962.'

The Khambas rejoiced in what seemed to be a great victory, quite unaware that the whole operation was a piece of treachery.

From this agreement the Chinese had gained two objectives. The first was a much-needed lull in the fighting, the second that by using the very terms of the Khambas' agreement they were able a month later to persuade the Dalai Lama to return to Tibet. For what the Khambas did not know was that once in India in November 1956 the Dalai Lama had told Nehru, who immediately told the Chinese, that he did not want to go back to Tibet. He had reached this decision because he felt there was nothing he could do there to halt the mounting rebellion in Kham which he feared would eventually spread to central Tibet, and therefore he felt that from India with the help of the Indian people he could better 'win back' Tibetan freedom by peaceful means.

Tipped off by their good friend Prime Minister Nehru, the Chinese rushed Chou En-lai back to India where he had been a few weeks previously to meet the Dalai Lama. Both statesmen set about persuading the Dalai Lama to return. The Chinese evidently could not stand the idea of losing the Holy Incarnation, who so far had proved their best asset in controlling central Tibet. To reassure him of Chinese goodwill Chou En-lai repeated to the Dalai Lama China's determination to withdraw its troops from Tibet and its agreement to postpone reforms in Tibet until 1962. In other words the Chinese Minister of Foreign Affairs spelled out to the Dalai Lama the terms that had been agreed upon by the Khamba commanders.

Reassured by these terms, the Dalai Lama decided to return to Tibet and when he had reached Lhasa the Chinese re-confirmed that 'reforms' would be postponed and the Chinese troops withdrawn, publicly repeating the articles of the Khambas' agreement but this time with two minor but crucial modifications. According to George Patterson one of these was that the Chinese would withdraw 'according to the desire of the people *and officials* of Tibet'. The Chinese added the word *officials*, having in the meantime persuaded Ngabo and other Lhasean officials to ask them to remain! But this was only one of their tricks for the Chinese now also asserted that the famous ten-point agreement concerned only Tibet *west* of Chamdo. In other words it no longer applied to Kham. Thus not only were the Khambas betrayed, but the Chinese now sent some of the troops they had started to withdraw from central Tibet into eastern Tibet to fight the rebels there, announcing later that all eastern Tibet was to be incorporated into the huge Chinese province of Szechwan.

Infuriated, the Khambas after the short lull in the fighting rose up again with renewed violence. They burned their houses and granaries and killed their cattle before taking once more to the hills. Meanwhile the Chinese in Lhasa renewed their pressure on the central Tibetans to send men to help them defeat the rebels in Kham. Although the Tibetans refused to do this, they nevertheless agreed to send a delegation of three monks and two lay officials to beg the Khambas to lay down their arms. It is hardly surprising that on reaching Kham, and learning the truth of what was happening in eastern Tibet (a truth well concealed not only by the Chinese but by the top Lhasean officials), the members of this delegation sided with the Khambas, never to return. One of its members, Namseling, actually became an influential rebel leader.

The very fact that not one official of the Tibetan government in those troubled years was willing to stand up for eastern Tibet illustrates how well the Chinese had succeeded in dividing the country. It shows also of what stuff the spoiled Lhaseans were made, concerned only with maintaining their own fortunes and privilege under Chinese rule. Indeed there are grounds for believing that, as Patterson said later, 'there was no official of the Lhasa government in India, and very few in Lhasa, who was prepared to sacrifice ten minutes of his time, let alone his wealth, position or life' for the cause of the Khambas or to fight the Chinese.

More than ever, the Khambas were convinced that to succeed they must by force if necessary overthrow the ruling clique in Lhasa and take over the leadership of the Tibetan world misled by the 'beautiful-mouthed aristocrats'. Consequently, while maintaining their positions in strife-torn Kham, the first rebels began to infiltrate central Tibet, determined to persuade the peasants to rise and join them in the ultimate battle for their common race, language and religion.

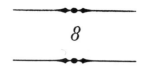

8

Lhasa and Loka

How it was that the Lhaseans were so blind to China's ultimate plans for Tibet, and so indifferent to the plight of the Khambas, is best explained by a glimpse at what life in Lhasa was actually like seven years after the Chinese takeover. Always a startling and paradoxical town, in 1957 the Forbidden City was more than ever strange and unusual. Side by side, living in apparent harmony, one could find the most flamboyant feudal theocracy and representatives of the world's most doctrinaire communist party.

The very fact that for seven years Lhasean society had been able to live cheek by jowl with communism is in itself little short of a miracle, unless one appreciates what rare and strange stuff Tibetan aristocrats were made of. Broad-minded, highly intelligent and therefore easily adaptable, this élite had already long before the arrival of the Chinese lived in a world of contrasts.

Tsarong's daughter, Betty-la, was a good example of the sophistication which characterized the Lhasean aristocracy. In Lhasa she lived a pleasant if not entirely carefree life such as few westerners could imagine. Beautiful by any standards, she led a busy social life, full of parties, at which her wit and humour (typical of the one country in Asia where women shared in all festivities on an equal footing with men) was much appreciated.

Betty-la's social life was not confined to the holy city. From time to time she would leave the problems of Tibet and travel to India. The Chinese never objected to these journeys. There, with her sister Tesla, she would grace the select enclosure of the Calcutta Turf Club, taking a passionate interest in the fine racing stable of her brother-in-law, Jigme Dorji, the Prime Minister of Bhutan.

None of the Europeans in Calcutta had any doubts that the Tibetan aristocrats who came there occasionally were by far the most refined and unusual personalities of the Orient. There was something in the grace and humour of Tibetan women in particular that could not be equalled in the East. This is possibly because women like Betty-la had never known the restrictions generally placed on oriental women.

In spite of her apparent fragility Betty-la was not a person to stand for nonsense. The future, anyway, was soon to prove her more rugged qualities.

In politics she shared her father's progressive views, and on this subject often disagreed with her husband, Taring, a small, dry man with a certain formality, a man less quick than his wife to grasp the subtleties of China's ever-encroaching grip on the Tibetan capital.

The aristocracy in Lhasa in 1957 was divided between those who sided with Ngabo and the Dalai Lama in the belief that Tibet's future (whether they liked it or not) lay in collaborating with China, and those who knew that China and Tibet had irreconcilable ideals which could only lead to a crisis. But even within these factions, few people agreed; for, just as in France, it was a standing joke in Tibet that two Lhaseans made a political party. Discord, endless discussions and especially indecision all explain how it came about that by 1957 the Tibetan aristocracy had been manoeuvred into collaborating with the Chinese and with a régime whose every value was the direct antithesis of everything Tibet had stood for.

As a result, while bloody battles were being waged by the Khambas to the east, life in Lhasa carried on much as before. It was a mad life, combining in the most contradictory and surprising way the sophistications of the modern western world with the traditional trappings of a feudal society directed towards the interest and advantage of a small aristocratic élite living in the shadow of the most puritanical and powerful of communist régimes.

For those in the West who look upon Lhasa romantically as a semi-mythical city of prayer, it may come as a surprise to know that for a few tennis was a popular sport in the holy city, a town which had seen its first automobile in 1927, and where large numbers of these vehicles now filled the streets, forging their way through the throngs of pilgrims leading yaks and mules past Lhasa's new airport or its first large cinema. From the homes of the rich in 1957 could often be heard the syncopated rhythm of the cha cha cha, as records purchased in Hong Kong enlivened the parties where young couples danced, dressed in the finest of Tibetan robes, yet fully familiar with our Western fads. Betty-la's cousin, Dundu-la, was earning himself the nickname of the Tibetan Elvis Presley and was famous among a small group of fun-loving nobles and their spoiled sons and daughters for his voice and his sideburns.

Like Betty-la, many of these young people spoke English, had been to school in Kalimpong or Darjeeling and acquired there, along with the more rigid principles of an occidental education, a taste for many of the trivial aspects of Western civilization.

The general austerity of the monasteries and the rigid daily life of the young God King contrasted with that of the secular heirs to great Tibetan names. Many houses in Lhasa were well stocked with whisky (purchased in Calcutta) and the products of Elisabeth Arden held no secrets for the women who, like Betty-la, graced the perfumed houses of rich men like Lahu, Ngabo or Tsarong.

This elite, though, had nothing in common with the usual run of oriental plutocrats: the aristocracy of Tibet was of a more realistic bent. There were no harems and no tyrannical eccentrics, only a smiling group of men and women given up to the milder pleasures of parties and drink and playing a sophisticated game of amorous intrigue. Divorce was frequent and scandals not rare. The young nobles and some of their wives indulged in love affairs which mingled the passions of Europe with the refinements of the East and the strong temperament of a race that, all told, remains one of the most rugged of our planet.

So it came about that while old Tsarong brooded over impending tragedy, his children danced with the unfailing optimism that characterises all Tibetans.

Compared with the fortunes of European and Asian plutocrats, those of the Tibetan aristocrats were relatively small, but the real standard of wealth was not gold so much as privilege and prestige.

It took hours for Betty-la's servants to do up her long brown hair on the silver and gold frames, studded with turquoise and amber, which rose high above her head, an obligatory sign of her noble birth.

The men, too, spent much time on their clothes. Gold and

saffron brocades filled their chests, for rank governed the smallest detail of their appearance: the right to wear certain knives and money pouches, and even the shape of the dress. Protocol even affected the accoutrements of one's horse. A lord would not hesitate to spend two thousand dollars on a gilded saddle, or to harness his mules with ivory and turquoise ornaments set in gold-trimmed silver buckles, if such was the extravagance required by his position in the complex governmental hierarchy.

Two thousand four hundred of Nepal's most skilled Newar craftsmen lived permanently in the Tibetan capital, turning out jewelled necklaces, snuff boxes and ornamental swords, along with the fine chalice-like silver butter lamps to be offered to the divinities.

Nevertheless, the greatest wealth in Tibet was in the hands of the monks, who were the most powerful and influential residents of Lhasa. It would be naïve to assume that the monks were above the petty jealousies and general weaknesses that curse all mankind. Lhasa, the Vatican of Tibet, also had its cardinals who ruled in great pomp over monasteries as large as towns, Sera, Drepung and Gaden being the largest. This last, with nine thousand inmates, was structured into a world of its own, a social pyramid of priests, at the apex of which were the gilded palaces and chambers of the supreme abbots. Here too prestige was equated with external signs of wealth. Those abbots who were incarnate lamas, selected from humble homes, hailing from the most distant pastures and valleys of U, Tsang, Amdo and Kham, were nevertheless quick to avail themselves of the benefits of their high position.

The majority were dedicated men of great virtue; yet some were less pure, and found in the delights of Sodom a relief from the sterner demands of their order.

Despite all this pomp, it would be unfair to believe that Lhasa was a decadent society. On the contrary, Tibet in the second half of our century was at the peak of its development. Everywhere new monasteries were being built and others enlarged. Artists abounded and new books were being printed. In the absence of foreign influence, Tibetan literature and fine arts possessed all the passion and vigour of the Renaissance. The same lords who so actively assumed the burden of the state's administration were also the most ardent spearheads of Tibetan culture.

When abandoned by the world in 1950, and faced with no alternative but to sanction the humiliating seventeen-point agreement that placed Tibet at the mercy of China, the Lhasean aristocracy, in good will, attempted to bridge the gap between their old way of life and the ambitious ideals of Mao's militant socialism. The wiser lords agreed that Tibet was due for a change, and although accustomed to a life very different from that of the modern world, some accepted quite willingly the first elementary reforms which, according to China, would spell justice for all.

'Immediately when the Chinese arrived, I volunteered to help set up a school, where I began to teach,' Betty-la told me. For her it was a great adventure, one in which nearly all Tibetans were keen, at first, to take part: the introduction of hospitals, of schools and of so many of the amenities of our age, all new and remarkable in Tibet.

In the fourth article of the seventeen-point agreement China had proclaimed that

the central authorities will not alter the existing political system in Tibet. The central authorities also will not alter the established status, functions and powers of the Dalai Lama. Officials of various ranks shall hold office as usual.

These promises, which included 'freedom of belief', respect for local customs and protection of the monks, along with the fiction of 'autonomy', had helped Tsarong and all the nobles of Lhasa to accept Chinese occupation when they were abandoned by the rest of the world.

Betty-la in particular agreed with the necessity for change, and her life soon became an amazing combination of Marxism coupled with feudal obligations, tempered by the amenities of the most sophisticated products of Western capitalism.

Even so, Betty-la could not condone her past way of life: 'Nobody felt that our privileges were anything but normal.' That some of Lhasa's beggars were her good friends never struck Betty-la as unnatural, any more than she resented working hours as a school teacher, expounding the doctrines of the Chinese. For her there was no incompatibility of creed, condition or culture. There was no gap to bridge. She only responded to her heart, a strange heart that would make her pity the poor Chinese soldiers, so unhappy in Tibet, where they suffered from the altitude, but allowed her to look indifferently on the face of a man whose eyes had been gouged out and his hands crippled for stealing one sheep.

Such was Betty-la, and the disturbing situation of the Lhaseans in 1957. In all the bustle of change, few realized how, slowly, the Chinese had begun undermining Tibet's promised autonomy.

The 14th Dalai Lama and his nobles had forgotten the warnings of the great 13th Dalai Lama, of whom he was such an inedaquate reincarnation. They forgot what he had written about 'the Chinese way'.

'The Chinese way', the 13th Dalai Lama had perceptively explained, 'is to do something rather mild at first; then wait a bit, and if it passes without objection, to do or say something stronger. But if we take objection to the first statement or action they urge that it has been misinterpreted, and cease, for a time at any rate, from troubling us further.'

Slowly, ever so slowly, China began eroding the prestige of the Dalai Lama, nibbling at the power of the lords, and undermining Tibet's promised autonomy. Alas, no one took exception. On the contrary, whenever a conflict arose between the Chinese and the Tibetans over a minor point, the Dalai Lama (the present 14th), not heeding the advice of the person of whom he was the reincarnation, voiced no objection. On the contrary the new Dalai Lama reasoned 'if we continue to oppose and anger the Chinese authorities, it could only lead us further along the vicious circle of repression and popular resentment ... a violent opposition was not only impractical, it was also unethical'.

By 1957 such ethical considerations had led the Dalai Lama officially to sanction most of China's anti-Tibetan policies. First he sanctioned the dismissal of his Prime Minister, Lungkhangwa, then he spoke out against the Khambas, consenting under Chinese pressure to brand them in all his speeches and edicts as 'reactionaries'. Next, the Dalai Lama agreed to send a delegation to beg the Khambas to lay down their arms, thus demonstrating his official opposition to their stand.

The young Dalai Lama, though, was not entirely insensitive to what was happening; he himself later admitted that he neared despair as every year he witnessed how the Chinese were exploiting him and how, as a result of his attitude, dictated by his naïve faith in abstract principles, he had managed to alienate many Tibetans. As the Dalai Lama wrote later in his autobiography: 'while the Chinese said the Cabinet [six ministers, including Ngabo, headed by the Dalai Lama] was in league with the Khambas, I have no doubts the Khambas believed the Cabinet was more or less in league with the Chinese.' Ill-advised, naïve and lacking decisive character, the Dalai Lama wished to abdicate his political powers and retire to India. As we have seen, when he visited India in 1956 for the two thousand five hundredth anniversary of the birth of Buddha, it had taken all the cunning and empty promises of Nehru and Chou En-lai to persuade him to return to Tibet. From 1957 on the Dalai Lama, in Lhasa, sought only to steer a veering course between postponement and acquiescence to Chinese demands, secretly hoping that he might soon be allowed to retire to prayer or to exile. It was a terrible position: to be, at twenty, both the God and the King of a land that had fallen into the hands of the materialistic Chinese; yet he could never be allowed to abdicate his sacred mandate.

While the Dalai Lama was near despair, Ngabo and the other members of the cabinet laboured to save their personal interests by giving the Chinese a free hand to fight the Khambas and to oppose the ever-increasing Khamba sympathizers within central Tibet, in particular the Mimang organization. This was a clandestine anti-Chinese organization which the Chinese themselves, strangely enough, had helped to set up. On entering Lhasa the communists had attempted to create 'people's associations' which they called 'Mimang Tsong-du' (many peoples association) hoping that these would eventually stand up and oppose the wealthy aristocrats. When these groups were organized the Chinese suddenly discovered to their surprise that they had, in fact, created the first cells of organized popular resentment against their presence in Tibet. These 'people's associations' openly criticized Chinese policies, declaring outright that as 'representative of the Tibetan peoples they wanted the Chinese to leave Tibet'. Hastily, but too late, the Chinese dissolved the 'Mimang' groups, which after being banned also by the Dalai Lama, went rapidly underground.

On two occasions members of the Mimang had slipped into

India to send petitions for help to the United Nations (petitions which, it is sad to record, went unanswered). Many of the members of the Mimang were imprisoned by the Chinese, suffering torture and death within Lhasa itself, without any of the ministers so much as raising a hand to prevent it. Worse still, the Dalai Lama and the Tibetan cabinet agreed in 1957 not only that the Mimang should be outlawed but also that all important Tibetans in exile, and those in Tibet suspected of anti-Chinese activities, be deprived of Tibetan nationality by official decree. Thus the Dalai Lama was persuaded to deprive his two brothers (Gyalo Thondup and Thubten Norbu) publicly of their nationality.

In his memoirs the Dalai Lama calls his decision to go along with China's request to brand his brothers as traitors to Tibet, and to call all Khambas 'reactionaries', a 'harmless acceptance of trivial Chinese demands' which he agreed to carry out because they caused no one any real 'inconvenience'. Alas, little did the Dalai Lama understand how valuable it was for the Chinese to be able to demonstrate to Tibet (and the world) that he, the God King, was backing Peking.

One after the other these blows hit the Khambas, and eventually in 1957 they realized that to succeed they must force the sanctuary of the Dalai Lama, if necessary with arms, weed out the Chinese sympathizers in Lhasa and take the God King under their control before leading the Tibetan people in a general revolt.

To oppose the Dalai Lama and his cabinet was a bold and dangerous plan, yet this was the only possible course if the Khambas were ever to free the Tibetan world; for at all costs, and by all means, they must have the Dalai Lama's support.

This was the Khambas' ultimate motive when, in 1957, they began infiltrating the richest province of central Tibet, Loka, the region stretching along the Brahmaputra south-east of Lhasa, an area known also as the 'granary of Tibet'.

By then massive aerial bombings of some three hundred towns and monasteries of Kham and Amdo had at last united all eastern Tibetan guerrillas and led the 'rebels' to organize themselves in a more military fashion. From the stray bands which had originally taken to the hills the guerrillas had grown into well-armed and efficient fighting units. Those whom the Chinese described as 'reactionary rebels of Sikang, Amdo and

Chamdo', and all Tibetans simply called the 'Khambas', were now the N.V.D.A., the National Volunteer Defence Army, known also as the *Ten Dzong Ma Mi*, 'the soldiers of the fortress of faith', a well-organized army of considerable proportions.[1]

It is difficult for the casual Western observer to understand how the Khambas could survive and prove so active, out-numbered as they were by the well-armed and trained Chinese People's Liberation Army. The Khambas' success in crippling the Chinese, and their ability to operate against such incredible odds can only be explained by taking proper account of their chief advantages: Tibet's size and incredibly rugged terrain.

However well-armed and numerous the Chinese might be, in Tibet they were far from being invincible. Only three roads cut across the inhospitable wilds of greater Tibet, three roads serving a territory as large as most of Europe. Because of the terrain, the Chinese were entirely dependent on these strategic highways along which their garrisons and outposts were scattered, fragile footholds difficult to supply and maintain. These garrisons were manned by soldiers physically incapable of wandering out into the surrounding country where the altitude ranged between 14,000 and 16,000 feet, forbidding any violent exercise, even after acclimatization. To walk a mile at such heights is an exhausting task; as for travelling ten miles, and fighting in the process, this was a feat beyond the capacity of most of the Chinese born in lower lands and more docile climes. Since the outbreak of the Khamba revolt, constant attacks and Khamba-provoked landslides very rapidly closed to all traffic the Kanting-Chamdo-Lhasa highway, the most direct link of the Chinese occupation force with their home bases. This greatly hampered the Chinese, whose garrisons were further isolated by the frequent attacks upon the alternative road across Amdo.

As a result, even after seven years of occupation, the invaders controlled, in fact, only small tracts of Tibet, garrisons sur-rounded by rugged peaks stretching out like a cruel sea over areas in which the Chinese rarely dared to venture.

Over ninety per cent of Tibet's vast expanse the Khambas

---

[1] The rebels were also known under the name of *Chu-shi khang-druk* ('four rivers six mountains') one of Tibet's ancient names from the days of Songtsen Gampo.

could circulate freely, with little to fear apart from air raids. And although the Chinese could pick a monastery at random and reduce it to a rubble, this was a quite inefficient means of destroying mounted men who were always on the move and could scatter at an instant's notice or seek shelter in caves, becoming impossible targets for fast-moving aircraft.

The Chinese air raids were only effective when directed upon large towns, such as Litang and Batang, where raids could be made to synchronize with infantry advances along the roads.

As well as the assets of Tibet's terrain and high altitude, the Khambas further benefited from their own long warrior tradition. To them, fighting was as natural as eating. They needed no training to become efficient guerrillas. Excellent horsemen, they also possessed the mobility so essential to guerrilla warfare. Not only were the loneliest trails their natural home, but they could also survive for months on the most barren steppes, drinking mares' milk and shooting gazelles, unhampered by problems of supply which plagued the Chinese.

The Chinese soon realized that they could never defeat the Khamba guerrillas by normal military tactics. In fact they began to wonder if they would ever be able to put down the rebels who, as Anna Louise Strong wrote 'would fight as long as they were given food', which in Tibet could well have meant for ever. This fact the Dalai Lama himself eventually understood when he wrote in 1962: 'In those impregnable mountains the guerrillas could hold out for years, the Chinese could never be able to dislodge them.'

These were some of the advantages which allowed the guerrillas to implement their bold plan of setting out into central Tibet, to extend their crusade into the realm of the Dalai Lama. In so doing they were ready to oppose not only the Chinese, but if necessary the Tibetan government and its troops.

Over the years, each of the large districts of Kham and Amdo had produced their own 'rebel' leaders, valiant commanders whose camps became rallying points for the ever-increasing number of eastern and later western Tibetans determined to give up their lives for their common country. In Chamdo there was Tsering; in Po, the Pangda Tsangs and their lieutenants. There was also Kesang in Litang, the Andrutsangs in Dergue, Nawang in eastern Amdo, Chime

Yudong and his father (before his assassination) in Jeykundo, Lobsang Yeshe in Changtreng, and Urgyen in Kongpo, alongside whom there also rose to power and influence such men as Kunga Samten, Thempa Thargyel, Amdo Leshe, Dawa Gyatsen and many others whose names are yet to be recorded. Each of these men also controlled a score of smaller units led by tribal chiefs, such as the old 'gap' of the Chengtu nomads.

There are still no accurate records, but it has been estimated that in 1957 there were over eighty thousand well-organized guerrillas in the N.V.D.A.; that is to say eighty thousand men constantly under arms and organized in a military fashion. To this number should be added perhaps ten thousand less well organized and equipped 'rebels', warriors and brigands determined to oppose the Chinese in any possible manner.

Despite the dispersal of the guerrillas and their lack of a single unified command, men such as Amdo Leshe and Kunga Samten soon became famous in their self-appointed roles as high commanders of the guerrillas.

Such was the force that, at the end of 1957, set out to conquer the heavily wooded yet fertile district of Loka, a vast territory south of the Brahmaputra, east of Lhasa, dotted with rugged fortresses, the 'dzongs' of central Tibet's momentous feudal past.

Osher was a member of one of the first guerrilla units to move into Loka. Since the siege of Litang he had been a member of the best organized and equipped unit in Kham, commanded by Amdo Leshe. In liaison with Formosa, Leshe's men had been among the first to receive air drops of American weapons and a radio transmitter. Ammunition was the only serious problem for Osher and his companions, a problem all knew would be partially solved once they controlled the province of Loka, whence innumerable trails led to Bhutan and the North East Frontier Agency of India, borders over which ammunition could be secretly shipped without too much trouble, forwarded by Khamba agents in Kalimpong.

After the siege of Litang, Osher's life took on the pattern which it was to follow for nearly eight years, until his death: the rugged life of a feudal soldier caught in a merciless war in which neither side took prisoners. It was a life unlike anything the soldiers of our more sophisticated armies are likely to experience, allying the rigours of Tibet's climate with the harsh discipline of the self-appointed, intransigent Khamba commanders.

Being very young, Osher suffered a good deal at first from the cool arrogance of his leaders, men hardened to war who ruled their camps with a stern hand. Rank among the Khambas was all-important. The Pombos, as the commanders were called, could only be approached with humble respect. Discipline was based on respect and the strict, unwritten code of tribal obedience. All soldiers were under solemn oath never to reveal their actions to anyone, even under torture. Insubordination was practically unknown in the *magars*, as the Khamba camps were called. When not on the run, the Khambas set up these camps in or beside lonely monasteries or villages dominating strategic trails, the yak wool tents erected over rectangular, coffin-like hearths of clay, upon which whole calves would be roasted at night or smoked for days to make the leather-hard dried meat on which one could chew for months while out in the open.

Ever since the outbreak of the war Osher had lived continually in the saddle, raiding, besieging, running and hiding. With a few men of his clan and soldiers from Po Dzong his unit soon formed a deadly instrument of war.

He had not been to his native district or heard of his old parents since December 1955, until he encountered Nyma, a girl who had been dragged into his camp to join the dozen women who followed the 'rebels', cooking, and also, it must be said, often yielding to prostitution, driven by the desperation of war.

Osher recognized Nyma as a girl he had known since childhood. From her he learned of the fate of his tribe: a Chinese guerrilla patrol had come to the plains in an operation to 'weed out reactionaries'. The old men of Osher's clan had fired at them and there had followed the useless massacre of many unarmed women and children. In the end the survivors had been led off towards the east. Nyma had escaped. That was all she knew. Never again was Osher to hear of his family. Until his death he was left to speculate whether they had died in Kham or struggled in deportation.

Anxious uncertainty was to be the lot of nearly all the Khamba soldiers. They could never hope to discover the fate of the parents, wives and children they had left behind. The lack of family names in Tibet and the absence of any form of civil records, or of any kind of address, made the fate of thousands the object of incessant painful speculation.

Although hardened to war and fearless of death, Osher was not immune to pain. The fate of his family burnt deep in his heart, as did the memory of his best friend, whom he had seen die in great agony at Litang from a bullet wound in the stomach. Like all Khambas, Osher's courage was bolstered by his faith in the holy charm he wore around his neck, a Bon charm 'more powerful' than those of the Buddhists, and which he believed would save him from violent death. The guerrillas spent fortunes on purchasing silver and gold boxes in which to carry their relics, whose mysterious emanations it was believed could deflect bullets. These relics were, for the Khambas, what the cross was for the crusaders, mementoes of their faith, symbols of their cause and reminders that even in face of death the just always triumph. It was with relic in hand that the guerrillas of Kham galloped into battle.

As well as their holy charms, the warriors of Kham also enjoyed the priceless asset of their remarkable horses, the secret weapons of Ghengiz Khan and of Songtsen Gampo's warriors, the powerful horses from Amdo with 'bones' from Sining: mares and stallions as tough as bulls and nimble as goats, tested daily by the men for their worth in races and bouts, the traditional pastime of Kham. These soldiers would pay thousands of silver dollars for their horses, for a warrior, as all knew, was worth 'little more than his steed'. Horse and rider were one, both wedded to the blade, and aided by ferocious Tibetan mastiffs, great burly dogs trained by the brigands for generations to kill – dogs that could knock any man from his saddle in one leap and tear open his throat.

The guerrillas wore no uniform other than the characteristic *chuba* of Tibet, draped Khamba-style, longer and lower than in Lhasa, with two pleats in the back instead of three. After 1956 parachute cloth in leopard camouflage was frequently made into high-collared shirts to replace the traditional raw-silk shirts of Kham. These 'sky-boat shirts' soon became the prized uniform of the better-organized Khamba units. In any case to all central Tibetans a Khamba was easily recognizable, not only by his clothes but by his features and his speech, with its slight nasal twang.

While life in Lhasa carried on much as before, and while Betty-la danced the cha cha cha, Osher with the men of his *magar* rode into Loka and the steep but fertile valleys south of the Brahmaputra, a rugged land whose wooded peaks and narrow gorges opened into fertile valleys where wheat grew in abundance, and in which even grapes were not unknown.

It was in the Loka region that the Phagmogru-pa kings, Lhasa's ancient rivals in the thirteenth century, had ruled. They were the first to build the string of forts that, from east to west along the Brahmaputra, raised their bleak battlements upon the jagged crests of impossible ridges, great fortified citadels whose names evoked the battles of days gone by. Over these forts, in 1957, the despised stewards still ruled for the Lhasean nobles who rarely visited their rich yet distant estates, from which they collected annually the subsidies necessary for them to maintain the standards of city living required by their rank.

The Chinese, on first coming to Tibet, had established garrisons in Loka in or around some of the region's great forts, and along the rough road which ran south of Lhasa, deep into Loka's forests, which the Chinese began exploiting for the timber so badly needed for building in the treeless areas around Lhasa.

In bold dashes and hazardous sieges the Khambas now successively stormed and conquered the Chinese strongholds of Gya-la Dzong and Guru Nakye Dzong along the Brahmaputra, before attacking the Chinese lumber road and wiping out the garrisons of Lhobu Dzong and those of the great forts of Towa and Lhuntse which controlled the precious strategic trails leading to Bhutan and India.

Incredible as it may seem, by the middle of 1958 the Khambas had made themselves absolute masters of all southeast Tibet. In Towa Dzong, behind the massive walls of the fort, Amdo Leshe (Osher's commander) set up his headquarters, from which his men controlled the richest province of Tibet and the precious trails running south, through narrow defiles and over high passes, across the four hundred miles of the border of Tibet with Bhutan and India's North East Frontier Agency.

In Towa Dzong Osher heard of the continuing fighting in Kham. There, despite the bombing raids and severe Chinese repression, the guerrillas had successfully resisted all Chinese attempts to reopen the two branches of the Szechwan-Chamdo highway.

All over Tibet the guerrillas were so active that the Chinese were obliged to ask President Nehru to postpone his visit to Tibet planned for 1958. Unfortunately this loss of face, proof that the Chinese barely controlled Tibet, passed unnoticed by the outside world.

The Chinese soon had to admit that their first offensive (of 1956) to check the 'rebellion' had been a failure. Neither propaganda nor jet bombers had been able to intimidate the men determined to free Tibet. As a result, in the corridors of the Central Administration in Peking the rulers of China were now searching nervously for excuses to explain the facts that nobody was willing to admit: the total failure of Mao's ambitions in Tibet.

Ever since Chou En-lai's declaration in 1956 that it would take fifty years to make Tibet communist, and Mao's official admission in 1957 that 'errors' had been made in Tibet, further 'confessions' of high party members told increasingly of the grave concern of the Chinese Central Government.

In a speech to the State Council, the commander-in-chief of the 'Tibetan Region of China' announced that 'difficulties had been encountered, that there have been grave misunderstandings in Tibet'.

This confession was further backed by a declaration of the Chairman of the communist-controlled Chinese Buddhist Agency at the National People's Congress in Peking, who declared outright that '*rebellions* in Eastern Tibet were a result of local dissatisfaction with communist policies'. Later, in December 1957, Fan Ming, the secretary of the Communist Party's Tibet Work Committee went as far as to declare that the cause of the apparently inexplicable rebellion of the Khambas was 'Great Han Chauvinism in Tibet manifested in the feeling of superiority of the Han [Chinese] race, and its repugnance for the backwardness of Tibet'.

This public proof should have enlightened the West about the Tibetan crisis but, out in the lowlands beyond the great peaks, nobody cared. Thanks to the active propaganda of Nehru, the world had been persuaded after the Sino-Indian Treaty of 1954 (although there was no legal justification for such a claim) that 'Tibet was an integral part of China'.

The Chinese failure to put down the rebellion in Kham, followed by the victorious advance of the guerrillas into Loka and their infiltration throughout central Tibet, obliged the communists, in 1958, to revise their attitude towards the Khamba uprising. General Chang Ching-wu, the commander-in-chief of the Tibetan military district, was recalled to Peking and a fresh offensive carefully prepared.

The basis of this new campaign to 'weed out reactionaries' was the further exploitation of the traditional mistrust by central Tibetans of the Khambas. The Chinese sought now by every possible means to revive the old spectre of Khambas as bandits and looters and potential rivals of Lhasean sovereignty.

For the third time the Chinese pressed the Dalai Lama to send Tibetan troops against the rebels. They had realized at last that only Tibetan soldiers could be effective in the mountainous regions where the Khambas were hiding. This time at last the Dalai Lama flatly refused, pointing out that Tibetan troops would most probably join forces with the rebels, just as the members of the earlier peace mission had done. However the Dalai Lama did agree to issue a new proclamation calling on all Khambas to lay down their arms and return to Kham, stating that they would suffer no reprisals from the Chinese if they did so. Needless to say, the Khambas laughed at his request, remaining all the more determined to seize the Tibetan cabinet and put a stop to its apparent collusion with the Chinese.

From 1958 onwards, with a view to further discrediting the Khambas, the dispatches of the New China News Agency published in Tibet and the world at large stories of alleged rape and murder, thefts and plunder committed by the 'rebels'. Among other crimes the Khambas were accused of desecrating monasteries and raping nuns. The better to implement this campaign, Chinese soldiers dressed as Khambas were sent into villages to steal horses and loot. In consequence, when the Khambas caught some of these disguised Chinese agents (who were immediately shot), it was decided that greater control must be established over the different guerrilla units: for the future all Khambas requisitioning animals and food were to present official documents, signed by their commanders.

When, by July 1958, the Chinese realized that their new

offensive had failed, orders were given that all Khambas found in central Tibet were to be arrested. Accordingly even people wearing Khamba clothes were jailed, or sometimes shot at. Although this extreme measure was never carried out within Lhasa, special agents of the Chinese secret police were sent to the capital to hunt down the rebel leaders. The army also began registering the names and family histories of all Khamba refugees in Lhasa. Fearing that this was a prelude to reprisals, hundreds of refugees began to leave the holy city, heading south for Loka. Yet all those who left Lhasa were soon replaced by ever more refugees coming in from the east with tales of how they had been shot at from the air by spotter planes as they made their slow and perilous journey towards the fragile shelter of the holy city. Many of the columns of refugees, weary from months on the road, were attacked just before they reached Lhasa by Chinese patrols sent out to 'greet them' some seventy miles from the holy city along the old trade routes.

Such repressive measures had, as one might expect, exactly the opposite effect from that hoped for by the Chinese. Increasingly the central Tibetans joined hands with the Khambas, and thousands flocked to their camps in Loka ready to fight. Nearly everywhere in central Tibet the Khambas found aid and refuge. In Lhasa itself, Mary-la, Betty-la's mother, as a leading member of the Chinese-approved Tibetan Women's Association, dared to organize relief for the women of Khamba guerrillas stranded in the holy city – a bold move which considerably angered the Chinese commanders who personally threatened the 'ladies' of Lhasa for their sympathies with those whom the Dalai Lama had officially branded 'reactionaries'.

In the east Chinese fury was also reaching a climax. From Amdo and Kham truckloads of children were being deported to China. According to one witness from Jeba, a village near Batang, forty-eight babies 'were taken to China in order, the Chinese said, that their parents would do more work'. When the parents tried to prevent it, soldiers went into the houses to take the children from their mothers by force. According to the same witness, 'Fifteen parents who protested were thrown into the river by the Chinese, and one committed suicide.' In Amdo, peasants were also bereft of their new-born infants and told that it was 'an order of Mao Tse-tung, and that the penalty for refusing was execution'. In all it was later calculated that fifteen thousand were taken out of Tibet, either by force or on pretence of educating them. To this day the fate of the majority of these children is unknown.[1]

Because of such actions, ever more women and old people fled from those areas of Kham which were controlled by the Chinese. By the end of 1958 over fifteen thousand families had set up their tents around the market of Lhasa, at the foot of the Potala and in the suburbs on the flat plain of the Kyi River, while thousands of young monks found an uncertain refuge in the 'regional' colleges of the great monasteries of Drepung, Sera and Gaden, reserved for visiting monks from the eastern provinces.

Even in Lhasa the refugees were no longer safe, since all Khamba men were hunted down by the Chinese secret police. They lived in perpetual terror, struggling for survival, begging or living off friends, as happened to Tsering's wife and his four children. Because the Tibetan government refused to give the refugees any assurances of protection, all were prepared, at a moment's notice, to flee south to Loka.

In spite of all this, by December 1958 Khamba guerrillas had begun infiltrating slowly into the holy city and after this sporadic gunfire became a nightly occurence. Tension began to rise in Lhasa, where the Chinese army was continually raiding houses suspected of sheltering 'rebels'. By day, the bodies of guerrillas were left exposed in the streets for all to see. Soon the situation became so tense that the Chinese hesitated to leave their garrisons. The Tibetan army was asked to police the city and the Chinese commander made the Lhasean officials responsible for ridding the city of 'subversive Khamba elements'.

In the last months of 1958 Khamba leaders approached members of the Tibetan cabinet continually, urging them to stand up at last in defence of their common cause. These delegations returned disappointed with counsels of 'patience' and orders to 'return to Kham and make peace with the Chinese'. In the end the Lhaseans and the Dalai Lama's administration overstepped the limits of reason and the Khambas' patience wore out. In December the guerrillas attacked a Chinese garrison of a thousand men, only twenty-five miles from the holy city.

[1] The report of the International Commission of Jurists lists 72 statements on the deportation of children to China.

In January, in the middle of all this agitation, Betty-la and her husband decided to go down to Kalimpong for a 'shopping trip and a little holiday'[1]. This decision is an index of the state of mind of certain Lhasean aristocrats during this tense period. Tsarong warned that matters would soon reach a crisis, but Betty-la's husband simply laughed at his advice. They would soon be back, he said. Betty-la promised to bring back toys from Calcutta for the children, and everyone waved happily as the jeep drove off. Betty-la remembers her smallest child (two years old) toddling behind the jeep, calling 'ama-ama'. It was not a sad departure. Betty-la was thinking of Calcutta's racetrack, of Kalimpong and its bazaar and the wonderful villa, Tashiding, with its bathrooms and British comfort. She also longed to see her Sikkimese cousins again and Tesla, the beautiful wife of the brilliant Prime Minister of Bhutan. It would, she thought, be a pleasant change from the tense life in Lhasa.

'Perhaps we should have brought the children,' she thought, as she and her husband sped down the strategic road that now linked Tibet with the Chumbi valley and Sikkim – so convenient for those aristocrats who now had jeeps to drive along the wonderful roads of the Chinese invaders!

Barely a week later two thousand Khamba guerrillas attacked the three thousand men of the garrison of Tsetang, the largest Chinese outpost on the south banks of the Brahmaputra, just thirty miles from Lhasa. After six hours of heavy fighting, the Khambas broke into the garrison; the Chinese scattered, most to be mowed down, others to be caught by patrolling horsemen who ran them to the ground or rushed them to a watery death in the turbulent Brahmaputra.

The Khambas now controlled access to Lhasa from the south-east and were solidly entrenched only one day's hard ride from the capital. The hour for revenge had struck.

---

[1] Betty-la's husband was officially going to India to buy tents for a pilgrimage the Dalai Lama was about to undertake in west Tibet.

9

The Chinese Theatre

The cavaliers of Kham were now ready to enter the holy epicentre of the Tibetan universe to compel the Dalai Lama, his cabinet and aides, his nobles and people, to stand up and oppose the Chinese openly and side with the cause of Tibetan survival, a cause to which the cabinet had been blinded by nine years of acquiescence to Chinese rule.

Secret emissaries from the holy city began to make their way into the Khamba camps to report that certain Lhasean nobles were sympathetic to the Khamba cause. How sincere were those who changed their minds at the last minute in this way, no one will ever know. Later, as refugees, all the Lhaseans shouted aloud their will to resist China, forgetting how for years they had opposed the rebellion of the warrior tribes.

Recently, in exile, Surkhang, the prime minister of the Tibetan cabinet, has been quoted as claiming (giving little or no credit to the leaders of the Khamba revolt) that he had been arranging all the time in Lhasa for certain arsenals to be made secretly available to the Khambas; but this claim is hardly borne out by the fact that the Khambas placed him under arrest as soon as they entered Lhasa.

Apart from the leaders of the Mimang, who came to place their own clandestine operations at the disposal of the Khambas, it would be fair to say that the majority of the influential personalities of Lhasa were jealous of the Khambas and afraid of losing to them their personal power and prestige. They preferred, along with the traitorous minister Ngabo, a certain collusion with the Chinese, who had so cunningly maintained them in a place of privilege that they could never have hoped to keep under a free Tibet led by the rugged warriors from the east.

The Khambas now fully appreciated that there was little or no chance of the Dalai Lama's ever standing up to the Chinese and preaching the general Tibetan uprising they longed for. As for the ten thousand soldiers of the Tibetan army, the Khambas knew that they too would never mutiny against their Chinese officers unless obliged to do so by the Khambas themselves. There was, it seemed, between Lhasa and the Khambas a basic incompatibility based on past history; yet however great the traditional mistrust of the Lhaseans for the Khambas, this could never justify the actions of those who, to the end, worked with the Chinese to oppose and hinder the justified cause of Tibetan independence. Hugh Richardson, although personally inclined to favour the Lhasean aristocracy he knew so well, wrote quite justly that

> If there had been trust and co-operation between the Eastern Tibetan leaders and the Lhasa Government from the start, the difficulties of the Chinese would have been many times greater. But the two were incompatible. For many centuries the policy of Lhasa had been to yield to force when it appeared irresistible and to look to time and patience to bring their reward. The Khambas' nature was quite the opposite. And so although there was some ground for their [Khamba] criticism of Lhasa officials as timorous and selfish it would be unreasonable to expect those officials to give unstinted cordiality and confidence to persons who had recently been plotting their overthrow.

During January 1959 more and more guerrillas filtered into Lhasa, many going about fully armed in broad daylight, swaggering through the streets for all to see.

By the beginning of February, preparations in Lhasa began for the Tibetan New Year. A New Year laden with evil signs and omens and which saw in Lhasa itself, guerrillas roaming the streets in defiance of the Chinese and in defiance of the God King's cabinet.

The impending crisis was now inevitable. Three distinct forces were thrown together that spring in the dusty streets of Lhasa, whose mighty temples and great palaces fluttered with countless prayer flags beating in a wind of change.

The first was the guerrillas, the men who for more than five years had been waging war against the Chinese in the name of Tibetan independence.

The second force was the Dalai Lama and his cabinet of six ministers, among whom the well-known Chinese sympathizers

Ngabo and Surten were included, assisted by a court of monks and aristocrats who for nine years had consented (at the expense of the Tibetan masses in the provinces and especially those of Eastern Tibet) to collaborate with the Chinese, to salvage their personal interests and privileges which the Chinese cleverly allowed them to maintain.

Lastly there were the Chinese, heavily garrisoned inside Lhasa and its suburbs and near its airport. They were headed by General Tan, then commander-in-chief in place of General Chang Ching-wu, who was absent in Peking. In the first months of 1959 the Chinese, having been hard pressed by the guerrillas, were afraid of the impending general revolt, which they had so far forestalled by their extremely capable manipulation of the Dalai Lama. They were firmly and quite rightly convinced that the Dalai Lama was their greatest asset and tool in maintaining their control over Tibet. They proved this by their behaviour towards the young God King in the coming days.

What happened in Lhasa between 16 February and 25 March was one of the strangest and most ill-understood coups of recent times. On 16 February, after the Khamba success in seizing the three-thousand-strong garrison of Tsetang, the rebels made their last official appeal to the Dalai Lama, giving him as it were his last chance to side with them. This plea was voiced by Chume Yudong, the much-venerated and respected incarnate Lama of Jeykundo. Noel Barber, whose book[1] on the Lhasean revolt is beyond doubt the most descriptive to date, gives us a detailed account of this appeal gathered from an interview with the Lama of Jeykundo, now living in London.

From his book one learns that the Lama arrived in Lhasa in early February after a harrowing four-month odyssey across the immense wilds separating Jeykundo in southern Amdo from the holy city. In the course of his flight to Lhasa the young Lama and his escort of a thousand armed Khambas had been under frequent attack by the Chinese. First his exhausted caravan was machine-gunned from the air while advancing along a ledge above a precipitous gorge. Many of the party had died in this attack, in which the Khambas succeeded in shooting down one of the Chinese planes. All were suffering from exhaustion when, just before they reached Lhasa, a detachment of Chinese fell upon them. In all, half the Lama's weary escort

[1] *The Land of Lost Content*

died before reaching the city, where the New Year celebrations were about to begin.

Once in Lhasa he was hunted by the Chinese as he made contact with rebel leaders in and around the city and awaited a personal interview with the Dalai Lama in which he was to try to secure official Tibetan support against the Chinese.

In the course of this interview, granted on 16 February, the Lama of Jeykundo calmly placed before the Dalai Lama an account of the atrocities committed by the Chinese on his people: how monasteries were still being bombed, peasants murdered and tortured and children deported. He then pleaded with the Dalai Lama to order the Tibetan army be sent into Kham to defend its inhabitants. This he flatly refused to do; whereupon the Khamba Lama asked the Dalai Lama to send at least a formal note of protest to the Chinese. But even this request the Dalai Lama turned down. Deeply upset by the Dalai Lama's apparent indifference, the Lama of Jeykundo dared tell the young God King 'that he did not think the Tibetan cabinet ministers realized just what the Chinese were doing to the Khambas and Amdowans'. But, as the Dalai Lama later confirmed in his memoirs, he and his cabinet knew full well all that was happening. Indeed, how could he have been unaware of the truth? He had been informed of it, officially, time and again since 1956 by Khamba dignitaries, and even through his own mother, whose servants were all Khambas and Amdowans.

His only reaction to the Lama of Jeykundo's requests was a promise to 'take the matter up with the Chinese generals in Lhasa', although when pressed he refused to give a definite date as to when he would do so. The infuriated Khamba Lama recalled later: 'I had the distinct impression that he [the Dalai Lama] did not want to go [and lodge a protest].' The Dalai Lama then repeated his declaration that he was against violence at any cost and asked the Lama and his followers, along with all Khambas, to return to their homes and make peace with the Chinese.

Exasperated by such an impossible and heartless request the young Lama told the Dalai Lama boldly: 'I would not be true to my people if I did not tell Your Holiness that many feel that the central government does not care what happens to them.'

Still, according to Noel Barber, 'Chime (the young Lama)

had the curious sensation that while the Dalai Lama secretly admired the Khambas in many ways, he might also be thinking that if there were no Khambas in Tibet, the task of working with the Chinese might be much easier.' His arguments exhausted, the Khamba Lama then said, 'But Your Holiness – you cannot expect my people to do nothing while the Chinese kill our women and children and plunder our monasteries.'

To this statement the Dalai Lama, apparently forgetting that he had been born in Amdo and that Kham had been, until the Chinese invasion, an integral part of his realm, answered, 'There is nothing I can do, I think your people (Khamba and Amdowan) should show a little more tolerance and try to abide by the seventeen-point agreement.' He then added: 'I may admire the bravery of the Khambas, but their actions do a great harm to those of us who are *trying to find a way of living with the Chinese.*'

This interview was to be the Khambas' final appeal to the young God King of Tibet. His total failure to back those fighting for Tibetan independence, along with his lack of comprehension of the situation, eliminated any scruples which might have remained in the minds of the N.V.D.A. about their decision to take the government of Tibet into their own hands. Certain that the Dalai Lama had been brainwashed by his traitorous ministers and by the Chinese, the Khamba leaders decided that the time had come for them to act.

Pity rather than anger is the proper reaction to the figure of the twenty-four-years-old peasant from Amdo who as a child had been made the God and King of Tibet. It is impossible not to pity him when we know that in those tragic weeks of March 1959, the most important of Tibetan history, he was, by his own published account, preoccupied above all by the religious exams he was about to take for his degree in metaphysics. He pursued his studies patiently, oblivious of the tragedy befalling his people, and apparently indifferent to the suffering of thousands of his charges, engaged in a war whose battles were being fought at the very gates of his capital where he was so studiously at work.

His Holiness was now to be carried away by the speed of events. The Khambas were determined to seize power. The stage was set. All that remained to be determined was how and when they would take control.

The opportunity was not long in coming. What later came to be called the affair of the 'Chinese Theatrical Performance' was already under way. Like every great crisis, that of Lhasa was triggered off by a trivial incident: an invitation from the Chinese for the Dalai Lama to attend a theatre performance at their headquarters of Yutok in Lhasa.

The affair began with an announcement by Radio Peking at the beginning of February that the Dalai Lama was to attend the National People's Congress in China. This news was greeted with surprise in Tibet, since the Dalai Lama had not yet formally accepted the invitation. It seriously alarmed most Khambas, who well knew that if the Dalai Lama went to China now he might be used for propaganda and become a Chinese hostage, as in 1954. This would be a serious handicap to their planned general rebellion in Tibet.

On 1 March, after this disturbing announcement, the Chinese sent two envoys to approach the Dalai Lama directly and ask the young God King to fix a date on which it would be convenient for him to attend the theatrical performance they had been planning in their headquarters in Lhasa. Although there was nothing remarkable in the Dalai Lama's being asked to attend such a function, which he had done before, the breach of protocol in addressing the God King directly was somewhat unusual.

On 7 March the date was fixed by the Dalai Lama himself in a telephone call for 10 March. On the morning of 9 March, Kusung Depon, the commander of the Dalai Lama's personal bodyguard, was called to the Chinese camp and informed that there was to be none of the usual ceremony attendant on the Dalai Lama's formal displacements. In other words, no soldiers or escort were to accompany the Dalai Lama beyond the stone bridge that led to the Chinese headquarters, with the possible exception of two or three unarmed members of his bodyguard. (The Dalai Lama's usual escort comprised twenty-five armed men.) When asked the reason for this, the Chinese spokesman, Brigadier Fu, told the commander of the bodyguard, 'Will you be responsible if someone pulls the trigger?' Why this strange remark – what could it mean? This remark, along with the new breach in protocol, was judged highly suspicious by Kusung Depon, and later by the Dalai Lama and the members of his cabinet. On the other hand it can be argued that in view of the existing tension in Lhasa, a formal visit by the Dalai Lama to the Chinese camp, accompanied by too much pomp and ceremony in a town full of trigger-happy Khambas averse to his apparent Chinese leanings could and probably would lead to unpleasant incidents. It is also quite possible that the Chinese may have feared a Khamba plot to abduct the Dalai Lama and place him and his ministers in a position where he could no longer continue to try to work out a compromise with the Chinese at the Khambas' expense. However, the affair became more suspicious when the commander of the Dalai Lama's bodyguard was asked to keep the whole matter 'strictly secret'.

However, although the Dalai Lama felt that this invitation, for which he himself had fixed the date, was quite unorthodox he agreed to go. To avoid the possibility of trouble and to acquiesce in the Chinese wish for 'discretion' the Dalai Lama asked the Tibetan police to announce that the following day's route to the Chinese camp beyond the stone bridge would be closed to traffic.

This public announcement, and the news that leaked out about the unusual Chinese invitation, sparked off the sequence of events which was eventually to set alight the already tense situation. The news that the Dalai Lama was to go to the Chinese camp in such unusual circumstances, coupled with the premature announcement about his departure for the People's Congress in Peking in April, was enough to set in motion a rumour that the theatrical show was a trap and that the Dalai Lama was about to be abducted. The Chinese had laid many similar traps for high influential figures in Kham, not to mention the one for the leaders of Chamdo in which Tsering had been caught at Jomdho Dzong.

As a result, on the evening of 9 March in the already tense city, crowds set out for the Dalai Lama's summer residence determined to prevent him from going to the Chinese camp. Among them, fully armed, were many hundreds of Khambas sent with orders from their commanders to stand by 'just in case'.

In a matter of hours ten thousand excited people had surrounded the outer of the two walls enclosing the various palaces, shrines and buildings of the Norbulinka, the Dalai Lama's summer residence four miles south of Lhasa, to which the Dalai Lama and his ministers had moved from the Potala Palace on 5 March.

Simultaneously, on 9 March the nervous Lhaseans laid siege to the Nepalese, Indian and Bhutanese consulates in a state of panic, calling on the consuls to cable their governments for help, and warning them of impending trouble. Indeed, to those Lhaseans who knew of the nightly shooting within the city it was clear that the inevitable crisis had come.

Meanwhile the general fuss raised over the theatre incident and the 'abduction scare' suddenly appeared to the Khambas as the best possible occasion for forcing the Dalai Lama and his ministers into open opposition to the Chinese. Consequently the Khambas took over leadership of the excited crowd of people who were surrounding the Norbulinka in ever-increasing numbers.

Inside the summer palace the minister Luishar and other court officials, including the chamberlain Phala, were endeavouring to persuade the Dalai Lama to appease the crowds by cancelling his visit. But he, reluctant to offend the Chinese, insisted on going. As for Ngabo, he had in the meantime gone to the Chinese camp, which he refused to leave when the Dalai Lama summoned him.

Why was Ngabo 'hiding', as it were, in the Chinese camp? This question has been answered by most historians of the crisis, with the hypothesis that he was one of the principal instigators of the so-called Chinese plot to abduct the Dalai Lama. The most probable reason for Ngabo's remaining in the Chinese compound was it seems that he had in Lhasa (and especially in the crowds surrounding the Dalai Lama's palace) thousands of heavily armed personal enemies: all those Khambas he had betrayed in Chamdo, who had heard him sing, and possibly teach the Dalai Lama to sing, China's tune for nine years. Ngabo the proud, arrogant aristocrat who had fled from Chamdo in disguise, who had capitulated and had blown up the Chamdo arsenal, had no friends in the milling, excited crowds through which he would have to pass to reach the summer palace – crowds which that same night manhandled two Chinese soldiers who went there to give the Dalai Lama and his ministers their 'invitation tickets'.

On the following day, 10 March, the crowds around the summer palace had grown considerably. Ever since dawn thousands more idle Lhaseans and as many armed Khambas had been marching over to the summer palace and crowding outside its main gate shouting the usual slogans: 'Chinese go home', 'Tibet for the Tibetans'. The crowd made it clear that it would not allow the Dalai Lama to go to the Chinese camp, even if this mean detaining him by force.

When at 9 a.m. a jeep drove through the crowds with Samdrup Phodrang, one of the Dalai Lama's ministers known to harbour Chinese sympathies, the mob rushed the jeep, overturned it, stoned the driver and knocked the minister unconscious. Samdrup Phodrang's life was only saved when he was hastily dragged into the palace gardens by one of the Dalai Lama's guards.

Surkhang, the Prime Minister, left his jeep and walked cautiously through the crowd into the summer palace from where by telephone he again called in vain on Ngabo to leave the Chinese camp and join him at the summer palace. This Ngabo, being no fool, steadfastly refused to do, as he would surely have met a violent death.

At 11 a.m. the Dalai Lama informed the Chinese commanders by telephone that 'regretfully, because of the crowds, he could not come to the theatrical performance'. This was true, because by then the Dalai Lama, along with four of his ministers (all except Ngabo and the unconscious minister Samdrup Phodrang, who had been rushed to the Indian hospital), was indeed virtually a prisoner of the crowd (led by Khambas) surrounding his palace.

An hour later, leaving the Chinese compound dressed in a Chinese jacket and wearing goggles and a dust mask, a high-ranking monk and good friend of the Dalai Lama took a bicycle and tried to make his way to the summer palace through the crowd. When he reached the main gates of the palace a Khamba ripped off his mask and someone recognized him as Phakpa, well-known for his pro-Chinese sympathies, and shouted that he was a traitor. At that moment the monk drew a pistol. Some claimed absurdly that he had been sent to assassinate the Dalai Lama. Certainly he was armed, being aware of the fate of the stoned minister. However his real reason for carrying a pistol will never be known because before the palace guards could drag him into the shelter of the wall surrounding the summer palace a Khamba grabbed him and stabbed him. He was then stoned to death by the mob.

Violence had begun; open rebellion was now to follow. Phakpa's bloody corpse was dragged by the feet into Lhasa and then set on a horse and paraded about the town. The body was a horrible but clear warning that it was against Tibetan traitors that the Khambas were now acting. It is no coincidence that this first victim was a Tibetan. The crowds of Lhasa were now on the rampage, supporting the Khambas in a mass movement of insubordination. For the Khambas the time had come to seize power from the 'beautiful-mouthed' aristocrats.

Outside the summer palace, the 'rebels' appointed a Freedom Committee of seventy members. A committee composed of Khamba, Amdowan and other 'popular leaders', along with leaders of the outlawed Mimang. (For fear of retaliation against those still in Chinese hands, the names of the members of this committee have not been released.) This Freedom Committee was to be the new government of Tibet, and it immediately made clear its intention of taking over from the cabinet. It ordered a unit of heavily armed Khambas to surround the summer palace and replace the Dalai Lama's bodyguard. In desperation, from a platform behind the outer wall, using loudspeakers, the Dalai Lama's Prime Minister Surkhang tried to make the 'rebels' disperse, only to hear himself jeered at by the crowd that chanted slogans against the Chinese and their sympathizers in the cabinet.

Fear suddenly struck the Dalai Lama and his entourage. The worst had happened: they were no longer the leaders of Tibet. The Dalai Lama understood that he would now have to negotiate directly with the members of the Freedom Committee. As the Dalai Lama puts it, he felt as if he was 'sitting between two volcanoes', the Chinese and his people. Once again, faithful to his long held and ambiguous policy, the Dalai Lama tried to appease both the Chinese and the angry crowd of Khambas and citizens of Lhasa.

To the crowd he promised not to go to the Chinese theatrical performance. This small concession proving unsatisfactory, the Freedom Committee demanded that the Dalai Lama should never again set foot in the Chinese camp. Reluctantly he agreed, yet at the same time he decided to send all his ministers over to the Chinese camp to excuse the crowds' behaviour.

But when the ministers tried to leave, the suspicious Khamba guards would not let them pass, allowing them to go only when they were assured that the ministers were simply going to refuse the theatre invitation. The Freedom Committee was unaware that this had already been done by telephone.

When the ministers were eventually allowed to leave the summer palace, the Khambas searched their car thoroughly, suspecting that the ministers were trying to smuggle the Dalai Lama into the Chinese camp. This minor incident (confirmed by the Dalai Lama) is good proof of the Khambas' contempt for the cabinet and mistrust of the Dalai Lama himself.

Once in the Chinese camp the ministers were openly abused by the Chinese generals who declared that they were helping the Khambas in their rebellion. This the ministers denied, promising the Chinese commander (according to the Dalai Lama) 'that they would do all that was possible to prevent an outbreak of lawlessness among the Khambas or any Tibetans who might be foolish enough to try and provoke a clash of arms with the Chinese occupation force'. Although the Dalai Lama states that 'the Chinese generals would not accept these assurances', this does not seem to be true, because by allowing them to return to the summer palace they showed that to some extent they trusted the ministers.

In the meantime the Tibetan Freedom Committee set out to the foot of the Potala Palace, the historic seat of the Tibetan government, the most famous of all buildings in the Tibetan world. There the Freedom Committee, as masters of Lhasa and the self-appointed government of Tibet, officially repudiated the seventeen-point agreement before a huge crowd of over thirty thousand people. Copies of the agreement were then burnt, an act which was repeated before the Jokhang, the great cathedral of Lhasa, the holiest place in Tibet.

The repudiation of the seventeen-point agreement on the grounds that it had been broken by the Chinese and had been ratified and signed by the hated traitor Ngabo was followed by an official declaration of war against China. The Chinese were ordered to leave Lhasa immediately.

When the Dalai Lama heard of this he was aghast. He felt that the rebels were endangering his life and sabotaging his policy of non-violence and his nine-year-long efforts to co-exist with the Chinese.

Towards 5 o'clock in the evening the Dalai Lama received the following letter, which had been smuggled past the 'rebel' guards. It came from General Tan, the Chinese acting commander-in-chief.

Respected Dalai Lama,
It is very good indeed that you wanted to come to the Military Area Command. You are heartily welcome. But since the intrigues and provocations of the reactionaries [read Khambas, as this was the official term to describe the Khambas, also approved and used by the Dalai Lama] have caused you very great difficulties, it may be advisable that for the time being you do not come.
Salutations and best regards
Tan Kuan-san.

This letter was the first of a secret correspondence between General Tan and the Dalai Lama. The letters were smuggled in and out of the summer palace, it being imperative that the members of the Freedom Committee should not know of their ambiguous contents. These letters, particularly the ones written by the Dalai Lama, are rather disturbing, because they reveal that it was indeed against his will that he was being detained within the summer palace, and that all along apparently the Dalai Lama was opposed to the actions of the Freedom Committee and the citizens of Lhasa.

Later on much fuss was made about these letters when the Chinese published them to prove that the Dalai Lama was abducted from Lhasa by the rebels, and to show that up to the last minute he was opposed to the 'rebellious' Khamba clique.

The Dalai Lama explained later that he wrote these letters to gain time, and to try and prevent bloodshed within Lhasa, and that the letters were mere strategems rather than the expression of his true opinions.

This is no doubt to a certain extent true, especially as regards the last letter, written on 15 March, the day before his departure. On the other hand the very tone of these letters would seem to prove that the Khambas were right in believing, as Stuart Gelder, a British journalist who visited Tibet in 1962, put it, that 'rather than having to fear a planned abduction of the Dalai Lama by the Chinese they [the Khambas] were right to fear that the Dalai Lama might himself go to the

Chinese camp in an attempt to stall the so long awaited uprising of the Tibetans'[1].

Meanwhile, before the Dalai Lama could answer the Chinese commander's first letter, the Khambas and all the population of Lhasa were living the exhilarating hours so many of them had looked forward to. All over the city on 10 March there were loud proclamations of the ultimate crusade, the general uprising of all Tibet against the Chinese.

It had taken six hundred years for the Tibet of Songtsen Gampo to stand up at last as one body, re-united after the factional dissensions of feudalism under the leadership of selfish aristocrats.

Thus the Lhasa rebellion became more than a general opposition to Chinese invasion. Simultaneously, as never before in history, a nation stood up to oppose both feudalism and communism, the two extremes of the political spectrum. It was a double revolution: first, the long overdue revolution against aristocratic privilege and the religious tyranny of the great abbots, and also against the equally dismal tyranny of imperialistic Chinese communism; the Hungarian and the French revolutions combined.

Faced with the spreading revolt of the Khambas, both the Chinese and the Dalai Lama were at a loss what to do. Neither of the two parties wanted the inevitable bloodbath, which would spell out to the world the double failure of Mao's communism in Tibet and of the Dalai Lama's policies of non-violence and co-operation with China.

At 6 p.m. [still on 10 March], to the great joy of the 'rebels' and the people of Lhasa, seventy officials of the Tibetan government and officers of the Dalai Lama's bodyguard met outside the summer palace and decided to endorse the decisions of the Tibetan revolutionary government and side with the Freedom Committee. The officers of the Dalai Lama's bodyguard declared that from then on they would no longer obey their Chinese officers or the Tibetan cabinet. They discarded the Chinese uniforms they had worn for so long and joined the rebels in Tibetan clothes. It was mutiny, at last.

Hearing of this, the Dalai Lama tried to intervene and use his personal authority, as spiritual and temporal leader of Tibet, to prevent the rebellion. But for the first time in the history of

[1] Quoted in Stuart Gelder's book *The Timely Rain*.

Tibet, even the highly respected and much-feared God King was powerless. As the Dalai Lama wrote later of his efforts to intervene, 'Their suspicion of the Chinese was so great that my advice seemed to have no effect on them at all.' It might have been more accurate to say that by then many Tibetans were also suspicious of the Dalai Lama.

If any doubts remained as to the intentions of the rebels, or as to who now ruled Tibet, these were soon cleared away on the next day, 11 March. That day, in open rebellion against the cabinet, the Freedom Committee sent six armed Khambas into the summer palace to place the four ministers there under house arrest. This act is proof of the real nature of the uprising, and also incidentally proof that Surkhang, the prime minister, was not, as he later claimed to be, the 'principal ally' of the 'rebels' within Lhasa.

The Dalai Lama was most upset to learn that the rebels had dared to place his ministers under house arrest, but he explains why they did so very clearsightedly in his biography when he comments that 'presumably they [the rebels] suspected that the Cabinet might make some compromise with the Chinese and so defeat the popular demand that the Chinese should leave Tibet'. Such was indeed the mistrust of the people for their government, a mistrust apparently justified. Even the Dalai Lama himself could no longer be trusted as he was again seeking to defeat his people's rebellion by secretly dispatching that same day the first of his three controversial letters to the Chinese commanders.

This first letter is self-explanatory and justifies the 'rebels'' suspicions as to the Dalai Lama's true intentions. The letter reads:

Dear Commander Political Commissar Tan,
I intended to go to the Military Area Command to see the theatrical performance yesterday, but I was unable to do so, because of obstruction by people, lamas and laymen, who were instigated by a few evil elements and who did not know the facts; this has put me to indescribable shame. I am greatly worried and at a loss at what to do. I was immediately greatly delighted when your letter appeared before me – you do not mind at all.

Reactionary, evil elements are carrying out activities endangering me under the pretext of ensuring my safety. I am taking measures to calm things down. In a few days when the situation has become stable, *I will certainly meet you.* If you have any internal directives for me, please communicate them frankly through this messenger.

The Dalai Lama
written by my own hand

Wasting no time, the mutinous Kusung Regiment opened its arsenals on the morning of the 11th and began distributing arms to the crowds around the summer palace and to those government officials and employees who had mutinied. These now began training inside the outer enclosure of the summer palace. Simultaneously, members of the mutinous regiment, along with Khamba soldiers, were sent out to man the mortars and light artillery on Iron Hill, a steep ridge surmounted by one of Lhasa's medical colleges, which overlooked the summer palace and most of what is known as the Vale of Lhasa on which stood the Potala and the Chinese military depot.

North of Lhasa the rebels also set up barricades, blocking the main road to the airport, where the Chinese had stationed tanks and armoured cars. All over Lhasa alongside the Khamba guerrillas, armed even with axes and picks, the masses prepared to face the Chinese.

General Tan, observing these preparations, promptly sent a second letter to the Dalai Lama:

To Dalai Lama,
The reactionaries have now become so audacious that they have openly and arrogantly engaged in military provocations. They have erected fortifications and posted large numbers of machine guns and armed reactionaries along the national defence highway, thereby very seriously disrupting the security of national defence communications.

On many occasions in the past, we told the Kashag [cabinet] that the People's Liberation Army is in duty bound to defend the country and to ensure the protection of communications related to national defence; it certainly cannot remain indifferent to this serious act of military provocation. The Tibet Military Area Command has sent letters therefore to Surkhang, Neusha Shasu and Phala [members of the cabinet in charge of defence and security, and Phala the Dalai Lama's chamberlain], asking them to tell the reactionaries to remove all fortifications they have set up and to withdraw from the highway immediately. Otherwise they will have to take full responsibility themselves for the evil consequences. I want to inform you of this. Please let me know what your views are at your earliest convenience.

Salutations and best regards

Tan Kuan-san

This letter reached the Dalai Lama shortly after news that two other Tibetan regiments, the Trapshi Regiment and units of the Gyantse Regiment, encamped to the north of Lhasa, had also mutinied.

On receiving this second letter from General Tan the Dalai Lama asked to speak again to the leaders of the Freedom Committee. He pleaded with the rebels to remove the barricades and stop their military activities. Naturally the rebels refused.

The young Dalai Lama was at a loss what to do. Not only was he conscious that his own life was in danger, but he also feared (in his own words) for the lives of the 'innocent unarmed Lhaseans' who might have to suffer for the rebels' actions. Yet the Khambas and Amdowans of the Freedom Committee could hardly have been expected to listen to the Dalai Lama's plea or to sympathize with his concern for the innocent Lhaseans when, just three weeks before, the same Dalai Lama had shown such indifference to the fate of the Khamba and Amdowan women and children who were being killed and tortured in eastern Tibet.

So great was the Khambas' mistrust of the Dalai Lama that now, in addition to the guards holding the ministers under house arrest, they appointed six soldiers to watch over the Dalai Lama. On this last act of insubordination the Dalai Lama writes:

The people became more uncompromising and appointed six commanders among themselves to strengthen the defence of the palace and announced that they would not leave the palace unguarded whatever happened.

This development distressed me very much; I felt it was one more step towards disaster. So I decided to speak to the people's leaders myself. I sent for them and all seventy of them came; and in the presence of the Cabinet and other senior officials I did my best to dissuade them from their actions.

To this plea the leaders of the revolutionary government did not answer directly. Rather than openly insult the young Dalai Lama they withdrew 'quietly' and held a meeting among themselves, after which they informed the Dalai Lama and his cabinet, still kept under 'rebel' surveillance, that they had decided not to heed the Dalai Lama's advice, but to stick to their decision to keep him under their watchful 'protection' in the summer palace and to proclaim again that 'the Chinese must leave Lhasa and Tibet, that now Tibet would handle its own affairs'. According to the Dalai Lama the rebel government then decided to move its assembly of leaders to the hamlet of Sho at the foot of the Potala from where 'they would send reports on their decisions to me and my Cabinet after each meeting'.

In other words the cabinet and the Dalai Lama were told that they had lost their power, that they were to remain under guard in the summer palace and await the orders and decisions of the Freedom Committee. The revolution the Khambas had wanted was now complete. The rebels were now masters of the epicentre of the Tibetan world.

On the pretext of ensuring the Dalai Lama's safety (from presumed abduction by the Chinese) the Khambas had made him and his cabinet their hostages; hostages they planned to keep under arrest and use to foster the general rebellion of all Tibetans.

That the Dalai Lama fully understood this situation may be judged from the second secret letter he sent on 12 March to General Tan:

Dear Comrade Political Officer Tan,
I suppose you have received my letter of yesterday forwarded to you by Ngabo. I have received the letter you sent me this morning. The unlawful activities of the reactionary clique cause me endless worry and sorrow. Yesterday I told the Kashag to order the dissolution of the illegal conference [the Freedom Committee] and the immediate withdrawal of the reactionaries [Khambas] who arrogantly moved into the Norbulinka under the pretext of protecting me. As to the

Khamba soldiers, the men who refused to capitulate.

Khamba soldiers, tall, arrogant and determined.

Well-armed Chinese soldiers capture two Tibetan officers emerging from a blasted house in Lhasa.   (*Chinese official photo*)

Lahu the one-time governor of Chamdo being denounced by a woman witness in a public trial staged by the Chinese after the fall of Lhasa in 1959.   (*Chinese official photo*)

The Dalai Lama and Nehru in India.

incidents of yesterday and the day before, which were brought about under the pretext of ensuring my safety and have seriously estranged relations between the Central Peoples' Government and the local government, I am making every possible effort to deal with them. At eight thirty Peking time this morning a few Tibetan army men suddenly fired several shots near the Chinghai Lhasa Highway. Fortunately, no serious disturbance occurred. I am planning to persuade a few subordinates and give them instructions.

Please communicate to me frankly any instructive opinions you have for me.

The Dalai Lama

It would be hard to find in this letter any form of 'lie' invented to gain time, for in it the Dalai Lama simply states the truth about what he was trying to do to stop the 'arrogant rebels' who opposed his wishes.

Regardless of anything the Dalai Lama may have thought about the rebels' endangering his life, the Khambas were in fact very concerned with the Dalai Lama's safety. While the Chinese with Ngabo were trying to devise some means of getting the Dalai Lama out of the rebels' hands, the rebels were thinking of taking the Dalai Lama out of reach of the Chinese. Whether the Dalai Lama wished to go or not was immaterial to the Khambas. The Dalai Lama had no choice but to obey the Freedom Committee.

It was decided immediately that he was to be taken to the Khambas' stronghold in Loka, the province they fully controlled.

The Dalai Lama's chamberlain was advised of this decision, and Khamba detachments, together with a detachment of the Dalai Lama's own mutinous bodyguard, were dispatched south from Lhasa to cover his route and prepare for the eventual escape to Loka. To reach Loka and Khamba-controlled territory there was only thirty miles of no-man's-land to cross, the distance between Lhasa and the rebel-held south bank of the Brahmaputra. Contrary to what the world press was to say later, the journey would offer no great risk or problem to the Khambas.

While the Khambas in Lhasa prepared to fight, the Chinese on their side were actively reinforcing their own garrisons.

Troops, tanks and armoured cars moved in on Lhasa from the surrounding depots. An armoured car was also seen to emerge from the Chinese garrison of Yutok, no doubt to inspect the situation. Its appearance further heightened the tension, which was soon made intolerable when the rebels learned that Ngabo had warned the Dalai Lama in a letter smuggled to him secretly on 15 March that the Chinese intended to open fire on the Norbulinka (now turned into a rebel fortress); and that he, Ngabo, would like to know where the Dalai Lama was hiding so that 'he would see that the Chinese certainly intend that this building not be destroyed'.

Everyone knew now that the Chinese were ready to attack. On the 16th the Dalai Lama, keeping up his secret correspondence with the Chinese commander, sent his last letter, the only one which can honestly be believed to have been written to 'gain time', as the Dalai Lama knew by now that he was to be taken to Loka. In the letter he wrote:

> I am trying tactfully to draw a line separating the progressive people among the government officials from those opposing the revolution. In a few days from now, when there are enough forces I can trust, I shall make my way to the military area command.

It can be argued that even this letter was sincere and that faithful to his stubborn determination to find 'a way of getting along with the Chinese' the Dalai Lama hoped to the last to prevent the inevitable onslaught.

But by now it was too late. The Khambas had decided that the Dalai Lama must leave Lhasa for Loka on the following night.

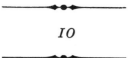

Revolt in Lhasa

Towards nightfall on 17 March, dressed as a Khamba soldier (rifle and all), an ironic disguise for a pacifist who had for so long opposed the men from Kham, the Dalai Lama, with his mother, young brother and sister (also disguised as Khamba guerrillas!), was taken out of the holy city. Along with him, smuggled out of the summer palace in the back of a truck, were the four members of his cabinet.

For security reasons the whole operation was kept secret. Neither the Chinese nor the Lhaseans were aware of his departure, which was planned and master-minded by the Khamba rebels and the mutinous captain of the Dalai Lama's bodyguard.

Considerable, and largely inaccurate, publicity was to be given to the Dalai Lama's alleged 'flight.' The perennial fascination of the semi-mythical 'land of lamas' was revived by fantastic accounts spread by eager journalists over the front pages of the world's newspapers. The lack of accurate information created a long suspense that further whetted the public appetite, already presented by the sensationalist press with incredible stories of the 'dramatic, miraculous escape of the young God King'. The entire world was kept breathless and astounded by his flight, so fixed was the belief that after nine years of Chinese occupation the communists must have all Tibet under control. The truth was never made clear to newsmen or to the public: that in fact a great part of Tibet in 1959 was under the absolute control of the rebellious Khambas, or that the 'flight' of the Dalai Lama before armed Chinese aggression was not a flight at all but the departure of the God King from Lhasa at the will of the Khambas, a departure not for India but to their strongholds in Loka.

Contrary to the general belief, also, the Dalai Lama's so-called flight involved little if any danger. The only dangerous part lay over a distance of less than six miles between the summer palace and the Khamba-controlled ferry of Rangsum, across the Kyi river of Lhasa. And even then, on the night of 17 March it was Khambas and citizens of Lhasa who patrolled the holy city and its environs, the Chinese remaining in their barracks, awaiting orders from Peking. Thus there was little chance of the Chinese successfully attacking the disguised party as it made for the ferry.

It was through compact, armed crowds of his own people, with nothing worse to fear than recognition by his own people, that the Dalai Lama slipped out of the summer palace to the ferry, veiled in darkness and further concealed by a duststorm (later called 'miraculous' not by the Tibetans but by the sensation-loving Western press).

At 10 p.m., undisturbed and still in disguise, the Dalai Lama crossed the Kyi river to be greeted on the southern bank by three of the Khambas' leading commanders. It was an historic meeting, and, surprisingly in the circumstances (reflecting how little panic attended the 'flight'), a formal one. There, on the low, sandy banks of the Kyi river only a few miles from the holy city, whose lights could be clearly seen in the distance, the rugged Khambas ceremoniously exchanged white silk scarves with the fur-hatted, Khamba-dressed God King of Tibet. It was an exchange full of unspoken significance for the 'rebels'. It was in a way a formal reception of their prize. The God King was now at last under their full control.

One of those present was Kunga Samten, the famous leader of the Khambas, now meeting the God King in person for the first time. With him were Thempa Thargyel and the young Kamba Wangchuk Tsering, a mere boy of twenty yet already a well-known and much respected head of a *magar*. And now, here before them, was the Dalai Lama, the very person who had obstructed their campaign for so long, who had outlawed them and called them reactionaries. In silence the leaders exchanged the white scarves of friendship. The moment was one of deep significance, one on which the life and destiny of Tibet and its God King depended.

Yet the moment was not ripe for formal reconciliation. The Khambas soon ushered the Dalai Lama on his journey south, Wangchuk Tsering accompanying his Holiness as far as the hamlet of Namgyalgang. There the party arrived at 3 a.m. and the Dalai Lama took a short rest while Wangchuk set off back to Lhasa with four hundred Khamba soldiers who had come up from Loka. These men were now to join the other two commanders on the banks of the Kyi river, to check any possible attempt by the Chinese to cross the river in pursuit. In a few days these soldiers would play leading roles in the historic battle of Lhasa.

From Namgyalgang three hundred other Khamba soldiers were dispatched southwards along the route the Dalai Lama was about to take over the fourteen-thousand-foot Chela pass leading to the north bank of the Brahmaputra. The Khambas, well prepared for the coming of the Dalai Lama, wasted no time in advising their guerrilla units all over Loka and Tibet. Already a commando was galloping down the road that led to India via Shigatse and Sikkim with orders to cut the telegraph lines between Lhasa and the Indian border and to spread rumours that the Dalai Lama would seek to reach India along this route.

In fact, contrary to what everyone was later brought to believe, there had never been any question of the Dalai Lama's going to India, much less of 'fleeing to India'. As he himself wrote: 'We could not tell where the journey would lead or would end.' It was the 'rebels' who had decided that the Dalai Lama should be taken to the shelter of Loka when they had planned his departure. India was not mentioned.

When I left the Norbulinka, [the Dalai Lama recalls] and throughout the first hectic part of the journey, I was not thinking of going straight to India; I still hoped to be able to stay somewhere in Tibet ... we were heading south and south east from Lhasa. In that direction there is a vast area of mountains without any roads [Loka], which the Chinese army would have found very difficult to penetrate in any strength; and the almost impregnable area [Loka] was one of the principal strongholds of the Khambas and the other Tibetans who had joined them as guerrilla fighters.

So it was to Loka that the Dalai Lama headed, escorted by his Khamba guards. It must have been a strange procession to watch on that first night and the following morning, as the disguised Dalai Lama travelled the forty miles from the comfort of his palace to the second great river across his route, the mighty Brahmaputra.

The circumstances now called for a complete reappraisal of his past policies. The Dalai Lama was a stubborn young man but he began to revise his opinion of the Khambas now that for the first time he saw clearly the faces and stern features of those arrogant warriors, their long hair blowing in the wind as they rode beside him. At every stop he was able to further his acquaintance with these so-called wild cavaliers, the defenders of the faith, the soldiers of the fortress of religion, that religion of which he was head.

During the first days of his journey south he began to understand that in certain cases violence can be justified, that negotiating with the Chinese had only led to his estrangement from his own people, alienating him from most Tibetans, including the rugged men now galloping at his side.

On the afternoon after leaving Lhasa the Dalai Lama crossed the Brahmaputra. Now he had nothing to fear. He was in Khamba-held territory. For a moment the crisis in Lhasa seemed a bad dream of the night. In broad daylight, as the God King crossed the ferry at Kyiling he could see on the other side the faces of more Khambas, a large crowd waiting to greet him as their new leader. In the crowd with the Khambas stood all the villagers of Kyiling, most of whom wore yellow arm bands and buttons, a sign that they too were proud to belong to the N.V.D.A., proud and happy too to see the Dalai Lama at long last among their ranks, one with them in his dress and, they all hoped, one with them in mind and intent also.

Twenty-four hours away from Lhasa the much dramatized flight became a regular, calm and well-organized journey. From Kyiling onwards the party travelled only by day, stopping in monasteries for the night. The slow procession was greeted along the way by enthusiastic crowds and ever more Khambas. From Kyiling the Dalai Lama went to spend the night at the near-by monastery of Rame. The next day he rode to Gyasang monastery, then on to Chenya. There he and his party were urged to push on to Chongya, some ten miles farther east, as this was a major Khamba garrison.

At Chongya, where he arrived early on 21 March, a large crowd of over a thousand Khambas awaited the God King. In the crowd was Osher, seeing the God King for the first time in his life.

At Chongya the Dalai Lama had his second formal encounter with the Khamba leaders, an encounter that none of
them would forget: the great encounter of reconciliation. There
the pact of Tibetan unity was sealed. The Khambas had
brought the Dalai Lama here against his original wish, and now
at Chongya, barely a month after he had refused the Khambas'
last official appeal expressed by the Lama of Jeykundo, with
advice 'to return home and show a little more tolerance of the
Chinese', the Dalai Lama formally made amends. It is best to
let the Dalai Lama describe the meeting for himself.

Before we left Chongya I had a most welcome chance to
meet some more of the leaders of the Khambas and talk to
them frankly. In spite of my beliefs, I very much admired
their courage and their determination to carry on the grim
battle they had started for our freedom and culture and
religion. I thanked them for their strength and bravery, and
also more personally for the protection they had given me. I
asked them not to be annoyed at the government proclamations which had described them as reactionaries and bandits,
and told them exactly how the Chinese had dictated these,
and why we had felt compelled to issue them. By then I
could not in honesty advise them to avoid violence. In order
to fight they had sacrificed their homes and all the comforts
and benefits of a peaceful life. Now they could see no alternative but to go on fighting, and I had none to offer.

The Dalai Lama then blessed the Khambas, whose crusade
now at long last had the benediction of the God King. The
tide had changed. Holy war was now declared, approved by the
saintly incarnation of Chenresi. The Dalai Lama (with a little
pushing perhaps) had in the end understood the justice of the
cause of the men from Kham. They could now ride out proud
and happy, their natural courage strengthened by the thought
of that blessing, which meant so much to all Tibetans.
The Khambas had achieved their greatest victory.

While the Dalai Lama was pursuing his journey into Loka
the Chinese in Lhasa began to suspect on the day after his
departure, 18 March, that he might have left the summer
palace. In an attempt to locate him, General Tan sent a
message to the Bhutanese, Nepalese and Indian consulates, ask-

ing permission to search their legations. When permission was refused, the infuriated Chinese commander ordered the consuls to vacate their compounds on the pretext of possible damage. This they declined to do, quite rightly understanding it to mean that the Chinese were now planning to bombard the summer palace.

This news further angered the aggressive crowds of Lhasa who for the most part were unaware that the Dalai Lama had fled, and were therefore prepared to lay down their lives to defend him.

Meanwhile, the Chinese were hastily fortifying the premises of the Transport Company, the cinema, the post office, the offices of the Working Committee, Shukti Lingka (a new palace just offered by the Chinese to the Dalai Lama, strategically located between the Potala and the Medical College on Iron Hill) and, of course, Yutok, the Chinese headquarters. Within the town the Chinese also set up mortar and machine-gun posts in various houses strategically located near the cathedral and on Lhasa's main streets. At the same time they brought tanks and more armoured cars into the city from the airport to reinforce the hundred trucks loaded with soldiers which had been stationed about the Potala since 16 March.

Ever since the beginning of the disturbances General Tan had been in constant radio contact with Peking, whence he had received instructions (according to Mr Gelder) 'not to retaliate against demonstrations, however provocative, unless directly attacked'.

The excuse the Chinese had been waiting for was not long in coming. At 3.30 a.m. on 19 March, in answer to gunfire from the summer palace now turned into a citadel, the Chinese let fly the full force of their artillery upon the Norbulinka. The Chinese claim that they only fired back at 10 a.m. is contradicted by the reports of all eye witnesses.

The rumbling of mortars and cannons in the dark night over the holy city soon jerked the citizens of Lhasa out of bed. Seized with the folly of desperation, believing their God King's life to be in danger, they marched out into the streets. Men and women, young and old alike rising up in arms, ready to 'lean over the bank'.

In their indignation, the crowds did not stop to think of the might of China and the strength of her garrisons. Years of pent-up frustration had revived the ancient warrior spirit of the Lhaseans and their traditional hatred of the Chinese. Along with the crowds, nobles Like Tsarong and Lahu prepared to fight, haphazardly taking up positions in their homes like Lahu, or, like Tsarong, going to the Potala, which was turned into a Tibetan stronghold along with the summer palace and even the sacred Jokhang, the cathedral of Lhasa.

As war broke out in Lhasa, there lingered in the minds of Tsarong and many other Lhaseans a vague and distant hope that perhaps at last the world beyond the great peaks would no longer remain indifferent to the plight of Tibet, a naïve hope that perhaps in the name of justice the world might at last come to Tibet's rescue.

This hope was based on the fact that on 9 March and again on the 12th an official Tibetan delegation had appealed to the world through the Indian consul, Major Chiba, the only foreign representative in Lhasa with means of communicating with the outside world. The Lhaseans had asked the consul to witness the Freedom Committee's declaration of independence, and although the consul had refused to accompany the Tibetan delegation as it delivered this ultimatum to the Chinese, Major Chiba assured the rebels that he would objectively inform India and the world of the Tibetan resolution.

A full week had now elapsed, a week in which (as witnesses have declared) the Indian telegraph was constantly kept busy night and day informing New Delhi (and, so the naïve Tibetans believed, the world) of what was happening in the holy city.

The Lhaseans could not foresee that in this their most valiant hour they were to fall victims of a shameful conspiracy of silence instigated by Prime Minister Nehru himself.

For this was indeed the case. All the cables with the news of what was happening in Lhasa sat in Delhi, but nothing ever appeared in the press about the dramatic plight of the inhabitants of the holy city.

Nothing except for a few articles, written in *The Daily Telegraph* by George Patterson, ex-missionary of the Plymouth Brethren, a man who had chosen to become, as he called it, 'God's fool', and who had been appointed by the Pangda Tsangs of Kham to be their spokesman to the world.

From Kalimpong Patterson had begun dispatching a series of articles to the British press. They told of a strange warrior race called the Khambas and the incredible story of how they had been successfully opposing the Chinese since 1954 and now, heavily armed, were on the threshold of Lhasa prepared to overthrow the Tibetan cabinet and ready to strike at the Chinese in their own headquarters.

In London, these articles read like science fiction. They were received with scepticism as just one more hocus-pocus story about the roof of the world. But the articles kept on coming, each more urgent and more violent than the last, telling, by March 1959, of an incredible revolt in Tibet and stating that any moment now fighting would break out in Lhasa.

Nobody believed these reports. Nobody except Jawaharlal Nehru, the Prime Minister of India. Nehru knew that these articles were telling the truth, because his desk was piled high with the long, urgent cables sent by Major Chiba from Lhasa, cables that told of the situation within the holy city, of how the rebels had seized Chinese garrisons within walking distance of the capital and had now taken over the town and officially declared war on China.

India, as Tibet's closest neighbour, was naturally the country best informed about what went on there, but India was then pursuing a policy of friendship with China; so Nehru, the great orator of Bandung, the spokesman for a neutral Asian block, the so-called defender of weak oppressed nations, chose to falsify the truth. Not only did he keep silent about Tibet's appeal but, when asked in parliament on 17 March (the very day the Dalai Lama left Lhasa for Loka) about the exact situation inside Tibet, he answered 'that the news of alleged unrest in Tibet' was merely 'bazaar rumours', that their propagator was Mr Patterson, who had already been warned that he would be obliged to leave the Indian border areas if he continued to send out 'exaggerated and misleading reports' about the events in Tibet. Then, as though to discredit finally any truth that might ever slip out of Tibet, Nehru added that the situation in Tibet was 'a clash of minds rather than a clash of arms'.

There are no valid excuses for Nehru's deliberate lie, and betrayal of the Tibetans. Despite the bogus, so-called 'two thousand years of Sino-Indian friendship', India's ancient religious, cultural and commercial ties with Tibet demanded that Nehru make public the desperate official appeal to the world of the Tibetan people, an appeal he had no right whatsoever to withhold.

Yet in spite of Nehru's attempts to blind the world, thanks to Patterson's courage and insistence the truth was slowly making its way out. On 21 March, while the dead lay in the streets of Lhasa, front-page articles in the British press announced that fighting had broken out in the Tibetan capital. This news was followed by a report to the effect that the whereabouts of the Dalai Lama were unknown.

Needless to say, the news came as a shock, although many people still doubted its authenticity. Without further details or official confirmation the press was now left to speculate on the Tibetan situation with the result that the wildest reports were printed, further increasing the tragic suspense of the whole Tibetan crisis.

Where was the Dalai Lama? Was he dead, was he fleeing to India, and if so could he be expected to succeed? Nothing more leaked through from Kalimpong. Quite naturally Radio Peking was silent about Tibet except for a broadcast on the building of a dam in Amdo, while Nehru, playing down the news, proclaimed as usual that the matter would soon be peacefully settled.

Meanwhile the fighting in Lhasa was brief and deadly. The crowds had all the passion and desperation usual in such uprisings. Men, women and children of the town armed themselves with home-made Molotov cocktails, picks, spades, swords and butchers' knives: crude instruments with which to oppose China's strongest garrisons, commanded by a veteran general with thirty years' experience in military and political warfare.

Much has been written about the uprising in Lhasa, making it appear to have been the showdown of Tibetan resistance. This is quite contrary to fact. The Khambas had never really hoped to overcome the huge Chinese garrison of the holy city in one attack. Although there were Khambas in Lhasa, they numbered only a little over two thousand men. Approximately a thousand of these were in the holy city only for the New Year festival, while the other thousand had been sent up from Loka to protect the Dalai Lama from pursuit by the Chinese. This represented only a minute proportion of the Khamba troops stationed all over Kham, Amdo and Loka. The revolt in Lhasa was not to be a battle in the classic sense of the word. It was to be only the first official and major clash between the central Tibetans and the Chinese occupation force, and not, by a long way, the last.

The battle of Lhasa, far from being, as the Chinese claimed, 'the end of Tibetan resistance' was in fact only the point of no return in the long struggle between the Tibetans and Chinese.

As with all popular uprisings, it is very difficult to follow the sequence of events in Lhasa on the three days between 18 March and 22 March. Only the Chinese were to employ any definite strategy against the disorderly Tibetan masses.

The number of Chinese soldiers in and around Lhasa at the time has never been known precisely. Estimates have varied from forty thousand to the exaggeratedly low figure of four thousand. As the strategic headquarters and administrative centre of the huge Chinese occupation force in Tibet, there is no doubt that the Chinese were well entrenched and numerous in the city. From the known number of tanks (fifty), the number of army trucks and armoured cars and the usual size of the Chinese garrisons around the town, it can be conservatively estimated that there were not fewer than fifteen thousand fully equipped Chinese troops opposing the uprising. To these troops must be added the four thousand armed 'civilian' Chinese technical personnel.

The Chinese, who had seen the uprising coming, had had time before 19 March to implement a definite strategy. This consisted of surrounding both the town of Lhasa and the out-lying valley on which stood the Potala, the Medical College and the summer palace, with tanks and troops, so as to cut off the Lhasa area from the outlying monasteries of Sera, Drepung and Gaden. This ringing of the valley cut off from the rebels the four thousand men of the mutinous Tibetan regiments, stationed near Sera monastery. By 19 March the only gap in this ring and the insurgents' only means of communication with the out-side was the Rangsum Ferry, controlled and defended by the Khambas of Kunga Samten.

When fighting broke out the Chinese further isolated the insurgents by setting up barricades at the foot of the Potala and before the Turquoise Bridge, cutting off the town itself from the insurgents in the Lhasa valley.

On either side of this line two very different and separate battles were soon to flare up. In the valley the fighting was an artillery duel between the Tibetans barricaded in the summer palace, the Potala and the Medical College, and the Chinese garrisons of Shukti Lingka. In the town the Chinese faced the repeated assaults of Khamba commandos and those of undisciplined thousands of outraged Lhaseans attacking the transport depot, the cinema, the radio station and other Chinese-held houses which had been turned into fortified outposts.

For five hours in the cold morning of Thursday 19 March the Chinese lobbed mortars into the gardens of the summer palace, killing many of the men entrenched there and hundreds of the crowd of civilians still hanging round its outer walls. The Tibetans retaliated from the height of the Medical College on the Chinese garrisoned in Shukti Lingka, who in turn were bombarding the summer palace and the Potala.

All day Friday the Chinese directed their guns against the Medical College and the Potala, slowly pounding to silence the old cannons of Iron Hill. In the later afternoon, they also attacked the rear of the Potala, using tanks to shell the massive walls.

By nightfall the rebels in the Medical College were practically out of operation, when seventy Khambas climbed Iron Hill from the summer palace to reinforce the position and carry up additional ammunition to man the last operational cannon.

That same Friday, according to Noel Barber's account of the fighting[1] within the city, the Chinese machine-gunned any civilians who dared run out into the streets in desperate attempts to flush the Chinese from the houses where they were entrenched. In the morning the Chinese also fired on a crowd of civilians demonstrating outside the transport depot, killing hundreds of women and children. Only with darkness did both sectors come to a standstill. Then at dawn on the 20th the artillery attacks in the valley began again with renewed ferocity. The Chinese now made two unsuccessful attempts to rush the summer palace. The moment they did this a detachment of Khambas coming from the Rangsum Ferry stormed Shukti Lingka and carried it in a desperate hand-to-hand struggle. This Tibetan victory was unfortunately balanced by the loss of Iron Hill, captured by a Chinese assault party late in the afternoon.

In the meantime General Tan sent troops with armoured cars to try and seize the Rangsum ferry. On 21 March, falling upon

[1] see Noel Barber *The Land of Lost Content*.

the reduced guards defending this only exit from the valley, the Chinese armoured cars did terrible damage to the Khambas, who charged the monstrous vehicles valiantly on horseback and eventually held off the attack.

Inside the town, early the same day, seventy Khambas succeeded in forcing the Chinese out of the cinema which commanded the road leading from Lhasa's southern gate into the valley. This victory, which reunited the Tibetans in the valley with those in the town, was followed by a mad influx of stranded Lhaseans back into Lhasa. Once within the narrow streets of the city, this disorderly mob was fired on mercilessly by the Chinese as they sought protection within the huge structure of the Jokhang.

By Saturday afternoon the fighting within Lhasa had reached a new peak. Tibetans and Chinese exchanged mortar fire from the rooftops above the heads of a wild crowd roaming the streets and lobbing Molotov cocktails into the Chinese-held houses. Great columns of smoke could be seen rising all over the town as fires gutted the houses, threatening to spread on the evening breeze.

Twice on Saturday the Chinese left their shelters and charged down into the streets. It was a fatal move, for they were instantly cut down by Khambas who plunged in, swords flashing, from the dark alleys and doorways, and displayed their indisputable superiority in hand-to-hand fighting.

The Chinese attempted vainly to silence the Tibetan mortars set up in the Moslem quarter and on the mighty Jokhang, from the roof of which the rebels dominated the town. The huge stone walls of Tibet's 'Holy of Holies' remained unshaken by constant Chinese fire, except when the occasional mortar crashed through the gilded roof, exploding among the women and children who cowered in the chapels below, beside the impassive golden images of past Dalai Lamas.

The venerable walls of the Potala, consolidated through the centuries, were practically unscratched by the shells that hit them, raining about the ancient stele on which were carved the 'beautiful words' of Tibet's most ancient treaty, words spoken in 882, and which after a thousand years still proclaimed in Tibetan and Chinese the empty promises of the Hans. Ironically the text recorded how the great religious king of Tibet, Ralpachen, and the Emperor of China, Mu Tsung, 'seeking in their far-reaching wisdom to prevent all causes of harm to the welfare of their countries', had engraved their agreement 'on this stone pillar to inform future ages and generations' that 'henceforth on neither side shall there be waging of war nor seizing of territory' and that 'between the two countries no smoke nor dust shall be seen'. Further: 'There shall be no sudden alarms and the very word "enemy" shall not be spoken. . . . All shall live in peace and share the blessing of happiness for ten thousand years. . . . This solemn agreement has established a great epoch when Tibetans shall be happy in the Land of Tibet, and Chinese in the land of China.'

By Saturday night (21–22 March) the Tibetans down in the valley, in the summer palace and the Potala, knew that they were fighting a losing battle in the face of the overwhelming Chinese artillery. Two days of bombardment had taken a heavy toll, especially in the summer palace, where many of the buildings in the 160-acre grounds had been hit. The bodies of the victims lay in heaps around the sacred walls.

The last defenders all knew by this time of the Dalai Lama's escape, but they knew nothing of the fighting in the rest of the valley and the town. The Khambas inside the summer palace realized quite clearly that they did not have a chance, unable as they were to come to grips with the Chinese. Consequently that same night the decision was taken to abandon the palace. Mortally wounded Tibetans were mercifully put to death by their friends, when in the darkness of Saturday night hundreds fled from the summer palace, leaving a reduced garrison which surrendered on the following morning (22 March) after a last brief bombardment.

Within Lhasa on the same Sunday the dust of the town's ancient streets was still bloody from the fighting, as in desperation thousands of Tibetans continued to throw away their lives in foolhardy attempts to take the Chinese strongholds.

Early in the morning three massive tanks crushed their way into the town, spitting fire, their diesels rumbling. Slowly rolling on, impervious to bullets, they were heading towards the Jokhang when suddenly one tank came to a shuddering stop and exploded. Khamba horsemen from the valley galloped wildly around the two remaining monsters as they rumbled on slowly into the cathedral square, crushing the victims of their own machine guns and grinding a shaky path over the Tibetan barricades. Then with a sinister thud one tank began ramming the great gates of the Jokhang while the other blasted the last Tibetan strongholds into silence. The tanks had tipped the scales; the fighting died down. At 2 p.m. on Sunday, obeying orders, the Chinese silenced their own guns, and an eerie peace settled over the city, broken only by distant sporadic bursts of gunfire. Then, breaking the silence from various parts of the town, a taped appeal was broadcast over loudspeakers. Everyone listened as a voice called for a cease-fire, calling on the insurgents to lay down their arms, promising that there would be no reprisals.

According to Noel Barber, after the first announcement a Tibetan then spoke out, saying: 'My name is Ngabo, as you know I am a member of the Kashag [cabinet]. All fighting must stop.' Ngabo carried on to say that this was an order from the Tibetan government which so he declared had agreed with the Chinese to end the revolt.

'The Dalai Lama has not been killed,' Ngabo then announced. 'He has been abducted against his will by the "reactionaries"!'

Hearing this, the tired, battered population of Lhasa ceased to fight, while the Khambas, faced with the futility of further resistance within the city, withdrew hurriedly over the ferry to join their units in Loka. Following the announcements hundreds of Lhaseans fled out into the country along with the Khambas.

So ended the fighting in Lhasa, while the great monasteries around the town, besieged by tanks, surrendered one after the other.

The Khambas had been misled once more by the 'beautiful-mouthed' Ngabo. But now they rejoiced, too, for at last they knew that they held the Dalai Lama. To most of the Khambas inside Lhasa, Ngabo's announcement was the first they had heard of their great tactical victory. The Dalai Lama, they now knew, was in their hands.

II

Abduction?

While Lhasa capitulated, the Dalai Lama was pursuing his journey south through Loka. Exactly what was to become of him was still undecided, when messengers arrived from Lhasa. They brought the bad news of how all fighting had come to a halt after three days, and how five thousand people had died.[1]

News of the Chinese victory in Lhasa was followed shortly by the news that the communists had dissolved the Tibetan government and were about to set up a new government headed by Ngabo. This measure decided the Dalai Lama to set up a new temporary government immediately at Lhuntse, the greatest fort in Loka, which he had reached on 26 March.

Six high passes now lay between the Dalai Lama at Lhuntse and the Chinese, passes that would be easily defensible in the unlikely event of any sudden Chinese advance. In fact there was to be no such advance or any attempt to recover the Dalai Lama, for the simple reason that to do so would have been impossible.

At Lhuntse, with as much pomp as was possible in the circumstances, and respecting the religious and secular traditions of Tibet, the Dalai Lama's new government was formally installed. Religious chants and prayers were followed by sacred dances of propitious fortune, enacted before the local dignitaries, three ministers accompanying the Dalai Lama and the Khambas of the Lhuntse *magars* and of the God King's escort.

Thus, while the world published weird rumours about the Dalai Lama's flight and even his death, in Lhuntse the ancient dances calmly sealed the establishment of the new Tibetan

[1] Although to this day detailed figures have never been issued about the number of victims of the street fighting and artillery duels, this figure is now generally accepted as a compromise between the ridiculous Chinese claim that not one civilian was killed and the more exaggerated reports of stunned survivors who claimed that over twenty thousand people had died in the streets.

'temporary' government, a government which now reaffirmed Tibet's ancient unity. The 'rebels' all rejoiced, for Kham, Amdo and central Tibet were now formally united as in the past, although a certain tension still lingered between the tough Khamba leaders and the sophisticated Lhaseans.

When news reached the Dalai Lama's escort that Chinese troops were setting out from the Sikkim borders in a sweeping move eastwards along the northern border of Bhutan, it became clear to all that his presence in Loka could only attract a concentrated Chinese attack. Air raids also were feared and since it would be foolish to mobilize much-needed guerrillas merely for the protection of the God King there was for the first time talk of his leaving Tibet. Exile in India, which had been in the back of the Dalai Lama's mind for so many years, was the obvious solution to the Khambas' problem. From there it was hoped that the God King could rally the support of an apparently indifferent world and help the rebels more successfully than from Loka; while to remain could only lead, as the Dalai Lama himself understood, 'to more fighting and more deaths of the brave men who would try to defend me'.

When the syncopated rhythm of the dances of propitious fortune had died away in Lhuntse Dzong, official letters about the setting up of the new government were given to messengers to be taken all over Tibet, along with gifts and an appeal to the second most important abbot of central Tibet, the young, controversial Panchen Lama. After carrying out these formalities it was decided that the Dalai Lama should retire two miles away to the less conspicuous monastery of Teulay.

It was here that after a brief discussion it was decided that in the common interest the Dalai Lama should go to India. This decision was taken with the full agreement of both the Khambas and the Dalai Lama.

Quite clearly, until the God King reached Teulay he had no definite plan for going to India, and while his journey was widely represented as a 'flight to India', this was not in fact the case. His departure from Lhasa had been brought about by the Khambas; yet once on the road to Loka the Dalai Lama had come to agree with and bless the Khambas' actions which he had previously tried to oppose in Lhasa. These were the precise circumstances of the God King's so-called abduction and flight, a journey carried out with maximum precautions, but with none of the undignified urgency lent it by the world press.

On 26 March, after the decision to go to India had been reached, a detachment of Khambas set out for the Indian border to seek asylum for the Dalai Lama. That asylum would be granted was not yet certain. India's known Chinese sympathies gave the Dalai Lama's party serious reason to doubt her agreement. The question may now be raised: what if Nehru had refused? In that case, the Dalai Lama would no doubt either have stayed in Loka or gone to Bhutan, the frontier of which lay only a few miles from Lhuntse.

As it happened, the Indian government, on first hearing that he had left Lhasa, had anticipated his wishes by giving advance orders to all border check posts to allow him entrance. Although Nehru knew such a decision would cause considerable annoyance to the Chinese, he must have hoped that it would be a good opportunity for his country to play its self-appointed role of mediator in Asian affairs once again. Consequently the Tibetan emissaries soon returned from the border to inform the Dalai Lama that he could proceed to India.

Two days later, on 29 March, the Dalai Lama and his escort entered Indian territory at Chutangmo. The same day Radio Peking admitted trouble in Lhasa and stated that 'the P.L.A. were ordered to take punitive action against a clique of traitors who had committed monstrous crimes'. This announcement was followed by the news that the Dalai Lama had been 'abducted by rebels and was now in India'. Thus it was in fact from the Chinese that Nehru first heard that the Dalai Lama was on Indian soil, because owing to the slowness of communications in the Indian frontier districts he was not to have confirmation of this from his frontier guards until 3 April.

The press was now quite delirious, because nothing was yet known for certain about where the Dalai had entered India. The rugged terrain of the Indian Himalayas of the North-East Frontier Agency which the Dalai Lama had entered presented no less of an obstacle than had the terrain of Loka. From the Indian border to reach the first roads of Assam the Dalai Lama and his party had to travel for sixteen days, sixteen days of additional suspense for the press whose correspondents were anxiously awaiting his arrival at Tezpur in Assam. Sixteen days, also, during which Nehru had time to think over what was to be done with his embarrassing guest. Already Nehru's welcome had been cooler than the world was led to believe. To begin with, the border guards had refused entry to many Khambas of the Dalai Lama's escort.

Indeed the situation was a most embarrassing one for India. Already China was clamouring about the Dalai Lama's abduction by an 'imperialist-financed rebellious clique', which, it was hinted, was operating from India. When the Chinese discovered that the Dalai Lama had escaped to Loka, and as soon as they re-read the letters sent by him to General Tan, they had immediately (as early as 21 March) jumped to what seemed a logical conclusion, that the 'Dalai Lama had been abducted by the "rebels" '.

This belief, a not altogether incorrect one, now became the basic slogan for the Chinese's third and most violent offensive against the 'rebels', an offensive aimed not only at the cavaliers of Kham, but at all Tibetan landowners and nobles, who were quite unjustly held responsible for the Dalai Lama's abduction.

The Chinese reason for wishing to shift the blame of the rebellion from the 'Khamba bandits' to the 'rich serf-owning aristocratic clique' was soon to become sufficiently obvious. Yet this further helped to mask from the world the exact role of the Khambas in the whole affair of the Dalai Lama's departure from Lhasa and the subsequent uprising. The Khambas' deeds were thus to pass practically unnoticed and the truth to remain veiled in the lies of Chinese propaganda and the understandable silence of the Dalai Lama and his ministers about the exact course of events in Lhasa that March.

To the world the name of Kham and the deeds of its soldiers meant nothing. Yet it was no coincidence that it was Jigme Pangda Tsang, the son of the great Topgyay of Po himself, who read out in English the vital and long-awaited first press release by the Dalai Lama on his arrival in Tezpur.

Proudly, before over a hundred of the world's journalists, the young Khamba lord read in English the arrogant answer of the cavaliers of Kham to the insidious propaganda of Mr Chou En-lai. To the Chinese foreign minister's sly declaration that 'although the Dalai Lama has been abducted to India, we still hope that he will be able to free himself from the hold of the rebels [Khambas] and return to the motherland' Jigme Pangda Tsang made it known officially that 'the Dalai Lama would like to state categorically that he left Lhasa and Tibet and came to India of his own free will and not under duress'. Although this was only partly true, the statement sealed a great victory for the Khambas. Now, the world could be told officially that the Dalai Lama was on the side of the men of Kham.

The Chinese were infuriated by this, the Dalai Lama's first official statement to the free world. They were never to accept it. A few weeks later, in Peking, the Panchen Lama, who had been taken to the National People's Congress in place of the 'abducted Dalai Lama' declared: 'The statement issued in the name of the Dalai Lama which turns things upside down, is a sheer distortion of the facts and a complete fabrication. It is obviously a result of coercion by the reactionaries, and certainly not the Dalai Lama's own will.'

But if the Chinese were right in believing that the Dalai Lama had in a way been abducted, they were wrong in thinking that he was still being coerced to back the Khambas. As it was the Chinese were never able to accept that he had been won over to the cause of Kham, that in fact he had in the end seen the real treachery of Chinese policies. It was as if the Dalai Lama had at last remembered that he was by birth, if not a Khamba at least an Amdowan, and therefore a member of the race of kings. Jigme Pangda Tsang's speech in Tezpur on 16 April 1959 closed the first chapter of the great Tibetan uprising of the cavaliers of Kham.

As for the world press, which understood little about Tibetan politics, it found the Tezpur statement tame and rather disappointing. Who were these Khambas anyway, and what was all this Chinese fabrication about an abduction? How could they understand? Consequently the flight of the Dalai Lama was made out to be just one more story of escape from the big red dragon of Chinese communism.

About the true situation even Nehru was in the dark. He had just seen himself ridiculed when the world found out that he had been lying about the situation in Tibet. Now he was to be further embarrassed when the Chinese, to support their account of the Dalai Lama's abduction, published the Dalai Lama's letters to General Tan. These letters Nehru haughtily declared to be a Chinese 'fabrication', only to be made to look even more foolish when the Dalai Lama himself admitted having written them. None of this added to Nehru's prestige, and his greatest critics were the Indian people, shocked at last by their prime minister's unpardonable attitude towards Tibet.

As for the hospitality extended to the Dalai Lama, it soon became known that the Indian government would not allow him to make any political statements or give press interviews. Already, when the Dalai Lama reached Tezpur, plans had been made to seclude him in Mussorie, as far away as possible in the Himalayas from Kalimpong.

After meeting the Dalai Lama on 23 April Nehru declared, 'We do expect him [the Dalai Lama] to keep in view the difficulties of the situation and speak and act accordingly'; adding, 'the Dalai Lama has more anxiety for conditions in Tibet, in a peaceful solution, not in giving press interviews', which amounted to an order for the Dalai Lama to keep quiet. As for the Dalai Lama being allowed to set up a government in exile, a question immediately raised by the world's press and a right generally granted to most exiled leaders, Nehru answered that, 'it was the ordinary right of any country, including Britain, to limit the function of foreigners who created difficulties with other countries'. In other words, the Dalai Lama could expect to see India place limits to his activities.

As for the Chinese, still certain of their 'abduction' theory, and desperate at the loss of the Dalai Lama, they officially declared that they 'awaited his return', and that in the meantime they would maintain him as the titular chairman of the Tibetan Autonomous region. This they did in fact for fully five years, never speaking a harsh word against the God King.

On the other hand, Nehru suffered the not-undeserved blow of seeing his relations with China deteriorate rapidly. The first indication of this was the Chinese declaration of 30 April stating that, 'Kalimpong had been used as a command centre', adding that the Indian town was a 'nest of spies'. This first note was followed by more aggressive statements about the actual collusion of the Indians with the Tibetan rebels. Unfortunately for the Khambas, this was quite untrue.

So it came to pass that the Dalai Lama, from the docile tool of the Chinese in Tibet became first the unwilling and then the willing hostage of the Khambas, to end up as the silent, restricted guest of India.

All told, the situation was so complex that, thanks to Chinese propaganda, Indian censorship and general ignorance, the world was soon brought to believe that all resistance in Tibet had ceased and that 'the rebellion was crushed'.

A few shed a tear for the end of their dream Shangri-la. The flurry over Tibet abated and then came silence; a silence in which no one so much as heard the war cries of the Khambas as they prepared to face the third and greatest Chinese offensive, and fight their most devastating battles against the armies of Mao.

12

'The Twinkling of an Eye'

By May 1959 many Tibetans had reason to believe that the exile of the Dalai Lama to India and the publicity about events in Lhasa would lead at last to effective assistance from abroad for the Tibetan cause.

But once again they were to be disappointed, for although the name of Tibet and the story of its plight had entered every home, there were no signs that any diplomats or politicians were stirred into action. On the contrary, the Lhasa uprising was misinterpreted as the death rattle of an already long-expiring land. Then the headlines changed and almost everyone forgot, all save those who offered to adopt Tibetan orphans or generously donated money to Tibetan charities; while to have an audience with the Dalai Lama became a social 'must', as tourists more frequently than statesmen sought to see the God King of Tibet, although visitors, especially influential persons, were openly discouraged by Indian officials.

Fearing to have angered her great neighbour, India spared no pains to patch up her alleged 'two-thousand-year-old Indo-Chinese friendship'. For a start, Tibet was sealed off as never before by a series of road blocks and police checkpoints that closed the Himalayan border areas to all foreigners, the term 'foreigner' being most often understood as being synonymous with Tibetan sympathizer.

India then assured Peking that she would again back her admission to the United Nations in September 1959. At the same time Nehru made it clear to the Dalai Lama that his country would obstruct Tibet's plans to place her problems once more before the Assembly of Nations.

This was the situation in May 1959 when I crossed the inner line to Kalimpong on what I hoped would be the first leg of a journey I was planning to Bhutan. In Kalimpong I went to Tashiding, the villa of that country's prime minister in Kalimpong.

Kalimpong, the gateway from India to Tibet, is wedged at the point where Sikkim and Bhutan meet, just below the high Tibetan Chumbi valley. Since the Younghusband expedition of 1904, by which the British had hoped to secure stable commercial relations with the kingdom of the Dalai Lama by the use of force, Kalimpong had grown into a great trading centre, unique in the world, a land-locked port from which for fifty years countless caravans of ponies and yaks had set out to weather the trails that stretched to the four horizons of Tibet, across the great open spaces of central Asia's highest plains: east to China, west to Samarkand and north to Mongolian Sinkiang.

There in the bazaar had lived the agents of the Tibetan merchant kings such as the Pangda Tsangs, of Muslim horse dealers from Sinning, as well as the representatives of nomad princes. All did a brisk trade based on messages sent by runners or carried in the breasts of the muleteers who linked the most remote corners of Asia with Kalimpong. Here was spun a fantastic medieval web of communications of a kind familiar to Marco Polo, and one whose intricate mechanism escaped the understanding of most, if not all, of the few Europeans living above the bustle of the bazaar, their flowery villas looking out at the snow-covered mass of Kangchenjunga, the impressive back-drop of that 'nest of spies'.

Soon after my arrival I discovered that most of the spying that spring was in the form of the 'tea-time espionage' so dear to small colonial towns. Comments were spilled over rummy and scones by a varied fauna of self-exiled anthropologists and missionaries, lovers of customs and lovers of souls, the backbone of Kalimpong's foreign colony: people with small but violent passions, surprised to see their once quiet settlement in the cool Himalayan foothills suddenly besieged by Tibetan refugees dragging useless ponies into a wheeled world.

The only real spies were Chinese and Indians, both out to break the back of the Khambas.

The Chinese operated from the huge, fully staffed offices of the Chinese Trade Mission set up in Kalimpong in 1954 with Nehru's blessing, and through which the Chinese shipped much-needed rice across the border, together with such strategic items as kerosene and petrol. It was later revealed by Dr

S. Sinha[1] of the Indian parliament that the Chinese even crossed soldiers from India into Tibet (via Sikkim) to attack the Khambas from the rear.

It was indeed far easier and cheaper for the Chinese to ship goods to its troops in Lhasa via Kalimpong, than to enter Tibet from China along their only operational road, which ran 1,600 miles across the deserts of Sinkiang and western Tibet.

In answer to the Chinese accusations that Kalimpong was the 'platform of the rebellion', the refugees who flocked there were hastily evacuated to Assam, where the infamous camp of Missamari had been set up. This was a sordid enclosure with all the appearance of a concentration camp, access to which was forbidden Europeans. Fifty per cent of the Tibetans interned there died in the first year as a result of neglect and of the hot, unhealthy climate, quite unsuitable for Tibetans. The affair of the Missamari camp was only the first of many untold scandals concerning the treatment of refugees, which eventually led to the declaration at the Dalai Lama's headquarters that 'many Tibetans [refugees] could hardly be worse off at home' (i.e., under Chinese servitude).

Although it was certainly true that Kalimpong had been and was still a major centre for the dispatch of what little aid the Tibetans received from abroad, what has been termed as Nehru's 'folly of appeasement' can hardly be justified.

Yet no one could actually stop the secret transactions being carried out by the rebels in Kalimpong, where smuggled cases of silver Chinese dollars were exchanged in the hovels of Marwari merchants for much-needed firearms of dubious origin and extravagant cost.

Tsering, coming down from Loka in April, directed these operations in conjunction with those Khambas who could be seen stalking about the town, swords sticking out of their belts, men standing head and shoulders above the sullen, emaciated Bengalis.

This trade was no secret to the Indian police, but no one dared to intervene, and with good reason. Shortly after my arrival, a police officer was foolish enough to intercept a shipment of Tibetan contraband. The next day, in broad daylight, Kalimpong's police station was attacked by Khambas come to release their jailed companion.

[1] In his book *Chinese Aggression*. New Delhi 1961.

Two days after reaching Kalimpong, my plan to visit Bhutan led me to Tashiding, the villa of its prime minister. There for the first time I heard a detailed account of the events in Tibet, from the only eye witnesses who spoke English, the refugee sons and daughters of the great lords of Lhasa who had made this villa their gathering point, as from Tashiding Tesla, the Tibetan wife of the prime minister, sister of Betty-la and eldest daughter of Tsarong, generously dispensed her hospitality and fortune to her unfortunate friends and relatives.

For the Tibetan aristocracy May 1959 was a time of rude awakening. Those who had made it to Kalimpong tried desperately to measure the scale of the disaster as they exchanged notes about missing friends and acquaintances. Where was Tsarong and his son George? Were they dead or alive? Nobody knew.

As for Betty-la, who had been down in India during the whole crisis, she now wandered about the bazaar like a ghost, asking every refugee whether they had seen her children, her five little ones left behind.

These were tragic times. Nobody knew what they should do, while those who attempted to join the Dalai Lama found themselves forbidden to go to Mussorie.

Nothing could ease the grim reality of the death in Lhasa of a way of life that had carried deeper than any civilization the privileges of feudalism into the age of space crafts. Many nobles felt guilty, some of them wept; it was mostly pity that they inspired.

Only the Khambas walked about serenely, their great booming voices and their impeccable appearance recalling that they alone had willed the situation. Such was Tsering, the day I saw him for the first time in the bazaar, and later at the house of Shakopa, the ex-finance minister whose son I had met in New York.

Shakopa, the leader of the ill-fated Tibetan 'peace mission', had not been back to Tibet since 1950. Now once again he had become a key figure, because, as many had come to know, he had been guarding the Dalai Lama's treasure all those years in India. Indeed, when the young God King had fled to the Indian border in 1950 as the Chinese entered Chamdo, the Tibetan cabinet had discreetly carried down into Sikkim one thousand mule loads (over five million U.S. dollars' worth) of gold and silver. All those nine years Shakopa had sat there taking care of the kitty, just in case. Now that case had arisen[1].

What would the money be used for? Already in Kalimpong tongues were at work. Some Lhaseans had brought their passion for intrigue with them. Would the Dalai Lama finance the purchase of arms for the Khambas? Was the past really forgiven? Was Tibetan unity truly complete? Few Khambas were allowed access to his Holiness to enquire, but on 20 June a journalist put the question to him. 'Would the Dalai Lama appeal for arms on behalf of the rebels?'

The Dalai Lama's answer was equivocal and diplomatic, 'Although I have no intention of leaving the National Voluntary Defence Army unaided, I am intending to help them by all means of a peaceful solution rather than military force.'

Were these 'beautiful' words? Tsering did not have time to find out, for he had his own cases of silver dollars to sell: Khamba coins shipped from Loka to pay for the arms and ammunition urgently needed, beyond the hills where the fighting was being carried on with new vigour. Thus, while I began taking Tibetan lessons with Betty-la, daily, to the tinkle of bells, the Khambas urged their loaded mules past the Chinese Trade Mission, past the Indian police station, heading north back into Tibet.

With one of these caravans – I never knew which – Tsering vanished, his boots gathering dust, his braids tight around his head, his leopard-lined *chuba* beating in the wind.

As the days dragged by, Betty-la's dilemma took a new, tragic turn. One morning Mary-la her mother turned up in Kalimpong, scarcely recognizable. Still under the shock of her frightening odyssey across Tibet, she explained in tears that she had had to leave the children behind. She had been cut off from her home during the fighting. Unable to rejoin her small grandchildren or her son-in-law, Taring, who was inside the summer palace, she had fled alone.

Eventually Betty-la's husband also arrived in India, having escaped from the summer palace before its capitulation, but he too came without the 'little ones'. In despair Betty-la, fearless of

[1] The Chinese quite rightly criticized this secret move, which in fact betrayed the frame of mind of the Lhasean ministers, who had foreseen exile all along. The Khambas were also to see in the affair of the treasure the sly double-faced policies of many Lhaseans.

death and the risks she would be running, pleaded to be allowed to set off alone back to Lhasa. No words could describe her anguish and the tragedy of her position. I, with others, attempted to dissuade her. By then still nothing was known of the fate of Tsarong, her last hope for the children. Then, unexpectedly on 24 June, a cable reached Tashiding from Peking. It read laconically: 'Tsarong has died in prison.'

What tragedy lay behind those words no one will ever know for sure. A communist report later stated that 'Another big "rebel", Tsarong, had been captured in the Potala surrender. His serfs demanded a "struggle meeting", but Tsarong was 70 years old [in fact 72] and died of a stroke before any meeting was held.' Frank Moraes[1] claims that in fact 'he committed suicide after being publicly beaten by some of his servants and a few pro-Chinese monks and humiliated before the people'.

Whatever the case, it was a tragic and undeserved end for an aged man known to all as the most progressive Tibetan.

Tsarong's death was not, alas, to be the last of those that stained with blood the hand of China in Tibet. Sixty-five thousand Tibetans (mostly Khambas and Amdowans), according to an estimate by the Dalai Lama, died between the outbreak of the Kanting Rebellion and 1959. This figure was soon to soar as the Chinese prepared for violent retaliation in Tibet, where already furious battles had broken out to mark the second decade of Tibetan resistance, the second phase of the long war born on the plains of Kham.

As soon as the last echoes of gunfire had died away in the still air over Lhasa, the Chinese swept into the town and rounded up the insurgents. No less than ten thousand people were imprisoned, according to the reliable estimate of Cha Teh, the pro-Chinese ex-mayor of Lhasa, the brother-in-law of Ngabo, who remained in the capital. In an interview with Stuart Gelder, Cha Teh declared that this represented 'one quarter of the town's population'.

This incredible figure, revealed by a Chinese collaborator, gives an idea of the scope of the repression in Lhasa, and

[1] See *The Revolt in Tibet*. New York 1960.

clearly contradicts China's claims that the 'revolt' had not been followed by the majority of the people.

Those imprisoned included rich and poor, men, women and monks. Among the rich was Lahu, the handsome, courageous ex-governor of Chamdo, who was to rot for five years in jail and 're-education through labour', after suffering mock trials in which he was publicly humiliated and charged with a dozen murders, including the assassination of Geda, that unorthodox lama who had died a mysterious death in Chamdo nine years previously. Geda was the Chinese envoy of whose alleged assassination Robert Ford, the radio operator of Chamdo, was also accused in 1950, and for which alleged crime he had already spent five years in Chinese prisons.

After the massacre of some five thousand people in Lhasa, the flight of many more and the arrest of ten thousand, life in the Tibetan capital came to a complete standstill. Then from Peking on 28 March Chou En-lai dissolved the Tibetan government by order of the (Chinese) State Council. Wasting no time, General Tan, in the midst of chaos, busily went about setting up a masquerade government.

It is hardly surprising to find Ngabo at its head and the other traitorous minister, Sampo Tsewan Rinzing; while the Panchen Lama, the second spiritual authority of central Tibet, one more docile than the exiled Dalai Lama, lent his weight as 'acting Chairman during the time the Dalai Lama is held under duress by the rebels'. Eighteen previous members of the Tibetan government were eliminated, all being declared 'traitorous elements' and replaced by sixteen hand-picked Chinese sympathizers. Also in the new Preparatory Committee for the Autonomous Region of Tibet were General Tan and eight other Chinese officers, giving Lhasa an effective Chinese military dictatorship whose decisions had nevertheless still to be approved by the State Council, which was entirely composed of Chinese.

In Peking news of the Lhasean uprising had come as a shock. The violence of the rebellion and the flight of the Dalai Lama were felt by the Chinese rulers as a severe loss of face, not only because the entire world had come to know that despite the strength of China and her high-handed methods, she had been unable after nine years to master the minute population of what was generally believed to be a land of feeble monks, but also because there had been extensive publicity inside China over the imminent arrival of the Dalai Lama to attend the National People's Congress, due to start on 17 April.

Infuriated, the Chinese decided to place all Tibet under the most rigorous military control and to adopt a ruthless policy of general repression. Consequently they began mobilizing all means at their disposal to subjugate unruly Tibet once and for all. Not only were the crack units of the Chinese army posted to Tibet, but with them were sent experts in subversive warfare, aided by young Tibetan 'cadets', fresh from indoctrination schools in China. Concerning these Tibetan 'activists' we have an interesting account by Mrs Strong, from whom we learn[1] that in May 1959 three thousand four hundred such students were sent to Tibet along with

> five hundred and fifty Tibetan cadres, civil servants in [from] autonomous Tibetan districts in adjoining provinces, being transferred into Tibet; of these one hundred and twenty-five had enough experience to become county secretaries or district chiefs ... staff for the reforms, prepared for eight years by Peking.

Continuing, Mrs Strong explains:

> In Peking I had seen the first group of returning students taken off by special train at the end of May [1959]. I asked the man who came from Lhasa to pick them, whether any of these could have gone to Tibet safely before the rebellion. He shook his head 'They would have been safe in our offices,' he replied, 'but they could not have gone safely into the villages for the armed retainers of the serf owners might have caught them, and they might have paid with their lives.'
> Now they can go safely with only normal caution.

To this clear illustration of Chinese tactics Mrs Strong adds, with candour,

> Looking back over eight years in which these events were prepared, one sees that all those years were needed.

So as strangers in their own land a few of the fifteen thousand children who had been taken away by force from their parents returned to Tibet; political pawns, out, so the Chinese hoped,

[1] *When Serfs Stood Up*. Peking 1965.

to help fight their 'rebellious' brothers and parents of the N.V.D.A.

To dissimulate the violence of this planned suppression of the revolt, and to counter her loss of face, China immediately began a vast propaganda campaign aimed at playing down the scale of the revolt and blaming it on a small élite of 'upper-strata reactionary serf owners'.

By officially blaming the Tibetan aristocracy for the rebellion the Chinese were to succeed cleverly in diverting world attention from their own oppression of the land· they had invaded. Although, given the facts, the Chinese claim is absurd, many were willing to believe it. It was difficult indeed for Europeans to understand that the Tibetan aristocrats had been the most powerful opponents of the general rebellion begun by the Khambas and backed by the popular assemblies of the Mimang groups, composed of common people. As the Dalai Lama wrote:

> They [the Chinese] could not allow themselves to recognize the truth that it was the people themselves, whom the Chinese claimed to be liberating, who had revolted spontaneously against their liberation, *and that the ruling class in Tibet had been far more willing than the people to come to agreement.*[1]

Yet everywhere communists, socialists and even liberals throughout the world accepted the Chinese bromide quite willingly, because everyone was persuaded that Tibet was a feudal country whose oppressed peasants could only welcome even communist liberation from their supposed terrible bondage. Illogically, in spite of the facts, the theory that the Tibetans are better off now than before has gained ground in the West. Yet how could a decadent aristocracy have succeeded in opposing the powerful armies of Mao for twenty years? Only popular support for the rebellion can explain Tibetan resistance. Yet it still seems impossible for many Europeans to understand this.

Thanks to a massive propaganda campaign the Chinese managed to hide in part their loss of face, by blaming incorrectly Tibetan aristocracy for the rebellion, acquiring at the same time a free hand and valid alibi for hitting out against the rebels under cover of seeking to exterminate 'serf owners'.

All 'rebels', regardless of their social class, were branded 'serf owners', even if this meant calling the entire population of

[1] Author's italics.

Lhasa serf owners, and similarly all members of religious institutions (who owned land) were also labelled as 'oppressive,
rebellious elements'. The Chinese justified their 'military
control' over Tibet as a crusade to defend the poor oppressed
Tibetans.

By killing Tibetans on the pretext of defending them, the
Chinese were now led to committing what in January 1960
the International Commission of Jurists called 'the most
ignominious of crimes' – genocide. But genocide, as the Chinese
were to learn, is a slow and difficult process, one impossible to
complete in fact when faced with such a rugged race as the
Tibetans, one third of whom were Khambas.

Although the Chinese now controlled Lhasa, their situation
was still critical outside the holy city. All over the country resolute
Tibetans sided with the Khambas and prepared to fight.

The new puppet government braced itself to meet the onslaught. Tibet was summarily divided into seven districts and
one municipality (Lhasa) for 'reasons of defence'. 'The central
task in Tibet at present,' declared the new government, 'is the
thorough eradication of the remaining rebels.'

To quote Anna Louise Strong again :

The People's Liberation Army [i.e., the Chinese Army] now
moved from Lhasa out into Tibet, to put down rebels in the
name, not only of the Government of China, but also in the
name of Tibet's new local government which, under the
Panchen Ederni, had declared for reforms. Wherever the
troops now went, they confiscated the great whips and
torture instruments from the monasteries and manor houses
and turned them in to the county governments under military
control.

Military control of all Tibet by the Chinese was indeed the
order of the day. For this purpose some hundred thousand
(eight Chinese divisions) fresh troops were sent into Tibet via
the Sinkiang road. On 7 April, over two weeks after the fall of
Lhasa, and after several severe battles against the Khambas of
Kunga Samten, the Chinese army was able to cross the
Brahmaputra in force at Kyirong and enter Loka.

If one listens to Chinese propaganda one is told that 'in Loka
the P.L.A. forces fought here forty-seven engagements in two
weeks and disposed of two thousand rebels'. By May the

Chinese were proclaiming that 'the rebellion was utterly routed in the twinkling of an eye, in spite of the national and religious sign boards held up by the rebels, the difficult terrain with high mountains and precipitous valleys and the many different kinds of foreign aid they got'.

On 20 July the Panchen Lama acknowledged these lies and thanked the Chinese for their success, which he said was 'inseparable from the entire body of the P.L.A., both officers and combatants, who had taken part in putting down the Tibetan rebellion'.

As usual, the Chinese were anticipating. Very soon they were going to have to admit that the rebellion in central Tibet, like that of Kanting of which it was the planned extension, was far from being suppressed. The decade between 1959 and 1970 was to prove more violent than ever, a time of constant fighting and severe repression, inevitably followed by ever-increasing Tibetan resistance, a period that eventually, against all probability, would see the Tibetan cause emerge as an international crisis.

To begin with, it was to take much more than the 'twinkling of an eye' for the Chinese to make themselves masters of Loka. Like Chiang Kai-shek in China, France in Algeria and the United States in Vietnam, the Chinese were going to learn the bitter lesson that there is no quick victory in a guerrilla war. More than two and a half years were to be needed before the Chinese could reasonably claim to have 'pacified' Loka, and then only after a major, long drawn-out military campaign, involving almost one hundred thousand troops, a campaign the outcome of which was to startle the world when, after mastering the 'rebel stronghold', the Chinese army marched down from Loka into the North-East Frontier Agency to invade India in October 1962.

Immediately following the Lhasean uprising, fighting flared up with renewed vigour all over Tibet. The Dalai Lama revealed in a statement from Mussorie on 20 June 1959 that general uprisings were reported north of Lhasa and in Kham. While these peripheral battles mobilized still more soldiers, the Chinese concentrated their main force in Loka.

Like all guerrilla operations, those of the Khambas in Loka did not conform to any specific strategy other than a fluid pattern of surprise attacks, followed by hasty dispersions. To understand the Loka campaign it is easier to follow the movement of the Chinese troops, who owing to the terrain and their eternal problem of supply were obliged to apply the cumbersome techniques of classic warfare.

The Chinese strategy consisted in entering Loka simultaneously in the north from Lhasa and in the south from the Sikkim border. From Lhasa the Chinese followed approximately the route of the Dalai Lama's flight, heading for Lhuntse to join forces there with the battalions advancing from Yatung along the Bhutanese border. These two sweeping advances, it was hoped, would eventually surround the major Khamba forces, whose only escape route west was, in theory, blocked by the strategic Lhasa–Sikkim highway.

The battle of Loka began on 7 April when, after defeating the Khamba rearguard commanded by Wangchuk Tsering and Kunga Samten, the first Chinese crossed the Brahmaputra at Kyishong on rubber rafts.

Some time was then lost while the Chinese repaired the ferry, damaged by the retreating Khambas, to carry their cumbersome yet deadly armoured vehicles over the mighty river. In a cloud of dust, their engines roaring, these made off slowly eastwards up the tortuous lumber road towards Tsetang.

According to the Chinese, forty-two engagements were fought during the first two weeks of the Loka campaign. Riding down from their camps of Dofug Cho Kor and Chongya, the Khambas raided the Chinese convoys.

The Chinese were able to retake Tsetang, the garrison post they had lost to the Khambas six months previously, with little trouble. This victory was greeted with great joy by the Chinese who now hastily pushed on down the lumber road, heading for the interior of Loka. Along this trail they were now frequently brought to a standstill by landslides and broken bridges, which were repaired under the constant threat of Khamba attacks, while the Chinese soldiers were obliged to fan out above the road to guard their vehicles. Yet despite these obstacles and continued harassment they soon reached the end of the road at the foot of the Yarto range. Here the advance came to a halt.

In the meantime, from the southern garrison of Yatung (partly supplied via Kalimpong), the Chinese had climbed through the countless hamlets sprinkled over the high wooded slopes leading to the great summits which marked the border of Bhutan. By so doing they were soon in a position to attack Towa Dzong, the headquarters of Amdo Leshe, Osher's commander, from the rear. Here they had hoped to win a major battle against the Khambas, but as usual they were to be disappointed. As soon as Chinese aircraft had begun bombing raids in Loka towards the beginning of April, the Khambas had abandoned their conspicuous headquarters in the old fort and taken to the elusive shelter of their tents again. So it was the Khambas who attacked the Chinese garrisons left in Towa Dzong, while other Khamba units set out to ambush the Chinese who were continuing their advance down the deep valley of the Manas river which rises in Tibet and flows southwards through a narrow defile into Bhutan.

Severe fighting was to follow in the Manas Valley, whose steep sides gave the Khambas trouble, because they were forced to abandon their horses and fight on foot. Eventually one group of Khambas was obliged to cross over into Bhutan, having been cut off from their major force after the Chinese had destroyed the perilous bamboo bridges that criss-crossed the river.

By August the Chinese were in complete control of the Bhutan border, which was further shut by Bhutan's bold determination to ban all commerce with Tibet – a severe blow to the Chinese, who had counted on Bhutanese grain to supply their troops. Bhutan's decision was to be the only formal act of any nation against China in that first year following the Lhasean uprising. Yet being a small country, possessing no diplomatic relations and belonging to no international organization, Bhutan, however much it sympathized with the Tibetans whose religion and language it shared, was obliged to refuse asylum to the Khambas and to Tibetan refugees, who were escorted down to the Indian border of their choice. Those Khambas who had entered Bhutan crossed over to Kalimpong, whence they later slipped back secretly into Tibet from the high unguarded passes of the Sikkim–Nepal border.

When the northern Chinese advance came to a standstill at the end of the lumber road, a large Chinese force set out on foot over the high Yarto Tag pass down to the Nye Valley, heading for Lhuntse, the fortress where the Dalai Lama had set up his temporary government. With little difficulty the Chinese were able to rout the Khambas there, who, like those caught in the Manas Valley, had no alternative but to back downstream into India, where they were intercepted by members of the Assam Rifles and disarmed.

When it became known that Khamba units had been intercepted and disarmed in India, the Chinese, previously so discreet about their Loka campaign, claimed for the second time that all Khambas in Loka had been defeated.

All told, the first months of the Loka campaign had been a costly operation for the Khambas. The monsoon clouds over the southern Himalayas had prevented their vital airdrops in May, June, July and August, while with the closing of the border of Bhutan and India's increased vigilance against the Tibetans along their North-East Frontier Agency frontier, they had seen their supply lines from the south successively closed.

Knowing their assets, the Khambas now determined to shift their headquarters and make central Loka their new stronghold. The *magars* regrouped around Yamdrok and Trigu Lakes, a region with a mean altitude of 15,000 feet overlooking the Brahmaputra to the north and to the south the valleys leading down to the low Tak district adjoining India.

In good cavalry country once again, the Khambas were able to pursue their harassment of the Chinese, who were handicapped by the first snow-storms of winter which brought their trucks practically to a standstill. This season, on the other hand, was favourable for the Khambas as rivers subsided or froze and once again the 'sky boats' began to return with supplies.

The news of the general Lhasean uprising determined Taiwan to increase (after the monsoon) her support to Tibet, now centred on dropping sites in the Yamdrok Lake region.

The Chinese communists were well aware of these airdrops, which they now openly denounced as flagrant violations of their frontiers, proof of 'Imperialist intervention in Tibet'. Later, when Sino-Indian friendship collapsed, formal protests were made to India for three hundred such violations of Chinese air space between 1960 and 1962. Captured weapons, parachutes and radio sets were displayed in a museum in Lhasa, with denunciations of 'Feudal Tyranny in Tibet', 'Imperialist Intervention' and 'Monastic Atrocities'. These exhibits were triumphantly displayed to foreign communist newsmen invited to the holy city to further implement China's propaganda campaign.

No amount of propaganda could conceal the facts indefinitely. The Chinese, although they had severely shaken many Khamba units in Loka, were far from having 'crushed the rebellion' or even dented the morale and power of the main Khamba force, further strengthened by the soldiers of Lhasa's mutinous regiments. As in Kham, they felt they could not rid the land of 'rebels' unless all the population united to help them. This was the futile dream the Chinese now tried to implement : a tactic applied also in Vietnam, as to win over the masses is still the only means known to stifle guerrilla action. But how could the hated Chinese ever have entertained the thought that they would find the sympathy in Tibet to achieve their goal?

So began 'the second phase of the Loka campaign, a political and military struggle combined. Notices were posted in towns and villages and meetings held among the people; announcing that no captured rebels would be killed' (an interesting and unintentional admission of past Chinese treatment of prisoners), 'that those who surrendered voluntarily would not even be imprisoned or accused in public meetings and rewards would be given for "meritorious deeds" in restoring order'.[1] For order was far from being restored, and bribes were certainly not the answer to the rebellion that was now, for many, nine years old.

The political and military struggle soon turned into the classic 'struggle meetings' for which the Chinese were famous. The public humiliation of officials, the mocking and beating of monks, all met with increased resistance.

Victim of their own false propaganda that only a handful of 'upper-strata reactionaries' were responsible for the revolt, unable to perceive the simple fact that the Tibetans wanted only one thing, independence from China, the Chinese now foolishly committed, not only in Loka but also all over Tibet, the same mistakes which they had made in Kham, with, of course, the same results.

How the Chinese succeeded in their 'political and military control' is shown clearly by the testimony of countless refugees. A monk from Tangya in western Tibet described to the International Commission of Jurists how, in December 1959, 'A meeting of the people was called. They were told that most of

[1] Quoted from *When Serfs Stood Up* by Anna L. Strong.

the reactionaries had now been suppressed, but that there might be some in the area. They should co-operate with the Chinese in searching for them. These people [they were told] would be mostly Khambas and the people of the wealthy class. The standard of the people was to be improved, the old system of the Dalai Lama's government abolished and they should speak out against it.' According to the same witness, 'nobody did so', and as a consequence 'road-building groups were organized and for this purpose all between the ages of eighteen and sixty were to be taken, whether man, woman, religious or lay'.

As a result, the political control that was supposed to see the 'serfs stand up' and denounce the 'rebels' only led to generalized opposition. Despite the renewed Chinese claim that 'the Khambas were robbing the peasants of their livestock and grain', popular resentment stiffened. Far from denouncing the 'rebels' or leading the Chinese to their secret camps, all those men who were able took to the mountains and joined the Khambas, while the old and infirm, whenever possible, took the road into exile, heading now not for Lhasa but for India. The few thousand refugees to be found in and around Kalimpong in July 1959 had seen their numbers increase to eleven thousand by the end of the year, a figure that was to soar to eighty thousand by the end of 1963. It is an incredible figure when one recalls the small population of Tibet and knows all the means employed by the Chinese to stop this mass migration; for the Chinese did not hesitate to fire on the refugees. They also declared all over Tibet that 'flight to India would be futile' because they controlled Kalimpong and could catch up with the refugees 'as far as Siliguri on the Bengal plain'.

Renewed Chinese attacks on the monasteries brought about a reaction far stronger than in Kham, since central Tibet possessed far many more monks. Every family sent one son to their local cloister. By attacking the monasteries, the Chinese were thus attacking every family. By attacking the gods, they were also insulting the whole land. By attacking the lords, even, they roused no sympathy. Nothing, the Chinese feared, could induce Tibet to play the role Mao had wished: to become a profitable and subdued annex of the 'great motherland' within the strategic heart of Asia.

Ten full years after Mao had decided to subdue central Asia's 'barbarians' he was still faced with open opposition, the first he had known since coming to power in Peking. Figures alone – the figures of the Chinese military budget for Tibet – showed Mao how he had failed. Tibet was becoming more than a costly experiment. It was occupying the best of Mao's army, matériel, planes and brains. To support one soldier in Tibet cost as much as to feed fifty in Peking. Transport by road over the 1,800 miles from China's border to Loka cost thirty yen (thirty-five American cents) a pound, practically the price of air freight. It took sixteen days for trucks to make their slow way across Kansu and Sinkiang, over the Frozen Sea into the terrible highlands of western Tibet, then down the Brahmaputra to Lhasa. Sixteen days one way, thirty-two days return, one month's salary for the driver, two tons of precious petrol that had itself to be trucked over at the same expense! Two sets of tyres to be cut to shreds on the jagged rocks, not to mention the wear and tear on the vehicles, which were forever breaking down. Yet there were a hundred thousand men to feed in Kham and Amdo; another hundred thousand in central Tibet, and still the requests arrived in Peking from Lhasa for fresh troops, while as sufficient food could not be imported over the road from China it had to be purchased from India at fifteen times the normal price: Tibet was now threatened with famine.

13

'Dry Bones'

1960 and 1961 were to prove bleak years for the Chinese in more than one respect. They were beginning to feel the disastrous effects of the 'great leap forward'. Communes, hastily set up, proved inefficient and ruinous and had to be disbanded, while heavy rains washed away in a matter of days the great dams it had taken years to build, proving to Mao that engineering and agricultural decisions could not be made on the basis of political theory only. Pig iron of poor quality lay rusting in stacks beside neglected fields, which in 1961 for the second consecutive year fell victims to exceptional floods followed by drought. Following these calamities, grain and oil were rationed, while reports from China claimed that 'most people were hungry'.

These setbacks added to the military defeat of China's 1958–9 offensive against the offshore islands of Quemoy and Matsu and her reverses in Tibet, where the Loka campaign was stretching out into a slow war of penetration. The Khambas were everywhere, lying in ambush, unexpectedly assailing each new outpost, each new garrison which the Chinese had pain-fully established, as, with the help of forced 'volunteer labour', they hastily blasted roads ever deeper into rebel-held territory. For these operations more troops were always needed, and daily thousands of ill-equipped Chinese peasants were trucked slowly over the freezing passes into hostile Tibet. The morale of these troops was low, so low indeed that many Tibetans were naïvely convinced that if they could bribe the Chinese leaders their soldiers would mutiny. This belief was fostered by the numerous defections among the Chinese occupational forces. Most Tibetans in exile reported their sympathy for these poor Chinese lads, whose lot was far from enviable as they fought the cold, pneumonia and the effects of malnutrition which dogged them along with the deadly shots of the elusive Khamba snipers.

Yet all was not well with the Khambas either. 1960 had

begun badly for them when serious disputes arose in India over the command of the N.V.D.A. and the appropriation of the Dalai Lama's treasure. According to a report by George Patterson published in the *Daily Telegraph* on 8 February:

> The Khamba leaders are infuriated with their vacillating Lhasean officials and their endless useless intrigues. . . . The traditional breach between devious Lhasa officials and militant Khambas which was temporarily healed last year [1959] is now widening into an unbridgeable gulf.

Behind this announcement was the question of what aid the N.V.D.A. should receive. The Khambas had hoped for money to purchase arms and medicines, but now it seemed that they would receive from the Dalai Lama only 'pacific aid', vocal encouragement, while the money of the national treasure was expended on members of the Dalai Lama's entourage sent abroad as representatives to the United Nations and to foreign countries.

The Pangda Tsangs, to whom the leadership of Tibetan affairs abroad should have been given by right, were slighted and brushed aside. Gyalo Thondup, the second eldest brother of the Dalai Lama, took over the leadership of Tibetan affairs, at the head of a small clique of Lhasean exiles who scorned the Khambas, whose actions in Lhasa they resented.

In disgust, the Khambas were obliged to turn once again to Taiwan for help. They were forced to continue accepting the double-edged assistance of their former enemies. In Kalimpong, Kathmandu and Mussorie, Nationalist Chinese agents eagerly recruited hundreds of Tibetan refugees spoiling to fight. These young men were flown secretly to Formosa where the distasteful prospect of being incorporated into Chiang Kai-shek's army awaited them.

Many of the Khamba leaders in India were left to finance their own struggle and their return to Tibet with Khamba recruits, young refugees opposed to working for Formosa, yet prepared to throw their lives away rather than moulder in refugee camps weaving carpets for tourists, or slaving at building strategic roads, a task to which many refugees were assigned by the Indian government for little or no pay.

Disappointing also for many Tibetans was the news of developments of Tibet's appeal to the United Nations in

October 1959, backed this time by the Republic of Ireland and Malaya. Yet in 1959 as in 1950 Tibet was to be shamelessly abandoned by the assembly of nations. To begin, Mr Kuznetsov, the Russian delegate, violently opposed the placing of the Tibetan question before the General Assembly in a speech in which he declared that 'Tibet was an inseparable part of China' and that the problem of Tibet 'was an internal affair of China'. Despite this speech, the Tibetan issue was placed before the General Assembly, but there it was sabotaged by India when Krishna Menon made a lame speech, deliberately ignoring the findings of the International Commission of Jurists, whose report 'Tibet and the Rule of Law' had shown to the satisfaction of International Law that Tibet had enjoyed legal 'de facto autonomy' from China until its invasion in 1950, and had stated officially that, according to all canons of international jurisprudence, Tibet had regained this independent status by the double breaking of the seventeen-point agreement by both the Chinese and the Tibetans in 1959. No country would take upon itself to raise the vital problem of Tibetan independence, and as a result the whole discussion was sidetracked to the theoretical problem of determining whether or not the Chinese in Tibet had violated the principle of the Universal Declaration of Human Rights. A point of pernicious casuistry, it was of no use whatsoever to a nation in arms about to become the victim of genocide.

Again in 1959 Great Britain failed sadly to make good her past treaty relations with Tibet or take a firm stand in favour of Tibet; and, worse still, the British representative, Sir Pierson Dixon, threw doubt over the whole Tibetan situation by declaring that he was 'unable to make up his mind'. Yet both India and Great Britain made up their minds sufficiently to abstain from voting, along with all western colonial and ex-colonial powers, while the entire Russian block voted against, leaving only the United States and forty small nations out of the eighty-two countries present to vote for the resolution.

The mild resolution which the United Nations eventually passed in favour of Tibet simply 'affirms its [the General Assembly's] belief that respect for the Charter and of the Universal Declaration of Human Rights is essential for the evolution of a peaceful world order based on the rule of Law', and 'calls for respect for the fundamental human right of the

Tibetan people and for their distinctive cultural and religious right'.

An affirmation and a call in the dark – 'beautiful words', said those Khambas who read the transcript of this piece of international hypocrisy in *Freedom*, the Tibetan newspaper printed in Kalimpong. Once again, Tibet had been let down by the world.

Yet inside Tibet more was needed to shatter the morale of the Khambas. Their success in Lhasa in developing their rebellion into a major Tibet-wide struggle encouraged them to struggle on, along with the stubborn certainty that eventually they would win. This blind faith in victory was not a mere product of fanaticism. The Khambas were taught from childhood that revenge was a sacred duty and that time was immaterial in its accomplishment. If not in this life, all felt certain that they would triumph in the next, death for the Tibetans having an undertone of hope, the belief in reincarnation assuring a continuity of purpose.

Tsering was of this mind, and while the disputes that now flared up between the Dalai Lama's court in exile and the Pangda Tsangs angered him, he had suffered too many betrayals to take the matter too bitterly. If Tsering had given up hope of ever returning to Chamdo, he knew that he would eventually be avenged, if not by his own sword, by those of his children. How often in Kham had even young girls sought out husbands in the only hope of producing sons to avenge their honour, as generation following generation inherited the same determination to seek justice in their traditional lengthy blood feuds!

From Kalimpong, Tsering had slipped into Tibet across the Sikkim border by the Donkya pass which led onto a vast barren plain above which rose one of Tibet's most impressive forts, Khampa Dzong, a place well named; for now this lonely central Tibetan fortress set on its spectacular crag became the rallying point of a large detachment of Khambas able to communicate by radio with the Khamba leaders garrisoned around Yamdrok Lake in Loka.

Although the Tibetans controlled the heart of Loka, the region had lost its strategic value now that the Chinese controlled the Bhutanese border. Consequently it was decided that the Khambas should extend their activities to the Tibetan province of Tsang. In other words, they were to penetrate the most populous region of central Tibet, the long, broad corridor running between the border of Nepal and the upper course of the Brahmaputra. In Tsang are Shigatse and Gyantse, the second and third largest towns of Tibet, along with countless settlements stretching all the way to the nomadic lands of Ngari (western Tibet).

This decision was to prove a clever move, for the cumbersome Chinese military machine, having concentrated its efforts and pride on pacifying Loka, was caught off guard by this extension of Khamba activity to the west. Further, the eight hundred miles of Nepal's northern border, marked by such huge peaks as Mount Everest, afforded a frontier across which the Khambas could infiltrate arms and evacuate their wounded undisturbed, since both sides of the border were inhabited by Tibetan-speaking peoples.

The success of the Khambas in their new operation was linked with the fact that in the most densely populated area of Tibet they could count on support from the local inhabitants. The Chinese on the other hand were quite unprepared for this move which allowed the Khambas to cut the Sinkiang highway time and again, temporarily isolating Lhasa and Loka from all approach by road. The reason the Chinese had not garrisoned Tsang heavily was that this province had been their most favoured region of Tibet – the province administered by the docile Panchen Lama.

From his huge monastery of Tashilumpo in Shigatse, the Panchen Lama had so far ruled the province to China's satisfaction. He was to all intents and purposes Chinese himself, having been educated by the communists and brought to Tibet by the People's Liberation Army in 1951.

In the West much confusion has clouded what has rightly been termed the case of the Panchen Lama, the holy reincarnation the Chinese had set up in Lhasa in 1959 as the head of Tibet 'until the return of the abducted Dalai Lama'.

The story of the Panchen Lama is indeed a confusing one, beginning forty years earlier when the tenth Panchen Lama fled from Lhasa to Amdo under the protection of Chinese troops after a disagreement with the thirteenth Dalai Lama. When, in 1927, the Panchen Lama died in Chinese-held territory, the affair of his successor began – of his successors, one should say, as two children were claimed to be his reincarnation: two children over whose heads a sinister drama of political intrigue unfolded that was eventually to lead both incarnations to a violent death. No more than the Dalai Lamas of the past were the young Panchen Lamas to escape the all-powerful hands of their tutors in those court intrigues that so disgusted the Khambas, born far away from the antechambers of the great abbots' residences.

Few Tibetans had any direct ill feeling for the 'Chinese' Panchen Lama. He could not, being only an innocent victim, be considered a traitor like Ngabo. He was a puppet with more excuse than the Dalai Lama for, not only was he of doubtful legitimacy, but he had been raised by the Chinese from infancy.

Even Chang Kai-shek, prior to 1949, had sought to use the Panchen Lama. In 1951 the communists had adopted the same policy and placed the present Panchen Lama on the diamond seat of Tashilumpo, disregarding the other (Lhasean) candidate who had conveniently disappeared, murdered. With the intention of dividing to rule, the Chinese had then restored territorial rights to the Panchen Lama, creating a Tashilumpo autonomous region within central Tibet, with its own preparatory committee such as that of Chamdo. The people of Tsang and Shigatse had fallen for this ruse which restored the prestige they had once enjoyed, when, in the eighteenth century, the Panchen Lamas had controlled much of Tibetan affairs during the minority of the Dalai Lamas.

Since 1951 the Chinese had been using the Panchen Lama to weaken the authority of the Dalai Lama. As a consequence of the privileges showered on the Panchen Lama's subjects, the province of Tsang had been spared much of the turmoil that other regions of Tibet had known. The Chinese had even endowed the monastery of Tashilumpo, already renowned as the wealthiest in Tibet, with further riches.

Two years younger than the Dalai Lama, the Panchen Lama had learnt the lessons of his Chinese advisers well; too well perhaps, or so at least it seemed to Stuart Gelder, who felt obliged to admit that 'when he spoke of politics and history, the Panchen Lama talked like a gramophone record which he could probably have intoned backwards without stumbling over a word'.

The docility of the Panchen Lama had caused the Chinese

to overlook somewhat their defences in Tsang, whose local population and countless monks it was naïvely believed could be counted on, with the Panchen Lama, to support Chinese policies.

It was to the relative peace and shelter of Shigatse that many of those fleeing from strife-torn Lhasa had come. Among these refugees were Tsering's wife and four children. While in Kalimpong, Tsering had been informed of their flight to Shigatse, so that while he planned in conjunction with detachments from Loka to strike at the Chinese in Tsang, he was worrying about the effect this might have on the safety of his own family.

The main Khamba objectives in Tsang became the towns of Tingri (north of Everest) and Shekar, reached by a small branch of the Lhasa–Sinkiang highway. These two towns were both due west of Khampa Dzong and Tinkya Dzong in which the Khambas, reinforced by Tibetans coming over from India via Sikkim and Nepal, were well entrenched.

In early 1960 fighting was intense in Tsang as, taking advantage of the cold winter weather, the Khambas set out in small detachments against the few Chinese garrisons. Their advance was greeted by uprisings in the monasteries, threatened like those in Lhasa with extinction. Rombuck monastery, south of Tingri, already the scene of considerable violence in August 1959, took up arms once more, while to the north a bloody battle took place between the Khambas and the Chinese at Tingri and in the west Khampa Dzong was 'attacked from the rear' by Chinese coming up from the border from Sikkim.

These attacks coincided with renewed resistance all over Tibet. On 15 March 1960 severe fighting was reported to have broken out in Chamdo and Markham, around which many uncontrollable Khamba nomads still roamed. In Lhasa itself, despite the severe Chinese military control, six party officials were assassinated in the same month. By spring most of Tibet was once again in arms. At first the Chinese were silent about this extension of the rebellion which they had allegedly quelled in 'the twinkling of an eye'. Yet the world press got wind of these events. On 3 June an article was published claiming that 'major armed clashes in Tibet were reported' and that 'lorry loads of Chinese dead had been seen coming down the strategic highway in the vicinity of Yatung'.

The situation was so much out of control that, probably on the suggestion of the Panchen Lama, his monks of Tashilumpo had to be armed to fight the rebels both in Tsang and Loka – a foolish move on the part of the Chinese, as these monks joined the rebels.

Anti-Chinese posters now reappeared all over Lhasa in what the *Daily Telegraph* termed 'reckless defiance'. Then, on 8 June, 'increased turmoil in the north west' was noted as fighting broke out on the high plains of Ngari. Meanwhile the roads joining Shekar and Lhasa, and Shekar and Tingri, were reported closed by the Khambas, who had wiped out the Chinese garrisons of both these towns before advancing two hundred miles north west to cut the Sinkiang Lhasa road at Sakya. On 25 June wounded Khambas announced in Nepal that the Panchen Lama's own father had joined in the fighting, though this news was contradicted by Peking. So serious had the situation become that B. P. Keriala, the prime minister of Nepal, saw fit to report on 27 June 'heavy fighting in Tibet and a trade halt as a result'. In their efforts to pursue the Khambas, the Chinese that same month sent two thousand men to within twelve miles of the Nepalese border near a remote region called Mustang. The Nepalese immediately protested to China, claiming a violation of the Sino-Nepalese friendship treaty that the prime minister had signed in Peking in April. The Nepalese government on 30 June officially asked the Chinese to withdraw their troops from the Nepalese borders. In reply, the Chinese at last had to admit to the world what they had concealed so well, when a Chinese note to the Nepalese foreign office announced that 'units of the Chinese army would withdraw to twenty miles from the border regions *immediately after the Tibetan revolt was crushed*'. Thus, a year to the day after having theoretically eliminated Tibetan resistance, the Chinese for the first time since 1959 admitted officially their failure to control Tibet.

The Chinese had been reduced to this humiliating declaration by the dramatic situation inside Tibet which until then nobody in the West had fully appreciated. Once again the Khambas were on the warpath; far from being wiped out (even in Loka) they had now increased their theatre of operations to the entire province of Tsang, while in Amdo and Kham fighting proceeded with renewed vigour.

The situation for China, difficult enough inside Tibet, was about to be made far worse by events in Sinkiang and the dramatic, quite unexpected turnabout of Russia against Peking. Indeed Russia had till 1960 looked with indifference on the happenings inside Tibet, and had even helped the Chinese in Tibet and Sinkiang by furnishing them with arms and occasionally with military advisers. Yet by July 1960, less than eight months after Russia's opposition to Tibet at the United Nations, China was being attacked by the U.S.S.R. and later by India and Nepal for its 'Imperialistic expansionist policies in central Asia'.

Why, one may ask, this sudden reversal? The answer is to be found in the behaviour of the Chinese themselves. That a large powerful nation in the twentieth century should attempt to crush an entire race, to eradicate its religion and to murder its population had caused little stir, but it was a different matter when China's claim to Tibet began to overlap the territorial claims of other nations.

The trouble began when the Chinese started taking seriously their own claim that 'Tibet and Sinkiang were an integral part of China', deducing from this that all Tibetan-speaking areas of central Asia were therefore integral parts of Tibet, and so also belonged to Peking.

As we have seen, a claim to Tibet in fact meant a claim to most of central Asia which had been Tibetan in the days of Songtsen Gampo. Consequently in 1960 the Chinese began asserting that they owned, as part of Tibet, much of the southern slopes of the great Himalayan range, in particular, great portions of Laddak and most of the North-East Frontier Agency and Sikkim, not to mention the Tibetan-speaking border zones of Nepal and those regions of Russia adjoining the Frozen Sea and Sinkiang. In addition, of course, to this provocation of Russia, the Chinese claimed Mongolia and thousands of square miles of disputed territory along the Russian Altai mountain borders. All these regions had been annexed, according to China, by the 'unfair treaties' of British and Russian Imperialists!

These claims were first brought up by the publication in Peking of maps showing over 16,000 square miles of Indian territory as part of Chinese Tibet and 12,000 square miles of Russian soil, taken from the frontiers of Russian Turkestan.

The West was slow at first to react to the Chinese claims. Not so the Russians.

Although the U.S.S.R. had until late 1959 openly admitted and declared repeatedly at the United Nations that Sinkiang, like Tibet, was an integral part of China, the Russians did not it seems truly believe this, as was shown by Khruschev's startling declaration in 1960 that Russia was favourable to the auto-determination of Sinkiang. Before the rest of the world, the Russians in 1960 had suddenly awoken to the dismal realization that, by claiming Tibet and colonizing Sinkiang, the Chinese were in fact gaining control of the strategic heart of the Old World.

Of the countries menaced by China's aggressive expansionist policies, India, still lulled by dreams of Sino-Indian friendship, was it seemed the last to understand the threat China represented, although Peking now had fortified garrisons less than two hundred and fifty miles from New Delhi. Garrisons from which Chinese soldiers could aim missiles at the Indian capital, in the same way as they could now attack at short range Kabul, the capital of Afghanistan, Samarkand and Tashkent, the great towns of Russia's richest Socialist Republic, Uzbekistan, not to mention the Russian atomic field of the Alma Ata region now within Chinese reach.

Reacting violently to the Chinese menace in the spring of 1960 the U.S.S.R. recalled all its technical personnel from China, asking them to take with them the blueprints of any unfinished projects. The Soviet Union then demanded that China repay outright all outstanding loans, even though (or because) the Russians knew that such a demand, in a time of famine and economic chaos, would cause China great trouble. (In fact it was to take four years for the Chinese economy to recover from this blow.) Then, overnight, all shipments of Russian planes, trucks, jeeps, tanks and weapons were halted, along with the export of spare parts, arms the Chinese had been awaiting to distribute to the ten divisions in Sinkiang and those in Tibet to implement China's wild new territorial claims.

The Sino-Russian break was sudden and irreversible, yet in the West little credence was given to it at first, although as early as on 15 March 1960 the first of a long series of violent armed clashes had broken out between Chinese and Russian armed troops in Sinkiang.

This was a pitched battle in the Altai region of Sinkiang between Russian-armed and -directed Kazakh herdsmen and the People's Liberation Army. It was the first of several little known battles that were expected, to use the words of Askaroff, one of the Russian commanders in Sinkiang, 'to fan into a large scale anti-Chinese (Sinkiang) national revolt' planned to unite the Uigurs, Kirghiz, Tartar and Tajiks with the forces of the original Kazakh insurgents.

From 1960 on, the Russians engineered constant turmoil and rebellion among the inhabitants of Sinkiang, so that, while the Khambas cut the only open Chinese road to Lhasa at Sakya, five hundred miles farther up in Sinkiang this same route was being similarly assailed.

The Russians were not slow to realize that the greatest military force and the one best able to oppose Mao in central Asia was composed not so much of the small national groups of Sinkiang as of the million-strong Khambas.

In August 1960 Dr S. Sinha of the Indian parliament and one-time Comintern agent in Russia, obtained in Moscow from Askaroff, one of the master minds behind the Sinkiang rebellion, the amazing admission that the Russians would have to 'co-ordinate the Tibetan revolt with that of Sinkiang. Without achieving this aim', Askaroff explained, 'we do not consider our eastern borders to be safe from Chinese threats'.

After China had lost Russia, her most powerful ally, on 23 February 1961, Nehru revealed to the Indian parliament details of the Konka Pass incident. Although not the first violation of Indian territory by the Chinese, this was to mark the beginning of India's reappraisal of the folly of its past policy towards Tibet.

The incident, kept secret, had occurred on 20 October 1960 while Krishna Menon was sabotaging Tibet's appeal to the United Nations. Early that October the Indians had at long last discovered that the strategic Sinkiang-Lhasa road had been built across a vast tract of Indian soil over part of the Aksai Chin desert. Consequently, Indian patrols were sent to investigate this road and the extent of Chinese encroachment. One of these patrols, sent out on 20 October, did not return. Immediately twenty Indian soldiers led by Karam Singh set out in search of these men. They soon ran into Chinese soldiers well within the Indian boundary. The Chinese called on the Indians to surrender. Karam Singh shouted that they were on Indian soil, upon which the Chinese opened fire, killing several Indians before the remainder surrendered. These prisoners were then taken and thrown into a pit and left for three days in the intense cold prior to being brutalized and tortured for twelve consecutive days.

The revelation of such inhuman behaviour towards Indian soldiers perpetrated many miles inside Indian territory rudely shook Indian public opinion. After this incident, Sino-Indian friendship naturally cooled, although not enough to make Indians take Tibetans off their 'suspect persons list'. Indeed Tibetans were still discriminated against to such an extent that as late as 15 April 1961 the Dalai Lama was obliged to 'appeal to Nehru to relax his recent move to seal the Indian frontier against Tibetan refugees' (*Daily Telegraph*).

To these Chinese blunders was added a third mistake, that of Mao's dealings with Nepal. In March 1960 Nepal had sent its prime minister to Peking, from where he returned with the statement that there were no border disputes between China and Nepal except some minor differences 'that would soon be resolved'. In fact, despite the treaty of Sino-Nepalese friendship which had been signed in Peking on 28 April, the minor differences were amplified by a quarrel over the ownership of Mount Everest, which the Chinese claimed was theirs (including the south face). Eventually it was conceded that half of Everest would be Chinese and the other half Nepalese. If this gave momentary satisfaction to Nepal, the intrusion in June 1960 of Chinese troops pursuing Khamba rebels into the twenty-mile demilitarized zone bordering Nepal led to more unpleasantness when the Chinese, while breaking into Mustang, actually fired upon Nepalese soldiers and killed an officer.

Despite Chou En-lai's declaration that this incident was a 'shortcoming' and 'not a breach of agreement', and despite Peking's apologies and payment of 50,000 rupees in compensation, this new affair caused grave concern in Nepal. The widely publicized incident, along with the Chinese declaration that they would only withdraw from Nepal's border when the 'Tibetan rebellion had been crushed', further brought home to Nepal the aggressive spirit and intentions of the Chinese, who were quoted again as claiming that Nepal, with Bhutan, the

North-East Frontier Agency, Sikkim and Laddak, was one of the five fingers of the (Chinese) Tibetan hand.

These incidents had slowly brought the world to reconsider the basis of China's presence in central Asia and to note the severe difficulties China had incurred through the break with Russia. Deprived of Russian technical assistance and the delivery of much-needed trucks, tanks and armoured vehicles, the Chinese were suddenly faced with a serious crisis not only in Tibet and Sinkiang but also in China itself. There the operation of the 'pruning of dangerous weeds' had met with serious opposition from the army, and in 1961 open rebellion broke out in the Honan province inside China where 'military officers and junior officials' had, according to Peking's habitual jargon, 'turned bandit'.

By early 1962 rebellion in Honan, in Sinkiang and in Tibet, in the middle of an economic disaster caused by three consecutive years of crop failure, had created for China a crisis as serious as that of 1956, at the outbreak of the Kanting Rebellion. The discovery of huge oil deposits in Sinkiang and vital rich uranium and gold deposits in western Tibet (natural resources that China greatly needed) made it more imperative than ever for the Chinese to put down the continuing rebellions in Tibet and Sinkiang. Yet how could this be achieved? The only answer was to stage major military operations; first to re-open the Sinkiang–Lhasa highway, and then to send still more men into Tibet. A feat easier said than done, for Khamba guerrillas were now pouring into the Chang Thang, the central plains of Tibet, from the east in their thousands, coming from Jeykundo and Chamdo. This fresh influx of eastern Tibetans across the Chang Thang caused new headaches for the Chinese, as these reinforcements tried to contact the main Khamba forces south of the Brahmaputra, while also opening a new front on the barren northern plains through which the Khambas hoped to be able to make contact with the Sinkiang Kazakh rebels. Lhasa's Dham airport was now the only sure link between the Tibetan capital and Peking; yet even that was not immune from attack, and it became known that rebels from Jeykundo had assailed the airfield in March 1961.

To add to the problems of the Chinese, and despite wild propaganda about 'bumper crops', in 1961 famine had again struck Tibet where, since the Lhasean uprising, the People's

Liberation Army had been obliged in many places to cultivate the fields abandoned by fleeing Tibetans. The situation inside Tibet had deteriorated so far that the Chinese, having claimed they were building 'paradise', had to admit officially in the spring of 1961 to a 'slowdown in Tibet' and that collectivization 'would be postponed' for the third time.

The Khambas in the meantime, taking advantage of China's predicament, continued their operations with renewed vigour, and reports of major fighting in Chongya in Loka were announced by the Dalai Lama. This Khamba stronghold in Loka held its ground until the summer of 1962, despite the intense concentration of Chinese troops in the area, and the near completion of two roads from Tsetang down to Lhuntse and Tsona Dzong along the Indian frontier, while another road was hastily pushed down to Towa Dzong near the Bhutanese border.

Towards the end of 1961 Amdo Leshe, in contact with other Khamba leaders, decided that the general headquarters of the Khambas should now be shifted from Loka to a region where it would be easier to receive arms and ammunition from abroad, a site with access both to Tibet and to some neutral country. The ideal region was found to be the little-known kingdom of Mustang, the same region which had been the scene of Chinese violence in 1960.

A fifteen-thousand-foot plateau overhanging the Brahmaputra and the strategic Chinese road from Sinkiang, Lo, as Mustang is called in Tibetan, appeared to the Khambas the ideal place they had been looking for. The six hundred square miles of Mustang project outwards from Nepal into Tibet like a thumb dominating western Tibet, far up beyond the great Annapurna and Dhaulaghiri ranges. In 1961 this region was, to all intents and purposes, independent, although in their desire not to anger Nepal the Chinese had conceded that Mustang should remain Nepalese on the grounds of a small annual tribute paid by the king of Mustang to the Nepalese kings. Entirely Tibetan by culture and language, the kingdom of Mustang, although officially considered part of Nepal, was administered by its Tibetan king, a man naturally favourable to the Tibetan 'rebels' and at the same time indifferent to Nepal, which had never in the past concerned itself with this remote region, situated twenty-four days' climb away from Kathmandu.

Being neutral and fearful of China, Nepal disapproved of the Khambas entering Mustang; but, like the Chinese, the Nepalese were soon to discover that there is no opposing the wish of a Khamba except by force.

Thus, while maintaining a token force in Loka, ten of the main Khamba *magars* moved off west across Tsang towards Mustang, and with them went Osher. Tsering, on the other hand, set out for Shigatse in search of his wife and children. Since 1960, in order to stop refugees fleeing from Tibet, China had issued all Tibetans with identity cards and had forbidden anyone to travel more than a day's journey from his home village without a special pass. With forged documents and dressed as ordinary peasants Tsering and three companions eventually reached Shigatse, the holy seat of the Panchen Lama.

This magnificent town with its monumental circular *chorten*, its palaces and Tashilumpo monastery, is dominated by a gigantic crenellated wall, snaking up the jagged crest of the semi-circle of mountains enclosing the sprawling city. Passing Chinese soldiers of the local garrison, Tsering made his way through the narrow streets towards the bazaar, turning the great creaking prayer wheels that lined the streets. Concealing his pistol within the back fold of his gown, he hung about the bazaar until he was directed to a group of Khamba refugees. In no time, these told him where his wife was living.

Tsering had not seen his family for nearly three years, and he had trouble recognizing his children, the eldest of whom was now nearly fourteen and the youngest almost six. Tsering's wife had settled in a little tea house where, with her children, she waited on customers. Like any Khamba woman, Tsering's wife showed little emotion at the sight of her husband, only her eyes betraying her feelings. Life in Tibet, a land with no quick means of communication, had long taught its inhabitants patience and resignation to fate. Since 1956 Tsering's wife had become accustomed to the dangers of her husband's existence and to the hardships of her own reduced condition. The days seemed far distant when she had ruled Ulag Dzong as the proud mistress of her husband's estate. Yet she never showed how much it had cost her to live alone and keep four children together in the turmoil of her successive journeys from Kham to Lhasa and then from Lhasa to Shigatse.

In Shigatse Tsering heard of the rumour, now making its

way by word of mouth across Tibet, that the Russians were fighting in support of the rebellion in Sinkiang. For years the Tibetans had maintained commercial relations with their northern neighbours, Moslems who shared in Lhasa a special district with other traders from Kashmir and who had even possessed a mosque in the holy city. Through these traders and their agents it was now learned that the Kazakh rebels were carrying out operations not only from the Altai regions but also from the shelter of the great mountains rising up to the feared Tibetan Chang Thang, that high plateau whose northern edge descended into the lower valleys of Keryia, Nyia and other towns of Sinkiang.

The Khambas knew and appreciated the valour of the Kazakh warriors, some of whom between 1950 and 1954 had already put up a strong fight against the Chinese; and in so doing had been forced to seek refuge in Tibet. To Tsering it became evident that the wilds of the Chang Thang would afford a second platform from which to oppose the Chinese, a sheltered region from which both Khamba and Kazakh rebels could operate jointly, attacking the Chinese on all sides. With the influx of Amdowans reported to be pouring into the Chang Thang, Tsering thought that it would be possible to establish there a huge, elusive nomadic community which could survive while fighting the Chinese jointly with the Kazakhs and which would eventually, it was hoped, receive direct help from the Russians.

Such a belief might seem wild to the Western political observer, but it appeared in no way unreasonable to the Khambas, who had been the first to realize the scale of the Sino-Russian break, which had so far been concealed abroad by Moscow and Peking behind the smokescreen of an apparently purely ideological disagreement, the Chinese calling the Russians revisionists, while the Russians attacked the personality cult of Mao, having themselves dismantled the image of Stalin.

To Tsering, as to many Tibetans, the idea of Russia coming to the rescue of Tibet appeared the last hope for their country. He may well have been right but he was somewhat anticipating events when he decided in Shigatse to set out himself for the Chang Thang, in the belief that this would be a better base than Nepal for opposing the Chinese.

Unaware that he was committing a fatal mistake, Tsering decided to take his wife and children with him. Securing, through friends, a permit to cross the Brahmaputra at Dronga, the great ferry crossing two miles from Shigatse, he set off in broad daylight past the town's check post over to the northern bank of the river. From there, leaving the main road with fresh pack animals and ponies, he headed for Namling Dzong in the first recesses of the trans-Himalaya.

So began the journey north which took him from Dronga to Namling Dzong and then on via Taknang monastery to the small hamlet of Neulung. Here Tsering and his party had reached the borders of the domains of the Naktsang nomads who grazed their herds up beyond the high Kyang pass, which Tsering reached eight days after leaving Shigatse. As they reached the summit of the Kyang pass, Tsering's party was met by a solitary horseman who came galloping up with news that a Chinese patrol, hard on his heels, had sacked La Ma Dzong. Unable to proceed north or return south, Tsering was obliged to head west into the barren wilds of Nagchuka, a desolate sea of craggy canyons and deep gullies sloping away northwards to distant salt lakes.

Fearful of running into Chinese patrols, Tsering and his men wandered for days over this desert, until eventually they encountered a small tribe of herdsmen, refugees from Amdo. For six months these nomads had also been dodging the Chinese, while slowly pushing their mangy herds westward. For these simple peasants their flight was, in a way, a flight to perdition, as they had wandered beyond the known limits of their universe, hundreds of miles from those distant eastern pastures they called home. They lived in constant terror, not only of the Chinese, but of the tribesmen into whose domain they had intruded. Many of the Amdowans had died on the way, and most were no fitter than their beasts.

Under Tsering's leadership the whole band headed for the shores of Kyaring Tso and eventually reached the small fort of Shentsa. They found it deserted, save for a few tents erected below the walls from which a handful of half-starved children and old men emerged to inform them that the Chinese had come and gone. As for the rebels, Tsering gathered that they were in hiding farther north. Since there was little fodder and no grain, Tsering decided to set out alone with his children, his wife and two of his companions in search of these guerrillas. He was still hoping he might encounter the Chengtu nomads, whom he had heard were somewhere in the area.

Tsering's party advanced northwards but, one by one, they found the encampments deserted, with not so much as a recent print to mark the trail. Long, exhausting marches, sustained by the ever-dwindling hope of finding help, placed a further strain on the party's yaks and horses which, one after another, became lame, collapsed and had to be killed. More and more Tsering was obliged to rely on his rifle to shoot gazelles and wild asses for food.

One night the first storm came, sooner than Tsering had anticipated: the short summer of the Chang Thang reached an unexpected end. Gale-force winds, laden with icy snow, battered mercilessly at the fragile door of the minute tent in which Tsering's children cowered, whimpering in the pale flicker of the yak-dung fire. For the first time in years Tsering prayed, his heart filled with fear, not of the Chinese but of the deadly forces of nature.

At last, near the hermitage of Ragu, Tsering's party came upon a large tribe of nomads setting up their winter camp. Fearful of the season, Tsering now gave up his plan to seek out the guerrillas. Trading his gold rings and his wife's necklaces, he purchased the best horses and yaks he could find and prepared to turn back southwards in the hope of reaching the warmer banks of the Brahmaputra before the full onset of winter.

In this enterprise Tsering was joined by a few Ba-Wa tribesmen. He left Ragu eventually with a party of fifteen men. Tsering now understood that there was little hope of his family surviving if he stayed in the barren wastes of the Chang Thang, where only the sturdy nomad tribes had ever been able to withstand the winter. Even the most rugged Khambas and Amdowans could barely expect to survive for long in the 'desert of deserts', an arctic Gobi, where the tallest plant to be found is a wild onion, growing painfully to a height of fifteen inches! Sven Hedin, the great Swedish explorer and the only foreigner ever to have penetrated the Chang Thang, has likened it to the moon – a region so little explored that it was only by photographs taken from a satellite in 1965 that the region was found to contain one of the largest lakes in eastern Asia. This vast inland sea (greater than Lakes Kokonor or Baikal) had until then escaped the notice of geographers.

Although they had been brought up to the hardships of the longest trails and the most rugged conditions, the winter of the Chang Thang, with the additional hazards of hunger, howling winds, polar temperatures, brackish water and lack of pasture, was soon to prove too much for Tsering's children as now they slowly plodded south through the snow towards the Brahmaputra.

One after the other, without complaint, Tsering's children weakened, fell ill and then died. In their father's own pitiful words the corpses were 'only light bundles of dry bones' which in despair he laid out to the vultures beside the carcasses of dead beasts that littered the trail. Exposed to scavangers, the bodies were believed to return to the wind of existence, one of the four sacred Buddhist components of man.

For Tsering this long march was the final trail of disillusionment, as he contemplated in despair the tortuous roads which had led him to the Chang Thang, now the grave of his last hope. Alone he pictured in his mind all the events that had driven him from Lhasa's betrayals to the bustle of Peking, from feudalism to communism, then back to wage the war of the just, from Chamdo to Loka, from Loka to India, and the turmoil of Kalimpong's intrigues. A bitter path, littered with the empty promises of communism, the indifference of the so-called democracies, and the unheard pleas of the Khambas' outraged innocence. On losing his children, who Tsering had always believed would one day avenge the cause he had tirelessly upheld, Tsering too lost his faith and courage, even his pride and self-respect. His once handsome, arrogant features were haggard, his fine frame so broken that the bones protruded through his taut skin. It was a wrecked man who eventually reached the southern slopes of the trans-Himalayas.

14

Disaster at Dhola

While Tsering prepared in despair to make his way across the Chinese-held banks of the Brahmaputra to the relative safety of Nepal, elsewhere in Tibet, in the winter of 1961–2, the war settled down to the pattern it was to follow for the next few years.

The Chinese had now succeeded in setting up garrisons in most of the major towns and villages of Tibet, while, out of their reach, well entrenched in remote valleys and high ridges, the rebels continued to form a parallel military force which could only be dislodged at the expense of large-scale military operations. Not only in Loka, but all over Tibet, this was the general pattern of resistance – a pattern similar to those found in Yugoslavia and in certain parts of France during the last war. The major difference here was that the pastoral, nomadic and warlike habits of the Khambas allowed them to be fully self-sufficient in their remote mountain hideouts, where they lived off the produce of the herds attached to each *magar*.

The poor morale of the Chinese troops and the great physical hardships they had to endure merely to survive in Tibet explain their reluctance to risk their lives in regions known to be occupied by the guerrillas. In most of Tibet the Chinese never dared to stray from their garrisons into the insecurity of the hills; except in Loka where their massive drive for local pacification still continued.

Apart from senior Chinese generals and policy makers, the most aggressive communists in Tibet in 1962 were not the Chinese but the fanatical young Tibetans educated and brainwashed in China to hate and despise their own kin. Yet even these, as the Dalai Lama later observed, often turned on their Chinese masters, numbers of them joining the Khambas, bringing with them detailed knowledge of Chinese policies and plans. They were not the only ones to defect to the rebels. Constant arrests of Chinese soldiers by the Chinese themselves told of the wavering fidelity of the communist conscripts, thousands of whom actually skipped their garrisons to join their former enemies.

With winter, Chinese attacks on Khamba positions almost ceased, although reports in November 1961 told of renewed jet bomber raids on some Khamba positions. The intense cold further obliged the Chinese to withdraw from many of their garrisons, in particular from those located in the high border zones of Laddak, Bhutan, Nepal and Sikkim. But while snow and ice brought Chinese vehicles to a standstill and howling winds forced the half-famished communist recruits to cower round their meagre fires, to the Khambas over most of Tibet this meant that the rivers were frozen and tracks were open to their hardy ponies and yaks.

With winter came also the clear skies skies favourable to parachute drops, which were renewed after the reopening in Taiwan of the 'Tibet Welfare Association' in 1962, which served as a blind for more direct Chinese Nationalist involvements in Tibetan affairs.

From their new headquarters in Nepal it was now possible for the Khambas to plan more effective resistance and co-ordinate rebel activity in Tibet. Increasingly Khambas could be met in Kathmandu – out to contact Chinese Nationalist and C.I.A. agents. (The C.I.A. had once again become involved in Tibetan affairs after the Russian-Chinese break.)

Abroad, by contrast, interest in Tibet had fallen to a low ebb. The country's name was being mentioned only in connection with the establishment of refugee villages and homes in Switzerland, Norway, Britain and France. No one was keen to publicize Tibetan military activities being carried out behind the backs of the Indians and against the will of the Nepalese, and so few people guessed the extent of the continuing Khamba resistance.

Even for foreigners living in Nepal a veil of mystery covered the actual course of events beyond the country's northern border, over which refugees were finding their way in their thousands, along with the Khamba rebels. By the summer of 1962 there were more than six thousand Khambas in north-western Nepal. The Nepalese might deplore this situation which endangered their good relations with China, but there was little they could do about it, because however massive the

Himalayan range might appear, seen from the low valley of Kathmandu, the great mountains were far from constituting a closed door to Tibet. More than twenty major passes led from Tibet to Nepal, and to these may be added the countless minor routes, familiar only to the local Sherpas, Lobas and Dolpo-pas and other Tibetan tribes of Nepal who had always lived, as it were, on both sides of the international line, grazing their animals in Tibet in summer and wintering on the warmer southern slopes of Nepal.

By religion, trade, language and race Nepal's northern inhabitants were linked and attracted to Tibet, and thus quite naturally they sympathized with the Khambas.

As a consequence of the Khambas' penetration of northern Nepal, Bodnath, the largest Tibetan Buddhist shrine of Kathmandu, had become the rallying point for those rebels present in the capital.

Bodnath is the most famous Buddhist shrine in Nepal, to which for centuries thousands of Tibetan pilgrims had flocked, some coming on their knees from the most distant regions of greater Tibet. At Bodnath ruled (and still rules) the Chini Lama, a man of dubious virtue, the abbot guardian of the holy place. Under this 'saintly man's' guidance the clatter of dice has come to accompany the rattle of prayer wheels, and from the fairy ring of small Nepalese houses surrounding the great Chorten prostitutes by the dozen smile down upon the pilgrims doing their holy rounds. A thousand ways existed to relieve the fervent visitors of their few silver coins and if they had no cash it was their bone rosaries and carved prayer wheels which became, under the abbot's guidance, the bargains eagerly sought by the tourists who from 1960 onwards flocked to Bodnath in increasing numbers.

Gambling also increased with the years as Tibetan pilgrims were replaced by refugees, not the poor wretches who wove carpets for the Swiss, but rebel soldiers who had made their way down to Kathmandu to find not only women and dice, but also the capable hands of doctors who on the ground floors of the brothels courageously extracted bullets in complete secrecy: Chinese bullets from a war which Nepal, India and the world still chose to ignore.

It was at Bodnath that I first met Osher, in the low upper room of one of the nearby houses, busily engaged in slamming dice on to a leather pad. Stripped to the waist because of the heat, Osher was playing with the young son of a Khamba merchant, my Tibetan teacher, whose father carried on with difficulty from Bodnath in the Nepalese Himalayas a trade he had once negotiated, with more spectacular success and higher profits, along the dangerous trade routes of Kham and Chinghai. Osher's long, silky, dark brown hair hung loose, untied upon his neck. His vanity (he was always combing his hair) contrasted oddly with the angular shoulder blades and thick muscles of his back which twitched with greedy anticipation as, with a shout for good luck, he lifted the dice cup.

Osher at twenty-seven, my own age, was everything that I admired in Tibetans: handsome, intelligent and reckless, both at ease with life and oblivious of death. We became friends at once; and from him, in the course of lengthy interviews, I learned, as I had from Tsering, much about the tragic destiny of Kham and of the operations on Nepal's borders.

With their characteristic disregard for the intricacies of international politics, the Khambas in Nepal had set out to stop all commerce between Nepal and China. Nepalese merchants were raided and sent home with a strong warning against any future attempts at such commerce. When some Takali merchants were foolish enough not to heed these warnings, two dead traders were found in the vicinity of Mustang. From then on the Khambas' reputation had spread like wildfire all over Nepal where *coolies* commented that the Khambas were the 'Tibetan Ranas' – an allusion to the much feared autocratic Maharajas who had ruled Nepal until 1950.

Nepal, unable to stop the Khambas' activities, had no choice but to ignore their presence and try and deny their activities. Only the International Red Cross was allowed to concern itself with the Khambas, otherwise declared officially non-existent by the Nepalese. The Red Cross had been taking care of all refugees in Nepal and by them the Khambas were treated as ordinary refugees, eligible for medical supplies, whether or not they were engaged in fighting the Chinese. For this purpose in 1962 a small airfield had been opened at Jomosom, a village south of Mustang, where small planes could land with Red Cross medical supplies, which made their way from there by mule back into the Khamba *magars* to the north. Unfortunately this boon was not to last.

The summer of 1962 marked a low ebb for Tibet and for the Tibetan guerrillas, as the desperate efforts of the Khambas to continue fighting met again with international indifference. Although this had little effect on the morale of most rebels, such as Osher, it was not without a tragic impact on some of their leaders, particularly on Tsering, who had reached Kathmandu in the sweltering month of June. Tsering never recovered from the tragic loss of his children and the disgust engendered by general indifference to the plight of Tibet. As a result the former lord of Ulag Dzong, member of the Chamdo Liberation Committee and ex-commander of the soldiers of the Fortress of Religion had become the wreck I was to meet once again in Nepal. Having shaved his head and discarded his grandoise robes, Tsering was a broken shadow of his former arrogant self, a desperate man slowly slipping into the torpor of alcoholism.

Osher, by contrast, was still full of naïve enthusiasm: it was with a broad, hopeful smile that he announced to me his return to Mustang. Unexpectedly, in the autumn of 1962 events were to justify his optimism. Early in October the start-ling news broke of the invasion of India by China, an event whose international repercussions were to advance considerably the Khamba cause.

The Sino-Indian war, so long misunderstood, only makes sense if examined in the context of the Tibetan crisis. By the summer of 1962 the Chinese in Tibet had at last made them-selves masters of Loka after a campaign lasting three full years and necessitating the presence there of a considerable armed occupation force. Partly unaware of, and for the most part uninterested in, Khamba activities in Tibet, the Indian govern-ment, equally ignorant of the Chinese military concentration in Loka, committed a major error when in 1962 it determined to revise its past policy vis-à-vis its borders with Chinese-held Tibet.

Having been strongly criticized by members of the opposition and much of the Indian public after the Lonju and Konka Pass incidents, Prime Minister Nehru suddenly decided to revive his waning popularity by pressing India's territorial claims along the Tibetan borders. Although much of this border had never actually been delineated by international treaty or even marked on the ground, Nehru refused Peking's offer to settle border claims by negotiation. He further declared before his parliament that India would never negotiate, claiming the borders of India as those sketchily shown on the maps inherited from the British. Not only would India not negotiate, Nehru had decided, but would set about effectively occupying the territories under claim by setting up military outposts in the remotest regions that India had unilaterally decided were hers. The Indians then began implementing their forward policy by infiltrating soldiers and setting up posts all along the Himalayan frontiers. Such a policy could only lead to trouble. And did so, effectively: in Laddak minor skirmishes broke out between Indian soldiers manning the new posts and Chinese patrols. By contrast the eastern frontier of Tibet with the North-East Frontier Agency was quiet, because here the Chinese had apparently accepted the international border known as the MacMahon Line. This border (unlike the frontiers of Laddak) had been clearly drawn on detailed maps, its latitude and longitude specifically determined, even though it had not actually been surveyed or marked along all its course.

In the summer of 1962, in accord with their new policy, the Indians decided to set up twenty new border posts along this MacMahon line. One of these was set up at a place called Dhola, close to the junction of the Bhutanese, Tibetan and Indian borders. Here the terrain was such that a high mountain ridge known as the Thag appeared to represent a better and more neutral frontier between N.E.F.A. and Tibet than the natural red-lined pencil mark of the official MacMahon line which ran a few miles south of Dhola and the Thag-la range. Thus, disregarding anything the Chinese might do or say, the Indians set up their Dhola checkpoint inside Tibet, north of the MacMahon line.

The Indians took this risk because they believed naïvely that the Chinese would never dare dislodge them any more than India had dared to dislodge the Chinese in Laddak. The Indians in fact thought the Chinese incapable of reacting to their minor encroachment into an area so far from Lhasa.

A month or so after the establishment of the military post at Dhola, sixty Chinese soldiers came over the Thag-la range and encamped before the post, telling the Indians that they were on Chinese soil north of the MacMahon line; which was indeed the case. Instead of withdrawing, the Indians foolishly let it be publicly known that the Chinese had 'invaded Indian soil in

N.E.F.A., south of the MacMahon line'. This deliberate lie was to have serious consequences, for now Indian public opinion, already roused by Nehru's biased treatment of Tibet and his bogus friendship with China, obliged the prime minister and his government to commit themselves to a firm stand, and to throw back the Chinese.[1]

When Umrao Singh, the Indian commander of the forces in N.E.F.A., informed New Delhi that it would be dangerous to provoke the Chinese by pushing them back over the Thag-la and that in any case the Indians were incapable of doing so, owing to the poor supply lines over the N.E.F.A. foothills, he was relieved of his command and replaced by General Kaul. This general was then instructed to implement 'Operation Leghorn', aimed at pushing the Chinese back over the Thag-la range, regardless of the fact that the Thag-la range, like the new Indian post at Dhola, was north of the MacMahon line. The Chinese, seeing a build-up of troops, warned the Indians on 3 October that any action on their part would be considered a serious provocation. Unheeding, General Kaul massed more troops in N.E.F.A., mostly under-equipped men of poor morale, many with nothing but their cotton uniforms and a single blanket, despite the mean altitude of 9,000 feet, and that the Thag-la range was itself over 14,000 feet high.

On 9 October, ignoring a cable from the Indian Consul in Lhasa stating that a division of artillery was massing south of Loka behind the Thag-la, the Indians sent fifty men up part of the ridge beyond the Dhola post to set up a position to the rear of the small Chinese detachment. Retaliating on the 10th, the Chinese attacked this advanced unit, having in the meantime brought more troops down to the border. The Indians were rapidly forced to retreat, and there followed an uneasy truce.

Ignoring this warning of Chinese determination, Nehru and the Indian commander continued to cherish the belief that they could eventually defeat the Chinese; consequently after the first border clash the Indians sent more troops into N.E.F.A., unaware that on the other side of the border the Chinese had at their disposal the huge force of the already well-acclimatized

[1] These facts, and a highly interesting account of the Sino-Indian war, are to be found in Neville Maxwell's enlightening book *India's China War*, published by Jonathan Cape.

Loka regiments, and that they could bring these troops down right to the frontier by road, whereas the Indian troops had to struggle up the mountains on foot from the head of N.E.F.A.'s only road, a small dirt track in the process of being built up to Towang, a town five days away from the frontier.

India's position in N.E.F.A. was a precarious one, politically as well as military, because the entire eastern portion of N.E.F.A. from the plains of Assam up to the MacMahon line, a region known as the Towang tract, was itself in fact Tibetan territory, since the Towang tract had been administered entirely by the Dalai Lama until 1951, from which date independent India, following the expansionist policies of the British, had for the first time sent Indian administrators into that part of N.E.F.A. These had thrown out the Tibetans, taking advantage of their war with China. Independent India had behaved towards the Tibetans of N.E.F.A. with the same brash arrogance as the Chinese had shown on entering Amdo and Kham. So tenuous were India's claims to N.E.F.A. that when the border incidents began in October 1962 Chiang Kai-shek (according to J. K. Galbraith) had the nerve to tell the United States that N.E.F.A. was neither Indian, Tibetan or Chinese communist, but Formosan, although no Chinese Nationalist had ever set foot there! This hollow relic of Chinese Imperialist claims was nevertheless to bother the United States when they later considered coming to India's rescue.

The Chinese had so far been patient in tolerating India's unilateral claim that the MacMahon line was her effective border, the more so since the Indians had now violated this very border in order to reach the Thag-la ridge and establish their post in Dhola. But China's patience was eventually exhausted. Ten days after the first skirmishes she determined to meet India's threats: the P.L.A. attacked Nehru's troops.

On 20 October the Chinese forces came over the Thag-la range at eight different points and, advancing first on the Indian positions, crossed the MacMahon line right into N.E.F.A. The Indian post at Dhola was rapidly overrun, while, bypassing it on either side, the Chinese surrounded the greater part of India's advanced troops. Those who could fled defeated down to the plains. Others escaped into near-by Bhutan, where they were disarmed.

The world was stunned. Lack of knowledge of the three-year combat of the Khambas in Loka, and the size of the Chinese army stationed there, had led Nehru and most international experts to make a colossal error of judgement.

Everywhere Indian troops were overwhelmed – either killed or captured – and only a few brigades succeeded in retreating in an orderly fashion before the Chinese, who now followed approximately the path of the Dalai Lama's flight from Lhuntse to Towang.

The Indian H.Q., still blind to the strength of the Chinese invasion force from Loka and still unwilling to believe that the enemy would dare to advance any farther south, ordered its troops to retreat halfway down the road that led from Tezpur to Towang (Towang being left open to the Chinese).

For a few days the Chinese halted their advance and offered to withdraw behind the MacMahon line if the Indians at last showed themselves ready to negotiate on their Himalayan borders. This second offer to negotiate India again rejected, on the advice of 'experts', and also because Nehru was now entirely committed to the folly of trying to repulse the Chinese.

On the other hand, swallowing his pride for once, Nehru, after preaching non-alignment for so long, begged the United States to give him arms. On receiving a promise of U.S. support the Indians prepared for a major battle which they hoped that Chinese would never undertake. The Chinese, however, faced with Indian stubbornness had decided to 'teach India a lesson' and show the world that now she and not India was the dominant force in Asia.

Consequently on 17 November the Chinese resumed their advance, attacking the Indians at the Bomdi-la pass and at the same time cutting off the retreat of the Indian troops stationed farther north on the Se-la pass. Surrounded on all sides, the Indians threw away their arms and fled in disorder to the plains. Owing to poor military tactics and poor judgement as to the number and strength of Chinese troops already in Loka, the Indians in N.E.F.A. suffered a humiliating defeat.

By now the whole subcontinent was in a state of panic. There were fears in Calcutta that the Chinese might bomb the city, while other Indians believed that the Chinese would actually invade Assam and join up with East Pakistan to seize the entire Brahmaputra valley, considered one of India's most productive regions. As a result refugees began swarming out of the

Annamese town of Tezpur, the place where three years previously the Khambas had read to the press the Dalai Lama's first speech proclaiming united Tibetan resistance to China.

Suddenly, in the middle of Indian chaos, to everyone's surprise, the Chinese halted their troops along what had been, until quite recently, the effective frontier of eastern India, i.e. the edge of the plains which marked the border of N.E.F.A. and Assam – the southern limit of the Songtsen Gampo's ancient realm. Not only did the Chinese stop and announce a ceasefire, they then declared themselves ready to withdraw.

Why the Chinese stopped and furthermore offered to withdraw *twenty miles behind the MacMahon line* was a question that mystified everyone, including the brilliant John Kenneth Galbraith, then United States ambassador to India, who confessed to his diary that the sudden Chinese decision to withdraw at the moment of total victory 'would all have been extremely confusing to Napoleon'.

Confusing it was indeed for all those who were ignorant or simply blind to the power and determination of the Tibetan Freedom Fighters, for it had been Khamba resistance that had from the start necessitated the stationing in Loka of such a large Chinese force. Khamba resistance explained also (in part) the necessity for the Chinese to withdraw, as her troops were still needed to fight the rebels inside Tibet. Indeed in November 1962, while the Chinese were scoring a victory in N.E.F.A., eight hundred miles to the west, north of Mustang, the Khambas mounted a series of violent attacks on the Lhasa-Singkiang road, succeeding momentarily in isolating from China the entire Chinese forces then invading India.

The contradictions between China's overwhelming victory and subsequent proposal to withdraw to twenty miles behind the MacMahon line are of course only partly resolved by a knowledge of the situation inside Tibet. To this reason must be added the fact that winter was drawing near, and also that China was in no condition, without a large air force, to conduct a long-drawn military campaign so far from home, especially one that could only lead to the rather dubious advantage of seizing a non-strategic portion of India.

Only one Indian commentator, G. P. Deshpande, took good note of China's situation when he asked, 'Can one power engage another power in ground warfare from a base which is heavily infested with guerrillas?' As for other historians and commentators, most seem to have entirely ignored the importance of the Tibetan rebellion in relation to China's invasion of India and sudden withdrawal. It was even suggested that China's invasion of N.E.F.A. was a sign that Khamba resistance was coming to an end 'or else, why did the Khambas not attack the Chinese from the rear when they invaded India?' A question, asked by George Ginsburgs and Michael Mathos in their work *Communist China and Tibet (the First Dozen Years)*, indicating that these scholars, like nearly all historians, knew nothing of the crucial developments of the Loka campaign. Napoleon would not have been at all confused by these events, unless like so many he had fallen victim to the combined voices of Chinese and Indian propaganda which had so successfully minimized the scale of Tibetan resistance.

Quite understandably, India received very little sympathy over the whole affair. After all it was she who, in 1950, had handed Tibet over to China and, four years later, signed the Sino-Indian Treaty which the Indian Socialist Party quite rightly called 'The first international document to set a seal on the abolition of Tibet's autonomy'.

Nehru's anti-Tibetan policy had backfired – while at last the myth of Sino-Indian friendship was exploded. Had not India, just a few years previously, allowed the Chinese to send troops through her territory to attack the Khambas of Loka from the rear? Now, with the Khambas at long last defeated in Loka, the very same Chinese troops had bitten the hand that had helped and even fed them. Although Krishna Menon was dismissed as a consequence of the Sino-Indian war, the greatest loser in the affair was Nehru – whose prestige and pride never wholly recovered. India emerged in her true light – as a weak country misled by Nehru, by his pride and the folly of his appeasement of China; attitudes and a policy which over the years had caused so much bloodshed and tears in Tibet.

Ironically, the only real beneficiaries of the whole crisis were the Khambas, who unexpectedly acquired India as an ally in their struggle against China. Furthermore, China's invasion of N.E.F.A. succeeded, in a dramatic way, in underlining the strategic importance of Tibet. It was suddenly made clear to all how, by ignoring Tibet and letting the Chinese establish themselves there, the entire safety of Asia had been endangered.

Looking towards Tibet and seeking how perhaps the Chinese could be dislodged, strategists now suddenly focused their attention on the cavaliers of Kham. For the first time in years, the United States, Russia and India agreed on one common point of international policy: that Tibet ought to belong after all to the Tibetans!

Logically the future should have appeared bright for the N.V.D.A. and the men of the lonely *magars*, yet this was not entirely the case. As well as the long-term advantages to the Khambas brought about by the Chinese invasion of India there also came certain drawbacks. Notably in Nepal, the government, frightened by China's aggression in N.E.F.A., began to take action in answer to Chinese protests as to Khamba presence on the border of Mustang.

Although there was little the Nepalese government could actually do to dislodge the Khambas from their frontier, they were nevertheless able to halt the flying of Red Cross medical supplies to Jomosom. Nepal then banned all foreigners from visiting the border areas by creating in 1962 an inner line similar to that which the Indians had used to stop Tibetan sympathizers from contacting the rebels.

Without medicines, the Khambas now had to send their wounded soldiers all the way down to Pokhara or Kathmandu for treatment – an exhausting and often fatal trek for the hundreds of sick men.

On the other hand, India's switch of policy with regard to China allowed more direct assistance to be handed out (in secret, of course) to the Khambas. Food, grain and funds were now shipped to Nepal directly from India, either through the good offices of New Delhi or through the services of the C.I.A. This aid reached the Khambas through various channels; either via Formosan or C.I.A. agents established in Nepal, or through competent members of the Dalai Lama's entourage.

In the political field, for a short time after the Sino-Indian war, a good case was made by the old Tibetan Prime Minister, Surkhang, who proposed a Confederation of Himalayan states – a project to group together Bhutan, Sikkim, Nepal, Kashmir, Sinkiang and Mongolia, into which it was hoped that Tibet could eventually be incorporated. The idea was a valid one, though premature, and indeed it might have solved many of the problems of Central Asian minorities, but of course it was unacceptable to Peking, although Russia considered it favourably.

Such projects did not however detract from the grim reality of increasing oppression in Tibet, and the continuation of severe fighting. For the Khambas, both on the borders and inside Tibet, the vital problem was still how to maintain an active guerrilla war against an ever-increasing Chinese occupation force, spread out over a territory as vast as Europe.

Perforce the guerrillas in Kham and Amdo could no longer be aided directly, so that resistance there remained on the level of the traditional looting and hit-and-run operations by rebel bands still encamped beyond the centres of Chinese occupation. The Chinese themselves as we shall see were soon to admit that these guerrillas in Kham remained remarkably effective.

In Loka, on the other hand, all Tibetan resistance had been curbed. To achieve this the measures employed by the Chinese had been so harsh that in late 1962 a new wave of thousands of refugees fled over into Bhutan and Sikkim.

In Lhasa too it seemed that all opposition had ended. At least there was little or no news of unrest in the holy city, where the Chinese were now planning a 'new Chinese town', to be built around the old to accommodate the ever-growing influx of Chinese officials and troops. Yet if all this seemed to suggest that Lhasean resistance had ended for good, this was soon to be proved wrong, for already the explosive fire that would lead to a violent new clash between Lhaseans and the Chinese had begun to smoulder.

Meanwhile in Tsang and western Tibet resistance remained particularly active, as major operations staged from Mustang against the Chinese garrisons along the Brahmaputra and the major highway continued, while at the same time constant attacks were made on the newly built strategic by-roads branching down to the Nepalese frontier.

How such Tibetan expeditions and attacks were organized and carried out no-one knew, not only because the Khambas were sworn to secrecy on pain of death but also because their leaders trusted neither Indians nor Nepalese, let alone other foreigners, so that even those foreign agents helping the Khambas remained to some extent in the dark about many aspects of the war they were supporting. This became evident to me when, on receiving permission to travel and perform an anthropological study in Mustang, I was approached by intelligence officers of major Western powers asking me to help them understand the complex Tibetan situation. Their propositions were a clear indication that even the 'top secret' files of their agencies were lacking much basic data concerning Tibetan resistance. Language problems were not the only explanation of their lack of information; another reason was the complexity of the situation, which had placed the rebels at odds with the Dalai Lama's entourage, to whom most governments had so far looked for information.

Not wishing to embarrass the Nepalese by abusing their trust and kindness in granting me permission to study in an area otherwise closed to foreigners, I naturally declined all proposals made to me in Kathmandu to gather information on the Khambas in Mustang. Nevertheless my relationship with so many Tibetans and deep sympathy for the Tibetan cause inevitably led me to take a keen personal interest in Tibetan affairs. Inevitably, too, I was to be the involuntary recipient of much information of the most secret nature while becoming a close witness of considerable clandestine Khamba activity in Mustang, information which I feel should now be known and made public.

Already from Tsering and Osher I had learned a great deal about the situation in Kham and Loka, while in India and Nepal I had over the years met dozens of other Tibetans from Lhasa, Kham and Amdo, including my travelling companion and friend Sonam Tashi, the Prince of Dergue's brother, Betty-la and my various Tibetan teachers, their friends and relations, all of whom had helped to give me a unique insight into the war being waged anonymously beyond the Himalayas.

For someone speaking Tibetan, Kathmandu was in 1963 (and to a certain extent remains today) one of the most fascinating towns in Asia. There could be found Lhasean aristocrats, Khamba warlords, princes of Amdo, guerrilla leaders, soldiers of fortune, Chinese officers who had defected to the Khambas, along with Tibetans working for Peking or lamas in disgrace – people from the four horizons of Songtsen Gampo's realm rubbing shoulders with Tibetan merchants, smugglers, notorious bandits and nomad chiefs great and small: a secret world, whose common bond was their language and their general concern for what was happening up there above the great peaks that shade the valleys of Nepal. As in Kalimpong, but perhaps even more so, the contrasts and variety of the vast Tibetan continent were concentrated in Kathmandu. Most of the refugees congregated either at Bodnath or in the small new Tibetan restaurants and hotels set up by the refugees. By a curious chain of circumstances, these hotels and restaurants have today become the refuge and headquarters also of many of the exiles from our own technological society – the hippies – so that one might drink *chang* (Tibetan beer) with a rebel leader while sitting alongside a 'flower child' from Chicago.

Through this complex world of exiled Tibetans there came and went the intelligence officers of the Russian, American, Indian and Chinese embassies to Nepal, brushing shoulders in their eagerness to get hold of the facts about the Tibetan crisis. The only consistent thread in the tangle of rumours and intrigues in Kathmandu led from the bazaar over to Bodnath, and from there by various and often secret routes north to Mustang and the Khamba headquarters, a trail forbidden to foreigners, open only to those members of the N.V.D.A. with business along the lonely tracks leading to their front lines. This was the trail I was now permitted to follow.

15

Magars *in Mustang*

One look at a detailed map of Nepal reveals clearly why the Khambas had selected Mustang as the site of their new headquarters. The realm of the Tibetan Kings of Lo (also known as the Mustang Rajas) sticks out like a rectangular platform 450 miles square into Tibet; where, from the mean height of 15,000 feet, it dominates the Brahmaputra river and the strategic Sinkiang-Lhasa highway. There being no difficult high passes along Mustang's northern border with Tibet, the rebels had easy access to Chinese-held territory. To the south, on the other hand, the mighty 26,000-foot Annapurna range shelters the region from the interference of inquisitive outsiders.

Located twenty-four days from Kathmandu and eighty days from Lhasa, the isolation of Mustang explains also how this minute kingdom (though officially considered part of Nepal) had succeeded in remaining virtually independent. His Majesty King Angun Tensing Trandul (the 24th descendant of Ame Pal, the kingdom's founder, who lived in the 14th century) spoke no Nepalese and still ruled his territory in 1963 according to ancient laws very similar to those elaborated by Songtsen Gampo.

To reach Mustang from Kathmandu is a far-from-easy proposition. I had elected to fly first to Pokhara, a Nepalese bazaar then beyond the reach of vehicles but possessing a small airstrip. From Pokhara the journey to Mustang is a three-day climb to the Kali Gandaki river and then a ten-day journey up through the great Himalayan breach between Mount Annapurna and Mount Dhaulagiri. In any circumstances it is a rugged trek, impassable during the monsoon because the bridges are often washed away. In 1964 it was a journey rendered all the more difficult and hazardous by the presence of large numbers of Khambas in the area.

From the moment I received my permit to go to Mustang my project became entangled with the Tibetan crisis. One after the other, the Nepalese cooks, servants and porters I contacted declined to accompany me, refusing to risk their lives in what they claimed was an unsafe area. The Khambas, they said, would certainly attack my caravan, perhaps kill me. When I laughed off these alarms and sought counsel and advice from my Tibetan friends in Kathmandu they simply confirmed the dangers of my enterprise, saying that there was no telling what the Khambas would do and explaining further that the Khambas believed that, since they were fighting a war, it was no one's business to be in the areas in which they operated. It was this policy which had made the Khambas drive away from Nepal's borders all those Tibetan refugees who had preferred the cool shelter of Nepal's high frontiers to the hot, unhealthy lowlands of Kathmandu. Likewise as we have seen, they had discouraged, stopped, and then forbidden most Nepalese trade with China.

Having previously had nothing but friendly dealings with members of the N.V.D.A., I was taken aback on the eve of my departure by their sudden reluctance to advise or help me. I naïvely believed that my Khamba friends would give me a 'pass' or some letter of introduction to their leaders in Mustang; but no one would hear of such a thing, let alone reveal the names of the Khamba commanders I might meet. Even Tsering turned down my pleas, only suggesting that to such Khambas as I might encounter I could mention his name – although he could give me no assurance that this would be of much use. Evidently no one was going to betray the secrets of the N.V.D.A., even to a friend.

Increasingly worried, I thought that I should perhaps join up with a party of Khambas returning to Mustang from Kathmandu. Every day I had met and occasionally chatted with such groups as they marched out of town along the dusty pilgrim trails; loud-voiced clusters of young men wearing assorted garments of varying shades of khaki, none were willing to let me travel with them. Osher had already left Kathmandu so he could not help me either.

Eventually a young Tibetan refugee from Amdo whom I had befriended agreed, against the advice of his friends, to accompany me. He was twenty and although a one-time 'rebel', he now greatly feared the Khambas because a few months earlier a dispute had broken out in Mustang which had temporarily split the soldiers of the N.V.D.A. The root of this dispute was Taiwan's recent attempt to take the entire control of all Tibetan resistance, while publicly claiming again that Tibet was Chinese Nationalist territory. Such a claim was of course violently opposed by nearly all Tibetans, who were mis-led into attacking the Formosan-paid rebel leaders (for the most part men from Amdo), the so-called Chinese province of Chinghai. The regrettable incidents that followed, in which Tibetans killed Tibetans, was the long-overdue consequence of the desperation that had obliged so many Tibetans to turn to their former enemies for help, only to discover that the Nationalist Chinese were taking advantage of them by claiming abroad that the Tibetan rebels were Chinese Nationalist troops.

When the Khambas got the upper hand of the Formosan-financed rebel leaders, Taiwan temporarily cut much of its aid and withdrew its remaining agents, leaving many Amdo rebels, like my friend Tashi, stranded in Nepal, penniless and under suspicion from most Khambas. Formosan actions had also suc-ceeded in reviving once again the ancient rivalry between Khambas and Amdowans, to such an extent that the Dalai Lama was obliged late in 1963 to call on all monks in and out of Tibet to hold services to pray for Tibetan unity and peace among members of the N.V.D.A.! Meanwhile the Dalai Lama's elder brother was rapidly dispatched to Taiwan to 'set things straight', and to persuade Nationalist China to drop its ludicrous claim to Tibet. Although the Dalai Lama's brother was not entirely successful, by early 1964 order was eventually restored. Nevertheless as a result of this sad affair the N.V.D.A. lost the much-needed cooperation of many courageous Amdowans, dishonoured by the Nationalists' clumsy manoeuvres and foolish claims.[1]

[1] It should be noted that even today Taiwan, with little or no sense of the ridiculous in its claims to be the true government of all China, has not yet entirely abandoned its claim to Tibet. It is a claim which has led the Nationalists, like the Chinese communists, to falsify documents to try and prove that Tibet belongs to China. Some of these falsifications are clearly revealed by the inquiries of the International Commission of Jurists, in particular the claim that the Tibetans had participated in 1954 in the Chinese National Assembly which drafted a Chinese constitution. This is one of many examples of the Chinese 'infinite capacity for misrepresenta-tion'. (On this matter see the Dalai Lama's depositions in the two reports

Tashi, who had taken part in Nationalist-financed operations over the Nepalese border into Tibet had good reason to
fear, as he prepared to accompany me, that in Mustang he
might be recognized as an ex-Nationalist-Amdowan agent, an
unpleasant prospect – the Khambas had recently manhandled
and even shot a number of Amdowans. In spite of the risks
involved, Tashi agreed to come on the journey that was to
take us for three months into the heart of the most remote and
strategic region of the Himalayas.

Needless to say, without a letter of recommendation to any
Khamba leader and in the company of an Amdowan considered *persona non grata*, I shared the age-old fear that the
very name of Kham had always inspired in the inhabitants of
the Himalayas.

It is beyond the scope of this book to recall the various events
of my expedition to Mustang and the many unusual and often
amazing aspects of life in a land still ruled in 1964 by a king
who was ignorant that the world was round, a region so remote
that even matches were unknown. These details I have recorded
in another book and in the thesis on the 'political and social organization of Mustang', the writing of which was the reason for my
expedition.

Yet in spite of the purely cultural nature of my journey, I
could not but foresee that my presence in Mustang would
inevitably lead to a close and possibly dangerous contact with
the Khambas entrenched there; consequently, to overcome any
problems, beyond the fact that I spoke Tibetan, I equipped
myself so as to be able to give the Khambas any medical
supplies they might need. I sincerely felt it to be scandalous
that medicines should have been denied to the Khambas.
Never, even in the worst moments of the last world wars, had
medical aid been refused sick soldiers, especially by members of
a neutral country. Yet this was the case in Nepal, where both
the Nepalese and the Swiss Governments were now refusing
medical aid to the Khambas in Mustang in fear of displeasing
China.

In early April 1964, a week before my departure, I met
George Patterson in Kathmandu. Patterson, the intimate

---

of the International Commission of Jurists entitled *Tibet and the Chinese
People's Republic,* page 309.)

friend of the Pangda Tsangs and the man who had done so much for the Khambas and the cause of Tibet, had arrived in Nepal accompanied by a young film director, Adrian Cowles. I had of course no idea then of his secret plans, yet I could hardly believe that such a champion of Tibetan independence had returned to the Himalayas with the sole intention, as he proclaimed, of making a film on Tibetan refugees. The future was to prove me right as Patterson prepared for a bold and dangerous mission inside Chinese-occupied Tibet.

On 14 April with Tashi I flew off to Pokhara. As soon as I arrived there I became aware of the Khambas' presence. Fifty yards from the airstrip, Tibetan banners fluttered in the wind beside the neat, low, whitewashed buildings of what a signboard claimed to be the Annapurna Hotel.

This building, known also as the Tibetan Hotel, is set on a small rise overlooking the airfield. To the casual observer it is in no way remarkable, beyond being a more pleasing sight than the assortment of shiny aluminium barracks next to it called the Sun'n' Snow Hotel.

Although on this journey I was only passing through Pokhara, I had time to meet Amdo Kesang, a tall, handsome Khamba from Litang whose broad smile showed impeccably white teeth framing, to its shiny advantage, a solitary gold one. In contrast to his smile, this man's eyes were as hard as stone; beyond this nothing at first sight betrayed him as the most important Khamba of the region.

Later I discovered how his hotel was the vital link between the Khambas of the frontier and the outside world. With the exception of a few foreigners, the hotel was at all times full of Khambas who drifted in and out to the tinkle of horse bells or the noisier shuffle of mule trains. Evenings at the hotel were punctuated by the clatter of ivory majong sticks, as seated crosslegged on a carpet Amdo Kesang engaged his transient guests in lengthy games in which considerable sums of money were gambled away, money whose origin is far more intriguing than the game the men play. Intriguing, too, is the conversation, and the contents of the messages written in Tibetan longhand which are exchanged or deposited at the hotel, letters grimy with the sweat of muleteers or flown in fresh from Kalimpong, Delhi, Dharamsala and all those other parts of India where the 'reactionaries' have contacts. Also at the hotel are piles of bills of lading and invoices of shipments awaited from Kathmandu or to be flown up directly to Pokhara from the Indian border. Plane loads of clandestine goods with no other immediate destination than the Annapurna Hotel. Cargoes carried in by the regular flights of Royal Nepal Airways or by special chartered flights whose pilots often unknowingly transport goods destined for the rebels. No questions are asked, of course, by the conveyors; or if they are they are never answered. Amdo Kesang simply collects the goods, shuffles the letters and sorts out the orders. Amdo Kesang, in spite of his name, comes from Litang; and of course few of the foreigners know that Litang was once the name of the largest monastery of Kham, which was partially destroyed by bombers after the memorable sixty-four-day siege. Amdo Kesang, who had been among the besieged, knows a lot more about America and international politics than most of his Western clients could ever suspect, as he is the first to receive the clandestine Tibetan newspapers and pamphlets, which he forwards to all those actively concerned with China and its war with Tibet.

Neither do the passing travellers suspect the length of the trails that flow like streams down to Pokhara and the airfield, trails which are the life-lines for the men of the distant *magars* lying high and far behind the huge Annapurna range which looms on clear days above the airstrip. Today for countless Tibetans the road to Litang now leads through Pokhara, the road to Lhasa also, the long trail of hope, also occasionally a trail of despair, a tragic trail of no return for many of the wounded who painfully reach Pokhara in desperate need of medical attention. These soldiers go to the mission hospital a few miles away which also caters for the members of Pokhara's two large official Tibetan refugee 'camps'. Quite naturally, nobody bothers or is able to distinguish a member of the N.V.D.A. from a refugee, although everyone knows. Carpet-weaving is not after all notorious as a source of bullet wounds.

Yet in Pokhara, as in Kathmandu, the Khambas are few and far between, only noticeable because of their size, their dress and also the way they ride their small horses; yet they remain a minority, and little betrays them as members of a large, operative and efficient army.

Not until three days later, when I reached the Kali Gandaki river, did Khambas appear in any large numbers. Before that

A fleet of Chinese trucks making their way painfully along the Kanting-Lhasa highway, the road most vulnerable to attack by the Khambas. *(Keystone)*

Ammunition for the rebels being transported across the frozen surface of Yamdrok Lake. *(Atlas Photo)*

The cave monastery of Lori, a Khamba refuge in Mustang. From similar caves in Tibet the rebels proved impossible to dislodge.

An elusive, unassimilable fraction of Tibet's population: nomads and their tents.

A company of Khamba guerrillas in Nepal.

we encountered a few on the trail, sick men coming down for treatment and two long caravans of a hundred mules each, whose unladen animals clattered and skidded past us for half an hour. Every group of twenty animals was accompanied by a Khamba muleteer, fingers in his mouth, whistling commands, or occasionally shouting, and more rarely biting the ear of a particularly stubborn beast.

Once we reached the mighty Kali Gandaki river we began to run into groups of five or six Khambas, and occasionally larger parties, some travelling on foot, others on horseback. Many were important officials, riding in the centre of the trail, arrogantly leaving it to others to move out of their way. Not even I, a foreigner, warranted so much as a glance from these men.

Two days up the Kali Gandaki river, I ran into a crowd of some fifty Khambas outside a house: tall booted characters who eyed me with a detached curiosity bordering on insolence. In spite of my private sympathy for the Khambas, my pride suffered a little and suddenly I began to question the basis of their arrogance, which I sensed even without speaking to them, and I began to feel the first serious pangs of fear. It was perhaps their air of confidence, all the more striking because in India and Nepal, not to mention most of Asia, the people one meets are generally shy and submissive. In the Khambas' expressions I saw an assured look of amused, fleeting interest. Nothing haughty or aggressive in their attitude, nothing vain and artificial, just a direct self-confidence, proclaiming a race of men of independent judgement. Only later was I to understand how that characteristic, shared by many Tibetans, was the true mark of a pure, rugged race, a race of men possessed of a calm self-confidence, not derived from petty pride or boastful vanity, but the legacy of a people free from the complexes that plague so many sophisticated societies.

I had so far admired this quality only in individuals, never before in a large group. Only now did I understand that what had attracted me to Osher and Tsering and so many other Khambas in Kalimpong and Kathmandu was in fact a national characteristic of their reckless race, a race whose like is perhaps to be met nowhere else. I could now imagine better how such people could inspire fear and also why the Chinese had built the Great Wall and lived for centuries in terror of the horsemen of Central Asia.

The track leading up the Kali Gandaki gorge to Mustang is among the most spectacular in the Himalayas, because the gorge itself is one of the most impressive natural features of our planet, a gigantic canyon, known as the Great Himalayan Breach, cutting three miles deep between Mount Annapurna and Mount Dhaulagiri.

The trail has to cling to the river bed or to the vertical cliffs, and in certain parts the footpath becomes a mere groove cut in the rock. At two points, where the groove has to round corners, the trail goes through man-made tunnels. These passages open onto giant stairs leading down to the river which is spanned by rickety bridges.

Until the arrival of the N.V.D.A. this track used to be closed for many months in the year. I soon found out that the Khambas I had met were in the valley to repair, enlarge and reinforce the track. They had not only cut new steps and repaired the damage done by landslides, but were also busy building bridges and dams, many of considerable size and span, so that their vital supply line could remain open all year round.

I thought at first that perhaps these men were working on the track by agreement with and paid by the Nepalese government, but I soon learned that this was not the case. The thousand Khambas who had been sent down from their *magars* to improve the supply route were acting entirely on their own, often against the wishes of the local inhabitants, who resented the felling of their trees and re-alignment of their fields to enlarge the trail. There was nothing in common between the efficient giants working on the track and the famished, over-worked Tibetan refugees who could be found slaving at road-building for little or no pay in India. The condition of these Tibetan road-builders in India was in fact so wretched in 1964 that it was rightly brought to the attention of the world's press (on 18 September 1964) by officials of the Dalai Lama's entourage that 'many Tibetans could hardly be worse off at home, under Chinese rule, than pursuing their laborious road-building fatigues in India'.

In contrast, the Khambas along the trail formed efficient commandos, busy felling trees above the river, then hurtling them down cliffs to construct massive wood-and-stone break-waters to divert the current from the stone piles of new bridges.

From these piles projected giant beams in successive cantilevers, forming arches closed by more tree trunks, the whole edged and guarded by a criss-cross railing. Monumental, magnificent bridges in pure Tibetan tradition, erected without so much as a nail or the use of a saw. One such was the large bridge of Lété beside which, on the fifth day after leaving Pokhara, I pitched my tents. Prayer flags and an arch of pine leaves testified that the bridge had just been opened. That evening, marching up from the sites where they had been working, a large crowd of Khambas invaded my camp.

This was my first encounter with men of the N.V.D.A. on what one could call their own ground. For there was no mistaking that even long before reaching Mustang, the upper Kali Gandaki was their territory, one in which they were the undisputed force in command.

The men pressing around my tents were dressed in an odd assortment of military gear in which parachute-cloth skirts, black army boots of Chinese origin and khaki Tibetan *chubas* predominated. These three characteristic elements of their attire gave these men the semblance of a uniform which made one forget the many strange and often incongruous garments some of them wore besides: Chinese caps, Tibetan fur hats, and American or Formosan surplus long-peaked hats, Chinese drill suits and occasionally Chinese zipped sweaters – garments purchased, or stolen, but the majority gleaned from the dead bodies of their victims. Occasionally I recognized elements of official Tibetan army apparel derived from the design of British colonial uniforms.

'Where are you going?' was the first and inevitable question put to me in a calm voice by a man who stepped forward from the crowd.

The fact that I could speak Tibetan seemed to take everyone by surprise. Nevertheless, the spokesman carried on with a quick cross-examination. What was my purpose in Mustang, was I a trader, what did my baggage contain? I remembered all I had been told about the Khambas as brigands, and while the men fumbled with my baggage I wondered what stopped them from simply picking up my things and leaving with them. Tashi, meanwhile, had disappeared, fearing recognition by men he had known in Lhasa or Kathmundu who could brand him as a 'Formosan'.

This was the first of my encounters with the troops of the 'fort of religion'. Every day, after that, the Khambas were more numerous, marching up or down the trail or settled in roadside houses.

A week after leaving Pokhara, owing to the slow progress of my porters, I reached Tukutcha, the limit of Nepalese culture and the point where one entered the Tibetan-speaking zones of Nepal on the northern face of the great Himalayan range. From here on the landscape was very like that of Tibet, bleak and treeless, and crowded with snow-covered peaks.

A day later, having changed my porters for yaks, I stopped in Jomosom, the only Nepalese military garrison of any size in that part of Nepal and the limit beyond which foreigners were not usually allowed. Fewer than fifty Nepalese recruits were stationed in a few local houses. Their commander, a captain who had served in a British Gurkha brigade, gave me his opinion of the Khambas, while confirming (what was every day becoming more evident) that the rumours in Kathmandu about a considerable force of N.V.D.A. soldiers stationed in the area were well-founded.

These troops obeyed no leaders but their own, men whose names the Nepalese officer did not know. He had orders to leave them alone, remarking that, as a soldier, he personally admired them and that anyway there was nothing the Nepalese could do to get rid of them. Of course they had caused the commander trouble, some of his soldiers had been robbed of their guns by Khambas, so that now, if his men left the check post, they did so unarmed! The old Gurkha admitted that there was no conflict between the Nepalese and the Khambas, and he expressed the secret opinion of most Nepalese officials, that the country's only real fear and concern was China, all the more so since the Chinese had recently let it be known among the local people that they considered Mustang and all the upper Kali Gandaki down to Jomosom (the check post) as land which should be theirs.[1]

At Jomosom an enterprising Nepalese trader had imported

---

[1] Jomosom is the Nepalese deformation of the Tibetan name Dzong Isam (Border Fort). The Chinese commander of the Likse garrison had let it be known that all place names in Nepal containing the Tibetan name Dzong (Fort) represented the true southern limits of communist Tibet and would be reclaimed as such, and more specifically Jomosom.

Tibetan gowns of khaki cloth from Kathmandu to sell to the Khambas. This small detail gave me an insight into the number and established nature of their garrisons to the north.

A few hours from Jomosom, following the mile-wide stony bed of the upper Kali Gandaki, we passed the small town of Kag. This was the first of the many typically Tibetan villages of the upper Kali Gandaki, built like a fort whose bastions are composed of the blank outer walls of the houses set one against the other. One enters the village by tunnels that burrow through the houses, and although Kag had long ago ceased to be one of the main defences of the old trade route to Mustang, its position at the meeting point of the track leading to Mustang and that bearing right from Muktinath had given the town a renewed strategic importance for the Khambas. In Kag the N.V.D.A. has established one of its three principal supply centres in the area.

It was at Kag that I first fully grasped the scope and implications of Tibet's continuing struggle against China. Until then I had never been really able to imagine the N.V.D.A. as anything but a romantic force of archaic warriors, men I associated inevitably with hazy visions of Genghiz Khan's horsemen. Only at Kag did it occur to me that such a force as theirs, to be capable of opposing China, had to be more than a haphazard collection of bandits or fierce tribesmen, but must necessarily constitute a vast and efficient military organization, one not only having its well organized hierarchy of officers but also efficiently equipped to cater for such needs as supplying its men with fuel and clothes, requirements just as essential as arms and ammunition.

With respect to supplies the Khambas settled in Nepal were remarkably well organized. The village of Kag was the centre for the distribution and supply of wood to all the local army camps, as its strategic location allowed it to serve not only the numerous *magars* of Mustang situated to the north, but also the large *magars* located to the east which could be approached by the northern route behind Mt Annapurna. One of these camps east of Mustang was the largest in all Nepal, with over two thousand men settled two miles from the shores of Lake Demodra Khund.

Seeing the uncomfortably large number of Khambas settled in Kag, I decided to push on to Tayen, a village set high up on a cliff above the trade route, standing between the gigantic ruins of two ancient fortresses. There, too, I found many Khambas, as this village turned out to be their transport centre, the base of the thousand-odd excellent mules needed to supply the *magars*.

At Samar, a day's march from Tayen, a village just below the southern border of Mustang, we ran into two hundred 'rebels' down from their camp located near-by. When I expressed my concern at the sight of all these soldiers, the yak drivers I had hired took the opportunity to enlarge on their grievances about the way the Khambas had come into their district as conquerors, appropriating for themselves the best grazing grounds and the little available firewood, the roots and branches of the stunted bushes and juniper trees. Although the local people feared the Khambas and resented some of their actions, they were sympathetic to their cause and resigned to their presence because, as they said, 'it is the wish of the Dalai Lama'.

At Samar I went through a second and more thorough cross-examination. The Khambas were particularly and, to my mind, unhealthily interested in what my cases contained; also they were incredulous when I stated that I was neither a trader nor had any intention of going over to Chinese Tibet, whose nearest border was now only four miles away, for we had just entered the narrow strip where Mustang projects into Tibet.

I felt the time had come to try and contact the Khamba leader, in the hope of obtaining a pass through to Mustang's capital. I therefore explained to the Khambas my willingness to distribute medicines to the soldiers, making this distribution conditional, however, on meeting the *Pombo*, their commander.

It soon became evident that the Khambas in my tent could not speak for their chief or even reveal his name, any more than their oath would allow them to tell me the exact number of soldiers they had in the district. Consequently the men withdrew, after asking for just a few pills for several of those present who were suffering from various complaints.

The following morning, on our way to the village of Geling, we passed below the local Khambas' large camp, partially concealed in the shallow of a 12,000-foot ridge overlooking the track. Prayer flags strung out between tall poles warned us of its presence, while the trail in its vicinity was clustered with soldiers. Towards midday three riders on fine horses passed us – important officers, to judge from their fine dress. One gave me a polite salute and a smile but did not so much as rein in his horse. Shortly after this I caught sight of a solitary rider galloping towards us. Reaching the head of our caravan, he pulled up and called to the leading man to stop. Advancing a little he spoke to Tashi, telling him that 'the *Pombo*' had ordered us to hurry on to meet him in Geling. Then he turned round and galloped off.

My immediate reaction was one of fear. I knew now that the most critical moment of my journey had come.

Shortly after we reached Geling two riders galloped into the village. I hurriedly entered my tent, where I had laid out carpets, and prepared to greet the Khamba commander. A few minutes later the tent flap was thrown aside and in walked Gyaltsen, a rebel officer from Kandze. For a Khamba he was short and stocky, with a deeply lined, sunburnt face. He wore army boots and khaki trousers and, instead of a *chuba,* a black leather jacket. Pinned to his fur cap was a solid gold medallion with a photograph of the Dalai Lama.

Gyaltsen, I found out, was only the commander of the *magar* of Samar. At first, he too was suspicious about the reasons for my presence in Mustang. When I told him of my purpose in the area and explained, not without difficulty, what anthropologists did, he asked my nationality. When I told him I was French, he seemed quite worried. The reason for this was that, as a result of the publicity over France's recent recognition of Communist China and the opening in Peking of a French embassy, news had reached the Tibetan papers in Kalimpong that France was now pro-Chinese. It was with the utmost difficulty that I demonstrated that France was not in fact unduly friendly with Mao and that much of the fuss over France's recognition of Red China was simply the product of journalistic exaggeration, catering to Chinese Nationalist and United States dissatisfaction. I then explained that in fact France's recognition was without great political consequence and that we remained a nation sympathetic to Tibet.

Although I had never been naïve enought to believe that a commander of the N.V.D.A. could be unaware of the subtleties of international politics I was nevertheless startled and also relieved to discover how thoroughly Gyaltsen, like Kesang, was familiar with them. Gyaltsen had good reason to be well informed, having gone through communist indoctrination in Kandze and then having lived in Kalimpong before sharing for a time the Dalai Lama's exile at Dharamsala.

When the conversation had covered the general problem of my presence in the area, I attempted once more to secure from this Khamba a letter of introduction to the leaders of the other *magars*. I also inquired who was the supreme commander of the Khambas in Mustang, but all to no avail. Each *magar*, I was told, was independent, with its own commander, and Gyaltsen could only speak for his own. On the other hand, however, he had taken good note of what I had told his men the day before because he drew from his pocket a long list of the names of those of his men who were ill and in need of medicine. The list was impressive, for he had six hundred men under his command as well as some thirty women and fifteen children in his camp! The women, I discovered, were army prostitutes, or rather 'temporary wives' as they are known in Tibet. Homosexuality, which is not rare in Tibetan monastic institutions, is practically unknown among the Khambas. These poor women who had followed the soldiers all through Tibet were involuntarily responsible for one of the most widespread afflictions of the soldiers, venereal disease. Owing to its isolation Tibet had been spared this affliction until a few years ago, but now, with war and the presence of the Chinese, it had begun to assume alarming proportions and because of the lack of medical treatment accounted for many deaths.

When Gyaltsen rode off I wanted to believe that my problems with the men of the N.V.D.A. had come to an end. But I still had no safe conduct or any guarantees, and the dangers attending my position were made rather brutally clear on the following day. At the summit of a high pass that marked the border I found myself looking into the muzzles of a sub-machine gun and a rifle. Two Khambas who had been coming up the opposite side of the pass stood before me. A few seconds of frigid silence elapsed while I wondered if they would fire. But without a word they lowered their guns, the man with the sub-machine gun endeavouring to conceal his weapon in the folds of his *chuba*, the other using his rifle to prod a small yak, probably stolen either in Mustang or over the border in Tibet.

In the two months after this incident I travelled all over

Mustang in the course of my anthropological studies; two months in which I came into daily contact with the soldiers of the N.V.D.A. and their commanders; two months in which I was able to gather much of the yet unrecorded material published here, and see for myself the hard reality of what from Kathmandu or abroad had appeared to be hazy rumours about the continuing struggle of the Tibetans.

I was able to ascertain that in Mustang, and the adjacent Tibetan areas of Nepal, Dolpo and Manang, the N.V.D.A. in 1964 had no fewer than six thousand men under arms. Their soldiers were well-established in twelve efficiently run camps, under the leadership of independent commanders, subject only to a high commission of generals who were in contact with the rebel supreme commanders in India and the agents of 'co-operative countries'.[1]

The separate camps were manned by guerrilla units from different parts of Tibet, men who remained united under the commanders who had led them through battle, or had risen to power in the early days of the rebellion against China. The men of these various *magars* were the survivors of what had often been much larger groups operating in Kham, Loka and central Tibet. Many of the men had come up from India, whither they had been obliged to flee in the course of Chinese operations.

In Mustang the *magars* were all stationed away from the villages, some, like those of Lori, Lo Gekar and Samdruling, near isolated monasteries, others nestling in hidden valleys such as those of Te and Kangra, and the very large *magar* of Demodra Khund. Small detachments of Khambas could also be found in the villages and towns of Mustang, men either too ill to stand the discomfort of living in tents on the windblown hills at 12,000 and 13,000 feet, or sent down to purchase horses, mules and yaks.

For three weeks in the capital, Lo Mantang, I shared lodgings with a young Khamba responsible for the purchase of horses. He was an unusually handsome man and reminded me of Osher who, since my arrival in Mustang, I had attempted to locate but without success.

All day long this young Khamba combed the neighbourhood in search of the best animals he could find, and every other

[1] United States, India, Taiwan.

night new horses would be stabled in the ground floor of the house where we lived before being taken away to the various *magars*. During the lengthy evenings we spent together I learned a great deal about the activities of the Khambas across the border in Tibet and how small raiding parties would slip over the border to attack the convoys which passed so close to it that they could be seen from several ridges inside Mustang. At night in fact it was possible to see the headlamps of trucks and the lights of the Chinese garrison of Likse quite clearly from the border itself, only a few miles away. Similarly, the capital of Mustang and much of its northern territory was clearly visible to the Chinese, who had established a look-out post on a ridge named Dzong Dzong, which loomed on the horizon as an ever-present reminder that the enemy was at hand.

Strangely enough, despite the tense situation, the border remained open to the local inhabitants who crossed it at will and often went into Tibet. No doubt this also allowed the Chinese to send agents into Mustang, accounting among other things for the Khambas' discretion and mistrust of many of the local people.

A few of the inhabitants of Lo Mantang spoke openly of their contacts with the Chinese and would often set out for Likse, to return a day or two later bringing back goods sold to them by the Chinese.

As far as raiding was concerned, the Chinese were at a disadvantage because they hesitated to pursue the Khambas into Nepalese territory, although at times they had done so, crossing the frontier, especially near Dzong Dzong, and coming down as far as the outskirts of the village of Sam Dzong.

The Khambas, of course, were not intent on attacking the main Chinese garrisons. Their aim was twofold: on the one hand to attack convoys, and on the other to stay by to help and supply the rebel groups inside Tibet. From the easternmost point of Dolpo to the region of Tsum, north of Kathmandu, they had a stretch of three hundred miles of Nepalese frontier from which they could cross over to Tibet and surprise the Chinese at any corresponding point on their main east-west highway and its branches running south to the Nepalese border. For these operations the Khambas could draw on all their reserves in Mustang and in other areas; and that spring they inflicted several serious and crippling blows on Chinese transport columns.

I never witnessed, much less took part in, any such missions, but on many occasions I was to have direct proof of these activities, notably through being called on to attend men wounded in the course of such operations.

During my stay in Mustang I learned that the commanders of each *magar* were subordinate to higher officers stationed in Mustang, who in turn reported to leaders in India. The men directing the *magars* and the military operations were stationed at Samdruling, a small monastery to the southwest of the capital, Lo Mantang. These leaders were a group of highly sophisticated soldiers. Several wore Chinese military uniforms and nearly all, in 1964, had close-cropped hair, having long ago discarded their braids, perhaps as long ago as the days when they had been officially communist-approved members of Chinese Preparatory Committees in Tibet.

To and from this headquarters came and went the various local commanders, easily recognizable by the small escort of soldiers who accompanied them. They were a splendid sight, riding the tallest and finest horses with elaborate saddles with gold-inlaid pommels, surmounted by brilliant saddle-carpets. Their bodyguards, carrying rifles, brought up the rear. My contacts with these men were few, brief, always courteous yet quite noncommittal. There was little to be learned from them about the nature of their clandestine activities.

Yet I was soon to find out that border raids and support for the rebels inside Tibet were not the only reasons for the Khambas' presence in Mustang. Another was their firm belief that sooner or later foreign nations would, at long last, come to their aid. With this in mind the Khambas wanted to be prepared and to have available a large force of men which could then act as the spearhead of a massive offensive against China. This explained why the Khambas continued recruiting young men in India to settle in Mustang.

The Khambas did not fully appreciate, apparently, that however sympathetic Taiwan, the United States and, more recently, India and Russia, may have seemed to their cause, in fact these large nations were by no means prepared to 'lean over the bank' and give them all the backing they hoped for. There is no doubt that the Khambas were the victims both of wishful thinking and of a calculated policy on the part of their presumed allies who, while intent on exploiting their nuisance value, were yet unwilling to endorse their cause wholeheartedly. Only the blind determination of the 'rebels' for the one ideal they cherished, the complete liberation of Tibet, explains their inability to see how they were being taken advantage of and kept, as it were, in reserve against a time when they might better serve the political interests of other nations.

Any thought of direct intervetion by foreign powers in Tibet was still generally regarded abroad as unrealistic and doomed to failure, although events inside Tibet were soon to prove that the foreign experts could have been wrong. Indeed 1964 marked the beginning of a new and violent period of unrest inside Tibet. The new uprising was a spontaneous reaction to China's enforcement of a sterner policy of repression.

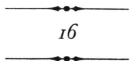

16

Anonymous Death

The first indication of China's new policy was expressed in arrogant protest notes to Tibet's neighbours. To begin with, the New China News Agency violently attacked India on 28 May 1964 for 'backing the rebels'. Then came more protests followed by the surprising news that Tibet was once again causing the Chinese serious trouble and that the situation there was rapidly getting out of hand. There were daily reports of Chinese convoys being 'plundered', military and civilian installations 'sabotaged' and personnel 'murdered'.

Had people in the West been aware of this, no doubt they might have changed their minds about the possibilities of successful intervention on behalf of Tibet. It was to inform the West of the true situation that George Patterson had come to Nepal, determined to bring back proof of effective Tibetan resistance in the shape of a film of military operations by the Khambas against the Chinese. To secure this much-needed document Patterson, while I was in Mustang, set out secretly with Adrian Cowles from Nepal into Chinese-controlled Tibet to film the attack on a Chinese convoy by a Khamba commando.

Patterson's action although much criticized was partially justified by the fact that world opinion' had once again entirely forgotten Tibet. The interest roused by the arrival of the Dalai Lama in India in 1959, followed by the stir over the Sino-Indian war, had now given way to the same indifference from which Tibet had suffered in the past.

As a result, everyone gradually forgot that conditions inside Tibet had not really changed since 1950. The Chinese there were still guilty of what the International Commission of Jurists had branded 'the gravest crime of which any person or nation can be accused: genocide; the intent to destroy, in whole or in part, a national, ethnical, racial or religious group as such'.

All evidence of genocide had been carefully suppressed abroad in order not to embarrass China. In fact any foreigner claiming the slightest interest in Tibetan affairs would have had his visas revoked by Russia, Nepal, India and Mongolia in 1964. The plight of the Tibetan people and the struggle of the N.V.D.A. was so ill-documented that many people even doubted the existence of the continuing struggle in Tibet. And when, from time to time, small articles were published about fighting in Tibet, they inevitably were branded either as propaganda or bazaar rumours.

It was to change this deplorable state of affairs that George Patterson determined to make his film of the actual fighting. Patterson eluded Nepalese police control and set out secretly for the Tibetan border with his companion. As Mustang was the best-known site of the various Khamba *magars* in Nepal and therefore the region most closely guarded by the Nepalese against inquisitive foreigners, Patterson chose to go to the east of Mustang to the Nepalese border district of Tsum. There he had no trouble in making contact with the local Khamba commander. Then, at the risk of their lives, he and Adrian Cowles crossed over into China with a Khamba patrol. After marching for two days inside Tibet, they lay in ambush and filmed the attack on a convoy of Chinese trucks.

There are few words to describe the courage needed to perform such a task and no good reasons to doubt the validity of the motives which inspired the making of such a film. Now at long last there existed the visual evidence the world needed to make it believe in the tragic reality of Tibet's plight, and the Tibetans' determination to fight for freedom. Although in other wars accredited correspondents have rarely been refused access to the front lines, when Patterson's feat became known it was treated as a major crime, first by Nepal, which jailed the two men, then, to a certain extent, by Great Britain, which obstructed the release of their film so that it was not shown until two years later.

The truth was undoubtedly embarrassing, because there on the film, for all to see, were the Khamba leaders and their men, armed and waging war. Through this film for the first time everyone could actually see the *magars* and the very faces of the Khamba warriors. Handsome, rugged, intelligent faces, not of legendary horsemen, but of business-like, matter of fact soldiers, competent and determined. Men still fighting in 1964 the soldiers of Mao. This was the evidence nobody wanted released.

The attack filmed was a small routine operation, one of many hundreds carried out that summer by the N.V.D.A. And if people were unable to see Patterson's film for some time and unwilling to believe in the Khambas' struggle, the Chinese themselves were soon to confirm the facts. On 10 July the New China News Agency announced that 'Liu Chun, Vice-Chairman of the Nationalities Affairs Commission of Communist China has said that anti-Chinese and anti-communist rebels belonging to the national minorities (Tibet and Uigurs) have been very rampant recently'. The report added in explanation that the 'reactionary elements' were supported by 'modern revisionists' (i.e. Russians). Liu Chun further specifically mentioned the giant provinces of Tibet and Sinkiang as centres of rebel activity, declaring that 'new measures are to be taken to root out reactionaries'. Three days after this announcement the Chinese once again accused India of helping the rebels with 'twenty-six plane intrusions into Tibet over the past six months'.

One may doubt a good deal of evidence about Tibet but it is difficult to discredit Patterson's film or to think that the Chinese would voluntarily fabricate news reports generally unfavourable to themselves, since they officially admitted China's failure to control the Tibetan rebels thirteen years after she had theoretically liberated that country, nine years after her claim to have put down the Kanting rebellion and five years after supposedly defeating the rebels 'in a twinkling of an eye'! But if no one could really doubt the Chinese reports, at least only a few read them, so that it was still considered wise to confiscate Patterson's film.

The film made by Adrian Cowles and George Patterson also showed some minor, yet not insignificant, aspects of the Khambas' courage and determination. It showed the Khambas' need for medical help, which led George Patterson to operate with the crudest of tools on soldiers of the N.V.D.A. suffering from bullet wounds and frostbite. It showed too, the amazing courage of one soldier who in the course of the attack rushed with his knife at two Chinese armed with machine guns, killing both, although not before one of them had sprayed him with machine gun bullets. Left for dead behind a rock when it was necessary to withdraw hastily after a Chinese soldier escaped to summon reinforcements, the 'dead' man reappeared amazingly three days later in Nepal, having travelled alone, despite his wounds, over several passes 16,000 feet high. Patterson's film shows where a Chinese bullet went right through the man's chest and came out at his back! Patterson later filmed the man declaring his impatience to recover and get back on the job.

The job? The Chinese press and to a lesser extent the international press give us a small insight into what this meant.

For the Chinese it meant 'new measures to root out reactionaries'. What new measures, one might ask? Had everything not been tried over the years? Perhaps so, but after all, the rebels had been 'very rampant recently'. Yet even the new measures of repression were to fail; for once again, in the autumn of 1964, general rebellion rocked Tibet.

The first sign of the storm to reach the West was in a rather unfortunate and contradictory article published by the *New York Times* on 19 July 1964, which claimed 'resistance to Chinese apparently wiped out even in south-east Tibet'. This piece of news was probably a transcription of the regular Chinese reports stating that resistance had been crushed, reports which inevitably followed any new outbreak of violence in Tibet. A month later the *New York Times* contradicted its original statement with a report that the New China News Agency had mentioned a 'student revolt in Lhasa'! Then, little by little, the Chinese communist press came out with more of its strange releases, symptomatic of trouble. In July, for instance, after proclaiming that the rebels had been 'very rampant recently' and that new measures would be employed to root out reactionaries, there was the mention of 'student riots', then, on 20 October, the Chinese admitted that they had 'committed many mistakes in their treatment of Tibet', putting the blame not on 'Great Han Chauvinism' as in 1957 but 'on their Soviet advisers' (it should be noted that there were no Soviet advisers in Tibet after 1960). The same dispatch then went on to explain that 'officials are being sent back to China for re-education', and that in the meantime a 'general amnesty is announced and a new policy to be followed'.

These declarations by the Chinese were following exactly the same pattern as in the past in trying to conceal a situation rapidly getting out of control. But now, after blaming Taiwan, the United States and then India for its Tibetan headaches, China had turned on Russia to save face. Yet very soon all these excuses were to prove futile when the seriousness of the new crisis in Tibet exploded with the startling news that the acting Chairman of the Tibetan puppet government, the Panchen Lama himself, had joined the N.V.D.A. and turned against the Chinese!

This unexpected news was greeted with understandable joy by most Tibetans. Unhappily, though, one person was never to rejoice at it or at the subsequent events in Tibet. This person was Osher.

While in Mustang I had tried vainly to contact my friend, whom I knew to be in the region. I had asked about him from all the Khambas I met but to no avail. For this the unfortunate custom by which most Tibetans bear similar names was mostly to blame. I had nearly lost all hope of meeting him in Mustang when I reached the village of Tangya towards the last week of my stay. By then I had visited practically every nook and cranny of the country, studying its people and culture. I had also visited all the area's *magars*: windblown camps of ill-assorted tents, where yak-hair shelters like those of the nomads stood alongside a few modern Chinese or Indian tents. Everywhere I had been impressed by the strict discipline of the Khamba camps; but most amazing of all was the toughness of these men who managed to live and look cheerful in the most god-forsaken, desolate recesses of a region which is itself one of the most barren of all the Tibetan highlands.

Remarkable, too, was the efficiency of the Khambas' organization. Besides depots for wood and transport in Kag and Tayen, they also boasted a large grain store in Gemi, one of the three small towns of the kingdom. This settlement was inhabited largely by Khambas, who in a very short time had 'rebuilt' many of its shabby buildings, giving the entire region a new look of prosperity. From Gemi food was distributed to all the *magars*, as the town was the destination of the endless mule trains which shuttled incessantly up and down the Kali Gandaki from Pokhara.

I was on my way to the village of Te, not far from the site of the Khambas' largest camp at Demodra Khund, when I stopped at the village of Tangya.

I spent the night there. In the morning a young Khamba called me to come and look at a friend of his who had been brought down to the village desperately ill. I had already been taxed beyond my competence in giving medical advice and had been pestered constantly for assistance, so it was with reluctance that I agreed to go and see his friend. It was a fine morning and the sun shone brightly with that golden clarity only to be found above 10,000 feet, which makes distant peaks appear almost within reach.

I tucked a few aspirins and pills into my *chuba* and, following the man, entered the village, a hive of interlocking houses beneath which I passed by means of small tunnels until finally emerging on to a flight of steps leading up to a sunlit roof. I was led through a low wooden door into a small, dark room. The contrast was so great that I was unable to see anything at first. After a few moments, however, I was able to make out the form of a man lying on the floor. A young man. I will never forget him. His eyes were bright with fever and, as I put out my hand to touch his brow, he lifted his own wearily to push mine away. At the same moment, our eyes met and I recognized Osher. Then his hand dropped, nothing in his gaze indicating that he had recognized me. His expression was one of panic, of fear. Then, a few minutes later, his eyes suddenly turned upwards, fluttering, and his mouth opened in the grim convulsion of death. Right before my eyes, Osher had died.

This strange and tragic coincidence affected me more than words can say. It was when I was outside again in the blazing sun that I resolved to write this book. More than anything, his death seemed to me symbolic of the Tibetan tragedy. Outside everything was so bright, while there, in that hovel, a young man of my own age had died, a friend, the victim of a war that nobody cared about, a war which had gone on for fourteen years and is still going on today, a war which had led Osher, the wild, arrogant, reckless man I had admired in Bodnath, to his premature, anonymous death, a lonely death in a strange land a thousand miles from the pastures he had called home, a thousand miles from where he had been born.

I shall never forget that look of fear in Osher's eyes or the morning sun that was his last.

He would never know the outcome of the struggle for which he had given his life or ever fully understood the reasons which had driven him and his people into war. Osher's death had come without even the glory of battle, and I felt as if his life had been wasted because nobody cared why the Khambas lived or died. I also saw that I too was among those who had preferred silence to the embarrassing truth, that I had been one with the collusion which had almost succeeded in erasing the facts of what must surely be remembered as one of the most valiant crusades of our times. A crusade that nothing, it seemed, would ever halt. A crusade that, shortly after Osher's death, was gaining a new impetus as Lhasa echoed once more to the sound of rifles and gunfire.

A year after President Kennedy's assassination, with the war in Vietnam escalating, there was little room in the press for the misfortunes of Tibet.

Once more, it was mainly on the reports of the Chinese themselves that we must rely for news of what was happening, reports far more accurate than those emanating from various sources outside Tibet, whether they were the over-enthusiastic bulletins of the Dalai Lama's office or the similarly optimistic ones of Taiwan.

Few of those who had fled Lhasa in 1959 would have recognized the holy city in 1964. The most obvious change was well described that same year by Israel Epstein, who wrote that

Lhasa is becoming a beautiful modern city. Not long ago, the Potala, the temples and a few mansions stood amid hovels and cesspools of medieval squalor. Now there are miles of well lit, asphalted streets and underground drains (whilst there was not an inch of either in 1959). Electricity is supplied to 90 per cent of all homes for illumination and often for cooking (ex-serfs and slaves get it free). A working people's Cultural Palace with a hall seating twelve hundred is used for meetings, plays and films; there are also two other film theatres. A State Emporium built this year, the biggest of many new shops and stores, sells everything from needles and thread to sewing machines, bicycles and transistor radios – all now popular purchases with people who were themselves so recently bought and sold.

Apart from the fact that no Tibetans were ever bought or sold, one wonders how truly popular transistor radios and sewing machines were with the so-called serfs. And as for the beauty of Lhasa, it had always been proclaimed by foreigners.

Of course technological progress is a good thing; but it was not exclusively Chinese property and, as the Dalai Lama has pointed out, the Tibetans had already planned and purchased the components of Lhasa's first electrical plant from Great Britain prior to the Chinese invasion, although its completion had been delayed during the first nine years of the occupation by the Chinese themselves, who were keen that the regime they planned to overthrow should have nothing to offer the masses.

How beautiful Lhasa had become is a matter of argument, not only for those not particularly keen on neon lighting and asphalt roads, but for the Tibetans who had seen the new Chinese towns of barracks spring up around the ancient city to accommodate the thousands of Chinese settlers who had taken over the capital, including its eleven prison camps where thousands of prisoners still lingered five years after the Lhasean uprising. Similarly underground drains could not conceal for ever the mounting dissatisfaction of the Lhaseans, who had seen their capital defiled and its monasteries emptied and desecrated, to be replaced by a cultural palace whose activities consisted mainly of indoctrination sessions, when it was not staging theatrical productions with gross political undertones.

So much appreciated were the Cultural Palace and new town hall that they became the first targets of Lhasa's new-found bellicosity. The so-called student riots of August 1964, it was revealed later, had been a popular rising which resulted in the city halls being 'burnt to the ground'. Shortly after this news reached India it was confirmed by the Chinese themselves, who, according to the *Hindu Time*s of 11 November, had declared that 'conditions were steadily growing worse in Tibet'. The unrest was blamed on 'reactionary elements' which had resorted to 'looting, arson and anti-state measures'.

Although earlier that year the Chinese had already blamed Russia for the trouble, a better excuse had now to be found. This time it was the Dalai Lama, who until then had been spared any direct attack in the Chinese press, no doubt for fear of popular reactions.

But now the worst had happened; and to save face, on 17 December the Dalai Lama was officially demoted from Honorary Chairman of the Preparatory Committee of the Tibet Autonomous Region' and declared 'a traitor who is an incorrigible running dog of Imperialists and foreign reactionaries, actively organizing and training remnant bandits [the new name for the N.V.D.A.] to harass frontier areas of mainland China'.

Yet to blame the Dalai Lama for frontier activities could not entirely justify unrest in the capital. Another scapegoat was necessary and was officially named on 31 December: the Panchen Lama, who was in turn demoted and disgraced for 'subversive activity'. The Panchen Lama himself, the greatest and closest ally of the Chinese, was now removed from the active chairmanship of the famous Preparatory Committee for Tibetan Autonomy and replaced by Ngabo, the hated and despised Ngabo.

With the Panchen Lama and the members of his cabinet the last monks went into disgrace, all of them people who until then had been among the few supporters of China.

The effect on the Tibetans of the disgrace of the Panchen Lama was of course quite the opposite of what the Chinese had expected. At the overthrow of their one-time greatest ally, even the most stubborn of the few communists in Tibet rose up in protest, triggering off increased violence all over the country. By early spring 1965, much of Tibet was once again in arms. Chinese officials were murdered by hundreds and when possible garrisons were attacked. Later that spring men of the N.V.D.A. issued reports that when Chinese soldiers had come to arrest the Panchen Lama, that young man, so long believed docile, had struck the Chinese official and cried 'Long Live His Holiness the Dalai Lama', the ultimate of insults to the Chinese who had just branded the Dalai Lama as a 'traitor and running dog', and who had for so long attempted to divide Tibet by playing the two young Incarnations against each other.

Any other régime would have put the Panchen Lama to death, but not the Chinese. Still obsessed by matters of 'face', they imprisoned him while they prepared a trial which they hoped would cover up their own shortcomings. At this trial, which lasted fifteen days, the Panchen Lama was publicly accused, having been singled out as the universal culprit, responsible for all China's failures in Tibet. The Chinese still remained blind to the fact that the Tibetans hated them, above all else, and still preferred independence to electricity, and freedom to sewers.

At the instigation of the Chinese, a woman was made to 'beat' the Panchen Lama, another attempt to discredit in the eyes of all his prestige as a holy Incarnation. It was a bitter moment for the young man who had been brought up by Chiang Kai-shek and then brought to Tibet by the communists and who had served the cause of Mao so well. Yet now he was able to prove at last what the Dalai Lama had always proclaimed, that like every young Tibetan who had temporarily inclined to communism, the Panchen Lama would never disown the blood in his veins, the blood of the race of kings. To the end, the Panchen shouted his pent-up hatred of the Chinese, unmasking their evil policies. Eventually the Chinese condemned the Panchen Lama for 'immoral behaviour and the murder of a junior lama' before taking him out of Tibet and throwing him into prison in Canton, as far as possible from his restless land. The trial of the Panchen Lama confirmed China's complete failure to muzzle opposition in Tibet.

After the trial, February 1965, the month of the Tibetan New Year, marked a new peak in Tibetan resistance. Anyone who still refuses to believe the reports to this effect issued by the Khambas or by the office of the Dalai Lama must accept the reports of the Chinese themselves.

Thus on 18 July 1965 Chinese-controlled Radio Lhasa announced that 'armed rebellion has broken out in several parts of Tibet'. The report added that the People's Liberation Army had surrounded 'seventy-eight bandits with machine guns who had rebelled against their motherland' and that 'five thousand reinforcements had been sent to South Tibet to quell the revolt'. The following day the same radio explained that 'the five thousand reinforcements were sent to Loka to quell a widespread revolt', adding hastily that 'the Chinese are mopping up the remnants of the counter revolutionaries' and that 'the Chinese have captured large quantities of arms and paraded the captured rebel leaders in the streets of Lhasa'. The Chinese also claimed to have 'restored peace in various parts of Tibet including the west'. Nevertheless, a general curfew was still maintained and convoys were still not allowed to move after dark.

Although the Khambas had attempted to publicize the news of the latest uprising, they received little or no attention from a world which preferred to believe that China had truly 'restored peace'.

And yet no amount of propaganda and indifference could

conceal for ever the massive N.V.D.A. operations and local uprisings of 1965, uprisings that spread even to Loka, the most policed and infiltrated part of Tibet. Loka, the base the Chinese had pacified a few years earlier and from which they had invaded India. Now, once again, Loka had come to the fore, although this was due less to the Khambas than to the courage of its own long-suffering inhabitants. The Khambas, on the other hand, carried the weight of their attacks north of Mount Everest into the vital Tingri-Shekar region. Fighting there was bitter and prolonged and the Chinese were once again obliged to use their air force in massive bombing raids.

Such had been the events of that spring, to which the Chinese referred in July when they claimed that 'peace had been restored'. Peace? Who could believe in that word now in connection with Tibet? Especially with the rebels, deep in preparations for a fresh offensive in August. In that month, the Khamba commanders made an official announcement of their intentions, stating that they had between fifty and eighty thousand men under arms inside Tibet, prepared to engage in military operations. They also declared that, taking into consideration the reasons which had caused their momentary set-back in 1956, they felt confident that from their new bases adjoining 'co-operative' countries they expected to be victorious with the aid of airdrops from 'interested sources'.

Shortly after this declaration one of the 'interested sources', India, was accused by the Chinese of three hundred air intrusions into Tibet, and blamed once more for supporting the guerrillas. It is interesting to note that this new Chinese attack on Delhi was followed, two days later, by an official declaration by the Russians stating that they 'would continue sending armaments to India': arms whose main use was the consolidating of India's Tibetan border defences. Later on 26 October the *Telegraph* revealed that 'the Dalai Lama was officially raising an invasion army trained in the use of modern arms to assist the Indian forces in the event of aggression.

17

Red Guards and Prayer Flags

So it came to pass that by 1966 the Khambas in exile were being openly recruited and incorporated into special Indian brigades armed in part by Russia, the same Russians who were eagerly helping the Khambas in the Chang Thang, where N.V.D.A. soldiers, along with the Kazakhs of Sinkiang, benefited from Russian air drops. About these air drops the Russians were far less discreet than Taiwan or India. Their embassies abroad openly discussed their support of the Tibetans.

Most of these developments, although drawing the outside world gradually into the Tibetan crisis, made little or no difference to the rebels who, unwavering in their determination, had now kept up practically alone their mortal struggle against China for more than fifteen years. As before, the Chinese were safe nowhere in Tibet, not even in Lhasa where, on 10 January 1966, the Chinese announced that they had 'discovered and destroyed a new secret opposition organization'. The situation of the Chinese was again made clear in an official press release on 30 January in which they were obliged to admit that 'Nationalist and traditionalist elements in Tibet are still fighting Chinese communists and have attempted to assassinate party officers in Tibetan villages'. The newspaper *China Youth* added in an article supposedly written by a young Tibetan girl that

> the reactionary serf-owners are not reconciled to extinction. They are trying by all means to wreck our new life, making use of questions of nationalities to carry out subversive and disruptive activities. Spreading rumours, they say the Hans [Chinese] are devils: Moreover they attempt to stage armed revolt in order to restore the old rule of serfdom. Manorial lords in our villages try to murder party cadres.

This was the situation in Tibet when, following Mao's memorable speech in Peking, the Red Guard movement swept

Lhasa, causing havoc among the Chinese to the greater benefit of the Khambas. The undisciplined Chinese youth did not stop to think of the disastrous effects their movement might have on a country where the P.L.A. was busy fighting rebels, for they now openly attacked the P.L.A. themselves, at the same time denouncing 'reactionary elements in [Tibetan] monasteries'.

Thus the Red Guards further stoked the fires of Tibetan resentment while at the same time attacking the Chinese People's Liberation Army, itself busily engaged fighting the Tibetans. The result was chaos. The Red Guards plundered Lhasa's temples and simultaneously fired at their own army in the streets. Outraged at seeing their most sacred objects destroyed or kicked about 'like a football' (as was done with the heads of a number of statues, including the seven-hundred-year-old figure of Songtsen Gampo) the Tibetans struck back at both the Red Guards and the army. Yet more men took to the hills to join the 'rebels' and by September the Chinese had to inform their own people and the world once again that there was 'revolt in the mountains'.

The year 1966 saw the beginning of a new phase of the long-drawn-out Khamba revolt in Tibet and for two full years the Chinese fought not only the Tibetans but violently amongst themselves.

While Tibet continued to experience the horrors of oppression and also to suffer the assaults of the Red Guards, bent on destroying the last remnants of their culture through the whole-sale burning of manuscripts, the ransacking of their religious buildings, the banning of everything Tibetan including long hair and Tibetan dress, in India another tragedy was unfolding. This was the tragedy of the Tibetan refugees.

In spite of the considerable financial aid given to Tibetans, seven years after the arrival of the first refugees in India the majority were still living under appalling conditions. The mortality rate in their camps was much higher than India's average, which is among the highest in the world.

The first reason for this was the nature of the Tibetan race itself, unable to face the hardships of the cultural and climatic changes from a healthy, cool climate and wide open spaces to the miserable, sweltering heat of an alien country, where they were camped in insalubrious buildings. The Tibetan aristocrats must be held partly responsible for this state of affairs, as they wasted no time in providing for themselves on a footing if not as superb as the one they had known, nevertheless grand indeed in comparison with that of their less influential compatriots who were left to struggle for life in unhealthy camps. The same petty intrigues which had divided the Tibetans in Lhasa were still to be seen in India. It is sad to remark that, with a few rare exceptions, the aristocrats in exile justified many of China's attacks against them as a ruling class. They further deserved contempt by posing to the world as the victims of China whereas in fact they had collaborated with the Chinese before fleeing in a flock after putting up little or no struggle, leaving most Tibetans behind to suffer in the name of abuses they alone had committed.

Many refugees were turned into a rugged, cheap labour force to implement India's new strategic Himalayan road-building programmes. The working conditions of these Tibetan refugees in the road camps fully justified the report of the Dalai Lama's office which stated that 'many Tibetans could hardly be worse off at home' (under Chinese rule).

The salary paid to the miserable labourers, three rupees a day, was barely enough to keep them from starving and the conditions under which they worked were worse still. Unable to bring up their babies by the roadside, mothers had to part with them if they were to survive. In their thousands, these 'orphans by necessity' were sent to the nursery school hastily set up by the Dalai Lama's sister at Dharamsala. It is hardly surprising that a few refugees preferred in desperation to return to Tibet and face the Chinese again.

As Hugh Richardson and David Snellgrove have so rightly remarked of the Tibetan refugees, the apparent good humour they showed and which always pleased Europeans was misleading, for their apparent 'equanimity and cheerfulness of demeanour often conceals an inner sense of utter hopelessness and loss of all purpose in life'. For indeed, the open, friendly faces of Tibetan refugees often hid the depths of the tragedy of nearly eighty thousand souls abandoned in exile with nothing to look forward to but premature death. Such a situation could well have been avoided had India been less suspicious and sensitive about its own Tibetan districts, such as Laddak and N.E.F.A., where the refugees could have found a home more suited to their customs, and a climate kinder to their health.

But India until 1962 was generally antagonistic to Tibetans and also keen on 'weaning away from Tibet' its own Tibetan population of the Indian Himalayan foothills.

For most refugees the only ray of hope was to be found, not, as the Dalai Lama claimed, in the 'compassion of His Master' and the illusion of pre-Nirvanic bliss, but in the knowledge that so many people in Tibet still fought on for the reconquest of their homeland.

In the course of journeys to Nepal, Bhutan and the Indian Tibetan border in 1966, 1967 and 1968, I was able to witness further developments in the Tibetan rebellion. Since my first journey to Kalimpong in 1959 little in the attitude of the West had changed as the Tibetan crisis continued to develop. As the years went by I saw many friends die or disappear. Yet, although Osher was dead and Tsering had met a fate as bad as death, there still remained Betty-la. Betty-la who until then had been a silent victim of the political and social upheavals of her country. The charming aristocrat of Lhasa, the delicate woman who represented the more fragile elements of Tibetan sophistication, had paid a heavy toll for the sins of her caste.

Betty-la had lost not only her titles, her fortune and her way of life, but also her four children. Yet she was now to lose even more. First her husband and then her health. Succumbing to tuberculosis in 1966, Betty-la lay in Calcutta, uncaring, in her own words, 'whether she lived or died'. Her life had become an infernal cycle of days filled with memories of the past and nights of tears, haunted by visions of her 'small ones' who were being brought up somewhere in Tibet to despise their parents.

That they were alive Betty-la knew, because she had received letters written by her eldest daughter asking her why she had abandoned them and why she did not come back, telling her how desperately she and her brothers needed her and begging her to be reasonable, to 'repent' her political sins and return. The letters, of course, failed to say where they were. Betty-la had tried everything in her efforts to locate them but in vain.

Betty-la had suffered indescribably. Her sensitive nature filled her with a sense of guilt, not only because she had left her children but for all the evils of her class. Better than anyone, she saw, knew and continued to witness in exile the arrogant folly of many Lhasean aristocrats, who wasted their time in rapacious intrigues in which money, and influence were the common coin. Her husband had abandoned her while her old friends despised her for her financial destitution. But Betty-la refused to play the game of intrigues, to benefit like many others from the Dalai Lama's treasure and the relief money generally showered on those who in exile continued to play for favours.

Although born a princess, she had retained the common sense and intelligence of Tsarong, her father, who had risen not by privilege of blood but through service. She knew now the best and the worst of four worlds: the luxurious, vain life of a Tibetan aristocrat; the austerity of a convent in colonial India; then communism; and finally the tragedy of exile. For weeks, there in Calcutta, her life was in danger. She felt she had reached the end of her journey. As an individual she had probably lost more than any, except for her life. This she was ready to see blow away. But nursed by her sister, the widow of the Prime Minister of Bhutan, the elegant Tesla, she slowly recovered her health. Then she understood that the true path lay not in complacency or tears, but along the trail marked out by those tall, handsome men from Kham, the so-called barbarians so often mocked by Lhaseans.

Betty-la now chose to place her person and her soft voice at the service of her country. And so her voice can now be heard on the Tibetan broadcasts of All India Radio. Daily the sound-waves carry her voice miles away to windswept *magars*, out to the lonely hamlets and nomad camps where Freedom Fighters and Tibetan patriots listen to her words of comfort. A cheerful, beautiful voice, recalling to all the men of Songtsen Gampo's realm the glory of their task. Few of the rough soldiers have ever seen her face, yet despite her sophisticated accent they heard for the first time from her lips Lhasean words of beauty, not just 'beautiful words'.

Today Tsarong lives on in the voice of the most fragile of his offspring, that of Betty-la, who since leaving Tibet had fathomed the well of despair.

It is Betty-la who now reads the news to all those intent on the future of Tibet. News which is not entirely discouraging. On the contrary, although what little of it seeps through to the rest of the world appears, as usual, so confusing.

It was all the more confusing because, after 1966, it became necessary to sort out the reports of two simultaneous conflicts in

Tibet. On the one hand, the Red Guards were fighting the conservative People's Liberation Army led by General Chang Kuo-hua, the Governor of Tibet. On the other, both the Red Guards and the army were attacking the Tibetan rebels.

Nowhere did China's cultural revolution show its true face so clearly as in Tibet. The origin of the movement had been Mao's proclaiming in Peking that the communist revolution should always be on its guard against 'bourgeois reactionary leanings' and that China's youth should renew the 'revolutionary struggle of communism'. Immediately after Mao's speech Chinese students in a sweeping movement of undisciplined enthusiasm set out on a massive witch-hunt. The army, the last rigid frame of order in China, soon fell victim to the wild crowds of slogan-shouting young fanatics; that same army which, as the Red Guards well knew, Mao himself had always slightly feared. In Tibet the army was all-powerful as, from necessity, the P.L.A. ruled the country. Consequently there the clashes between Red Guards and the army were particularly severe. The Red Guards of Tibet were composed mostly of young Chinese technicians and bureaucrats stationed there. This corps of expatriates represented an élite, a handful of resolute intellectuals only too delighted to get to grips with the army they despised. The very fact that Tibet was still the scene of violent Tibetan rebel activity only appeared to the Red Guards as evidence of the army's incompetence. To prove this point and demonstrate their zeal, the Red Guards went about carrying out their own private campaign against the Tibetans who, having been attacked already as feudal, were now branded as bourgeois. Disobeying the orders of the military commander, who already had enough problems with the N.V.D.A., the Red Guards stormed the monasteries and threw their contents out into the streets, regardless of any effect such actions might have on the already explosive population.

Outraged Tibetans all over the country renewed their attacks on the Chinese and flocked in greater numbers to the mountain retreats to join the rebels.

Faced with both the Red Guards and the rebels, the P.L.A. began making massive arrests. In Lhasa thousands of young Tibetans were imprisoned in the hope that the leaders of the new Tibetan rebellion might be among them. By 1966 a new generation of rebels had emerged, young men who had been educated in China and who had been only children eight years earlier when Lhasa had first resolved to oppose China. The soldiers who had originally fought in Chamdo in 1950 were now, by Tibetan standards, nearly all old men. A whole new generation of Tibetans had been born under Chinese occupation, a generation very different from their fathers, bred on indoctrination and yet in whose veins the same blood flowed.

Many of these young Tibetans had succeeded in rising to power inside the clandestine new Tibetan Freedom Committees throughout the land. The older rebels were mostly to be found in Mustang and on Tibet's borders, preferring to leave internal matters to the more sophisticated new leaders.

By September 1966 Loka was once again teeming with rebels. Bands of young Tibetans seeking shelter and organizing resistance in the same ravined hills from which the Khambas had launched their assault on Lhasa.

In December 1966 the *Daily Express* reported that 'two thousand Chinese soldiers had been killed in the course of encounters with Khambas, rebels and other Tibetan irregulars reacting against Red Guard actions in Tibet'.

The rebels had even spread to the north-east, where they again captured the Tsiwa pass on the Chinghai-Lhasa Highway, for long a favourite target.

Large attacks were carried out simultaneously by Khambas in far western Tibet, whose capital Gartok was stormed.

Reports reached India of shooting in Lhasa itself. Once again a dusk-to-dawn curfew was clamped down all over the country by the old General Chang Kuo-hua.

This news Betty-la relayed with enthusiasm along with the news that in Kham itself, a region so long silenced, fighting had flared up once more.

So began the new storms that were to rock Tibet in 1967, when a full-scale battle broke out among the Chinese themselves before the astonished and delighted eyes of the Tibetans.

Behind the trouble was Chang Kuo-hua, a soldier who had risen from the ranks during the famous 'long march'. He was a man who liked to consider Tibet his private domain. After all, he had handled Tibetan affairs since the earliest days, having negotiated the famous seventeen-point agreement with Ngabo in 1950, which he had signed on behalf of the Chinese. Subsequently he had lived through all the events of the long war against the Khambas and the N.V.D.A. Quite naturally, this old veteran was determined to stand no nonsense from the young Red Guards. Little did he care if this meant being branded officially as an anti-Maoist. General Chang Kuo-hua had little personal esteem for Mao. Mao was China's mastermind of politics and ideology, subjects General Chang Kuo-hua had little time or respect for, as he had shown in his dealings with the Dalai Lama and the Panchen Lama in the past.

Consequently, when the pseudo-intellectual Red Guards began meddling with his job of controlling and running Tibet, he was furious. He cared very little what Peking might think when he ordered his soldiers to open fire on the Red Guards. General Chang Kuo-hua's behaviour is a good illustration of a little-known aspect of the Chinese régime. In China all high officials were quite independent of Mao. They were leaders in their own right and not lackeys of the top administrators.

Such insubordination would have been unthinkable in Stalin's Russia, but not so in China where Mao might be the figurehead but was not, so to speak, God Almighty to his top officials, men who had risen with him as co-leaders of Communist China from as far back as 1933.

Since Tibet was a long way from Peking the Commander-in-Chief of the Tibetan military district, who was also the supreme Chinese administrator in Tibet, could act according to his own judgement without fear for his position. Thus the rugged general did not hesitate to distribute ammunition to his men garrisoned in and around Lhasa and to order a couple of armoured cars to force an entry into Lhasa, not to the old city, but to the new Lhasa, whose Chinese population of advisers and technical assistants outnumbered the Tibetans two to one.

With expert efficiency General Chang took command of the situation. The bodies of the Red Guards killed in the fighting were hastily cleared off the streets. The old general had won his first victory, although elsewhere in Tibet Red Guards were still causing trouble.

Meanwhile the Tibetans stood by in utter amazement. Although similar situations had arisen all over China where the army had come to grips with the Red Guards, nowhere had the fighting been so violent, or its implications so serious, as in Tibet. Observers from Peking and abroad began to fear that the general, sure of his power, might break away completely from mainland China and try to build up an independent Tibet on his own. After all, all he had to do to achieve this was to come to terms with the N.V.D.A.

Peking was quick to react to such a prospect. Three divisions were sent to Tibet at top speed to try and bring General Chang Kuo-hua to reason. He was hurriedly demoted and recalled to China. But to the surprise of everyone, before the troop arrived General Chang Kuo-hua left Tibet for China of his own accord.

Too hastily perhaps the Red Guards acclaimed his departure over Radio Lhasa, which they had seized, as a great victory.

But the army, even though their leader had left (to be liquidated, as some thought), refused to side with the Red Guards, so that army and Red Guards fought each other once again, while thousands of Tibetans fled to India, telling of Red Guard atrocities and also of the heavy casualties which the Khambas, taking advantage of the chaos, were now inflicting on the Chinese. The Tibetans were soon causing so much trouble that, to the surprise of all, General Chang Kuo-hua was suddenly announced to be returning to Tibet, sent back by Lin Piao to restore order.

The fact that it was Lin Piao himself, the declared successor of Mao, who sent back the anti-Maoist General Chang to restore order in Tibet, came as a severe shock to the Red Guards, indicating as it did the extent of· the general's influence and, more particularly, how concerned the Chinese were that Tibet should have a strong man at its head to hold the Tibetans in check.

When the Red Guards heard that their arch-enemy was returning, they prepared to kidnap him on his way into Tibet, at the same time hastily striking out at his best friend, the despised Ngabo, whom they deposed. Ngabo, who had betrayed his country to serve his own interests and position, who had put his faith in Chinese communism, suddenly found the ultra-communist Red Guards calling him a 'running dog'. Justice had caught up with him at last. Ngabo the superb, who had successfully survived so many crises, was liquidated. At long last this controversial and hated figure disappeared from the Tibetan political scene to moulder in some unknown jail, perhaps even the same prison in Canton where the Panchen Lama sat meditating on the impermanence of Chinese friendship and the dubious advantages of Chinese rule in Tibet. No one wept for Ngabo.

As for General Chang Kuo-hua, he was another matter. When it became known to his soldiers that on his way back he had been arrested by a wild group of intellectuals they set out to attack the Red Guards and liberate him, then bore him in triumph into Lhasa, which became the scene of a fresh blood-bath in October 1967. Daily, battles rocked the city, from which the anti-Maoists eventually emerged victorious.

However, the Red Guards were not prepared to accept defeat so easily. For a whole year Lhasa was the scene of disturbances in which, to quote the Dalai Lama, 'Tibetans took part on both sides', since they had everything to gain from such discord.

At the root of the crisis between the two Chinese factions was the question of partial restoration of private ownership in China. General Chang was for such a measure, siding with Liu Shao-chi, the famous 'heretic' Chinese minister and the only member of the top Chinese cabinet ever to have been 'liquidated' (although he was not actually killed).

Meanwhile, the world as usual paid little attention to the plight of the Tibetans, being far more interested in how the events in Lhasa might prove to be the first signs of a collapse of the entire Chinese communist régime.

All through these troubled years the Tibetans remained the losers and suffered the most, especially from the actions of the Red Guards who associated all Tibetans with the opposition. Once again Han chauvinism had reached a new peak. Chinese costume was made compulsory, although for lack of adequate materials this measure was never fully implemented.

There was now not one monk left in the holy city or one Tibetan in any formal official function in the land. Regional autonomy for Tibet had come to mean absolutely nothing, while the very word Tibetan was now synonymous with 'enemy'.

It would appear logical to believe that by 1968 Tibet had at least been vanquished, as one after another, over the years, the fearful prophecies of the 13th Dalai Lama had come to pass.

It is chilling to read now all that the great 13th wrote in 1931, two years before his death. In his testament the previous Dalai Lama stated: 'The present is the time of the five kinds

of degeneration in all countries. In the worst class is the manner
of working among the Red people.'

He then described what had happened to Mongolia under
Russian rule, adding the terrible prophetic paragraph that,
word for word, has proved true:

> It may happen that here in the centre of Tibet, the religious
> and secular administration may be attacked both from the
> outside and the inside. Unless we can guard our own country,
> it will now happen that the Dalai and Panchen Lamas, the
> Father and the Son, the holders of the Faith, the glorious
> Rebirths, will be broken down and left without a name. As
> regards the monasteries and the priesthood, their land and
> other properties will be destroyed. The administrative customs
> of the Three Religious Kings [Songtsen Gampo and the two
> most famous of his descendants] will be weakened. The
> officers of State, ecclesiastical and secular, will find their
> lands seized and other properties confiscated, and they them-
> selves made to serve their enemies, or wander about the
> country as beggars do. All beings will be sunk in great
> hardship and in overpowering fear, the days and nights will
> drag on slowly in suffering.

By 1968 every detail of this tragic prophecy had come true.
As a consequence there were many who proclaimed abroad that
'Tibet is dead'. What, one wondered, could be left of the Land
of Gods? Had not the Russians themselves confirmed in 1968
the most sinister rumours about the Tibetan tragedy, when
Radio Moscow attacked the Chinese for turning Sinkiang and
Tibet into 'a prison of non-Han nationalities', a place where
according to the same report 'force has become the direct
instrument in effecting the "withering away" of differences
among the nationalities of China'? In September 1968 Russia's
Tashkent International Radio Service added: 'today Tibet is a
huge military camp; the number of regular Chinese troops is
said to exceed three hundred thousand'.

'Genocide', the 'withering away'. It seemed as if the whole
world was ready to agree that Tibet had at last been defeated.
Such a conclusion after all these years did seem logical, if one
forgot that the same conclusion had already been hastily reached
many times before, as in 1950, when 120,000 Chinese soldiers
overran the 8,500 men of the Tibetan army. It was a logical

conclusion to reach again in 1956, when the Chinese bombed Litang and first routed the Khambas. It was a conclusion reached by nearly everyone in 1959 when Lhasa was over-powered, an obvious diagnosis in 1962 when Loka had been 'pacified', or again in 1964, or 1966 with the Red Guard atrocities. To declare that Tibet was dead would indeed have been logical all through the twenty bitter years which followed the fall of Chamdo, had not the victims of Chinese aggression been a race driven by a force stronger than all logic, a force drawn from the eternal winds of nameless pastures, a wind of conquest which had produced a race of men more powerful than reason could understand. A race which again and again, with flintlocks and horses, had proved superior to the power of numbers and machines, stronger than the venom of vindictive theories and ideals.

Far from being dead, in 1968 this force was still very much alive. Nothing had dented or dampened the determination of the Tibetans, those same Tibetans who had overcome the obstruction of India, of Russia and the indifference of most of the world, surviving betrayals 'from within and without', always proving wrong the calculations of strategists, the con-clusions of experts. No more than the Great Wall, had the soldiers of Mao yet been able to contain or conquer the spirit of the barbarians of central Asia.

In 1968 the prayer flags of countless *magars* still fluttered in secret all over the immense expanse of Tibet, and on the borders of Songsten Gampo's realm the flags of men waiting in ambush for the grey hours of dawn, the dawn of hope.

18

'Till the Crows Turn White'

If in appearance by 1968 Tibet had changed it was still far too early to proclaim that Tibet was dead. Not all the changes had been detrimental to the cause of the Tibetans as a race, even if over the years time had left its inevitable mark on Tibet and its people.

Much had indeed changed since that distant morning of the fateful Iron Tiger year when, for the first time, the Chinese had invaded the territories of Lhasa. It is true that the Tibet of old, the Tibet of the Dalai Lama, the hazy Shangri-la so dear to romantics, had disappeared. That strange world on which explorers and adventurers, historians and novelists had thrived was gone for ever. In war and struggle, under Chinese occupation, the whole country had experienced a technological revolution. Cars drove where yaks once used to plod; yet, sad as this might seem, pigtails and prayer wheels, along with all the land's archaic customs, had little to do with the real reasons why the Khambas had risen up in arms. On the contrary, retrograde feudalism, the oppression of the 'beautiful-mouthed' Lhaseans, had been one of the basic evils the Khambas had always sought to combat, so that the land might regain its rightful place in the world as a strong, united nation.

In turmoil and tears, and in spite of Chinese rule, the Tibetans had over the years finally regained the lost unity of Songtsen Gampo's days, the unity called for, and also predicted in the 13th Dalai Lama's testament. Indeed it seems that nothing will ever really succeed in extinguishing the true spirit which had animated the most rugged of Tibetans in their crusade. It is this same spirit which today, in the hands of the young, carries high the banners of revolt against China. In this respect nothing inside Tibet has changed.

Evidence proves that in Tibet today a whole new generation of rebels has been born, young technocrats whose education in

China, like that of Tsering, has in no way weakened their combative spirit.

It is time to understand that the fires which, tonight as every night over the past twenty tragic years, burn in the hidden *magars* of the rebels and in the heart of every Tibetan, are not the fires of the romantic cavaliers of a dead Shangri-la, but of men belonging to a race which still shames the world by daring to stand up alone and challenge our planet's largest nation. It is time the world knew and appreciated fully that today, at this very moment, all over the immense realm of Songtsen Gampo, a bitter war is being waged against China, a war whose actions are still revealed in brief and incomplete reports from China, testifying to the amazing courage and crippling efficiency of the Tibetan Freedom Fighters.

Reports by the New China News Agency on 5 March 1969 told how 'many Tibetans died while resisting the desecration of temples and their sacred places'. A few weeks later China again reminded the world of the grim reality of the secret war in central Asia by accusing 'the C.I.A., India, the Dalai Lama and his brother' of sending 'traitor bandits into Chinese territory to carry out harassment and sabotage activities'. On 23 September of the same year a refugee reported 'Khamba activity in the middle sector of Tibet and in Kham'. This statement was published in the *Hindu Times* side by side with a complaint from the men of Mustang's *magars* that now 'Nepal was joining hands with the Chinese to bring the Khambas to heel'. China was exerting pressure on Nepal while also widely blaming all nations for the continuing unrest in Tibet. Thus even Switzerland found itself in 1969 openly accused by China, accusations which were completely unfounded, as the true cause of China's troubles rests only with the Tibetans' invincible determination to fight, as proved on 24 December 1969 by the Chinese announcement that once again a general curfew had been ordered over Lhasa after the killing 'of a high ranking military officer and four soldiers *by the rebels*'.

In 1970 more acts of anonymous heroism came to light, small fragments of the unsung epic of a war about which nobody cares, sparse evidence that conceals a thousand other deeds never reported. Far from being vanquished, the Tibetans, according to a Chinese report on 17 March 1970, were still engaged in 'subversive activities, harassment and sabotage in the Sino-Indian border area and in the Tibetan autonomous region of China'. When one considers the reluctance of any nation to publish news of open opposition within its frontiers, the Chinese dispatches deserve close attention. Each of them betrays China's exasperation at her inability, despite the fantastic means employed, to master Tibet. If in 1970 the Chinese were again putting the blame for Tibetan violence on 'the reactionary Indian Government' which according to Peking had 'intensified its collusion with the Chiang Kai-shek bandit gang entrenched in Taiwan and instigated and assisted the Tibetan traitorous bandits', this was too much praise for the nations of the world, who with the exception of Russia had in fact reduced their support to Tibet. It was a support that was never wholehearted or disinterested, and it remains quite insufficient, little more than token assistance dispensed, in great secrecy, to those Khambas still entrenched in Mustang, sealed off from the world by Nepal's inner line, and the victims of Nepalese pressures, directed to thwarting Tibet's legitimate struggle for independence.

In 1970, to serve the defence of its own frontiers, India officially incorporated more Khambas into its 'special task frontier force'.

Russia on the other hand had increased her activities in Sinkiang, and consequently widened the Sino-Soviet breach, leading to a massive military build-up on both sides of the Sinkiang border. The Urumchi river incidents were only part of the general military unrest in central Asia. Russia is now more than ever determined to bring about the eventual 'auto-determination of Sinkiang'. She has not hesitated to sound out her European satellites, and even the Western diplomats, about their reactions to a possible 'Atomic War' in Sinkiang. In this respect it is easy in the West to forget how the pro-Arab, pro-Moslem attitude of Russia in the Middle East is much more dictated by her central Asian policy than by any consideration of opposition to the West. Sinkiang is predominantly Moslem and the Russians have not abandoned the desire, so dear to Stalin, to reunite the central Asian Moslem states, and in particular Sinkiang, because the Russians fully appreciate that however one looks at the map of the world Sinkiang and Tibet remain the strategic heart of Asia, and nothing will ever alter the fact that China has no place there, either in Tibet or in Sinkiang.

Events in Vietnam, if they have now made the United States reluctant to consider any future intervention in Asian affairs, should also teach the United States that if their troops have proved ineffective, despite their arms and equipment, against the North and South Vietnamese National Liberation Front, so, in the same way, China can never gain the upper hand of the National Voluntary Defence Army, the troops of Kham who today, aided by the entire Tibetan nation, are still fighting for freedom in Tibet.

Shortly after 27 April 1970 when the King of Bhutan made public his belief that the Panchen Lama had died in a Chinese prison, it was learnt from the Dalai Lama's office that there had been a 'renewal of rebel activity in Tibet' and it became known that buildings in Lhasa were covered with posters demanding Mao's execution and Tibetan independence.

As late as 22 and 23 December 1970 the London *Times* was to publish a report by a young Tibetan by the name of Paljor who had recently escaped from Lhasa where he had worked as a news correspondent and a member of the Chinese intelligence service in Tibet. From this young man we have come to know how in 1969 eight hundred Tibetan rebels stormed a major Chinese garrison thirty-two miles from Lhasa before retiring to secret camps in the hills, having killed two hundred and fifty Chinese, and how in 1970 'all over Tibet small groups of guerrillas are operating'.

Chinese-controlled Radio Lhasa has explained further how, in July 1970, 'taking advantage of exceptional floods Khamba rebels in Chamdo had risen and cut national defence highways': in Chamdo itself, where, twenty years ago, it had all begun with the uprising of the 'cavaliers, wild and accustomed to living by loot', men who have succeeded in shattering what Mao had called 'his most sacred duty', the liberation of Tibet. Mao to all appearances has failed, failed before what some have called 'an insignificant tribe'.

History in Tibet is now repeating itself and, although a day may come when it will be possible to write, in full detail, an account of the secret war being waged in Tibet, yet it is time now for the world to face the cruel realities of a struggle that can no longer be ignored. It must be known and understood that although Osher is dead, and Tsering sunk in despair, their struggle was not in vain. For there are thousands of men born to replace them, men and women like Betty-la, determined to fight and to win. These are people animated by a force which not all the might of China, not all the power of her sophisticated civilization, her new-found technology, even her atomic bombs, will ever be able to contain, any more than the Great Wall or the spells of her magicians were able in the past to oppose the spirit of this race of kings.

Fragne and Cadaques 1971

Select Bibliography

Barber, Noel. *The Land of Lost Content.* London 1969
Bell, Sir Charles Alfred. *Tibet Past and Present.* London 1924
Bull, G. *When Iron Gates Yield.* London 1957
Dalai Lama XIV. *My Land and My People.* London 1962
Fisher, Margaret W., Rose, Leo E., and Huttenback, Robert A. *Himalayan Background.* New York 1963
Ford, Robert. *Captured in Tibet.* London 1957
Galbraith, John Kenneth. *Ambassador's Journey.* London 1969
Gelder, Stuart and Roma. *The Timely Rain.* London 1964
Goyal, Narenda. *Prelude to India.* New Delhi 1964
Legal Inquiry Committee on Tibet. *The Question of Tibet and the Rule of Law.* Geneva 1959
Maxwell, Neville. *India's China War.* London 1970
Mitter, J.P. *Betrayal of Tibet.* New Delhi 1964
Moraes, Frank. *The Revolt in Tibet.* New York 1960
Norbu, Thubten J., and Harrer, Heinrich. *Tibet is my Country.* New York 1961
Pannikar, K.M. *In Two Chinas: Memoirs of a Diplomat.* London 1955
Patterson, George N. *Tibetan Journey.* London 1954
              Gods Fool. London 1956
              Tragic Destiny. London 1959
              Tibet in Revolt. London 1960
Peissel, Michel. *Mustang: A Lost Tibetan Kingdom.* London 1968
Richardson, Hugh Edward. *A Short History of Tibet.* New York 1962
Richardson, Hugh Edward, and Snellgrove, David. *A Cultural History of Tibet.* London 1968
Sinha, S. *Chinese Agrression.* New Delhi 1960
Strong, Anna L. *When Serfs Stood Up.* Peking (2nd edition 1965)

Taring, Rinchen Dolma. *Daughter of Tibet*. London 1970

Teichman, Sir Eric. *Travels of a Consular Officer in Eastern Tibet*. Cambridge 1921

Winnington, Alan. *Tibet: Record of a Journey*. London 1957

Index

Alma Ata region, 180
American Society for Free Asia, 78, 79
Amdo province, 4–5, 7, 13, 29, 52, 55, 57, 102, 104, 118, 170, 178, 187, 207; Chinese road across, 52; rebellion in, 71–2; 'rebel' leaders, 104; deportation of children by Chinese, 111–12; guerrilla fighting in, 202
Amdo tribe, 88
Andrutsangs, the, 104
Angun Tensing Trandul, King of Mustang, 205
Annapurna, range and mt, 184, 205, 210, 212, 215
Askaroff, 181
Associated Press, 59

Barber, Noel, 116, 117, 143, 146
Batang, 5, 13, 22, 31, 45, 60, 61, 70, 104: Chinese enter, 27; recaptured by Khambas, 68, 71; bombing of, 74, 86
Betty-la, 1, 2, 3, 16, 18, 250: life in Lhasa under Chinese, 95–7, 99; goes to Kalimpong, 113; life in Kalimpong, 157, 158; her despair, 237–8; illness, 238; as 'voice of Tibet' on radio, 238, 240
Bhutan, 17, 71, 105, 108, 155, 156, 182, 191, 201, 202
Bon religion, 49, 107
Brahmaputra, the, 4, 78, 79, 105, 113, 135, 136, 163, 165, 170, 188, 189, 190, 198, 202, 205; floods, 31
Britain: relations with Tibet, 11–12; fails to help Tibet, 24, 76, 173; obstructs release of film, 224
Bull, Geoffrey, 27

Calcutta, 80, 81, 95, 198, 238
Dum Dum airport, 80
Cha Teh, 159
Chamdo, 5, 12, 13, 14, 24, 27, 29, 32,

38, 40, 45, 52, 55, 60, 68, 69, 70, 75, 76, 94, 102, 183: news of Chinese invasion reaches, 19, 20, 21; earthquake shakes, 31; ceremony in, 36–7; falls to Chinese, 41–3; People's Liberation Committee, 46, 52, 55, 60, 62, 64; anti-Chinese sentiment in, 62–3; besieged by Khambas, 70, 71, 77; fighting round, 177
Chang Ching-wu, Gen., 59–60, 110, 116
Chang Kuo-hua, Gen., 239–43
Chang Thang desert, 5, 71, 183, 188, 189: Khambas in, 234
Chen Yi, Marshal, 92
Chengtu Drokpas, nomads, 21–2, 48, 66, 105, 188
Chiang Kai-shek, 9, 12, 13, 79, 172, 176, 197, 232
Chiba, Major, 139, 140
China: menaced by Khambas, 11–12; claims to Tibet, 17–18; invades Tibet, 38–9; first impact on Tibetans, 44–6; plans for uniting Khambas, 45; colonizes Kham, 56–7; 'a great leap forward', 68, 171; extended borders of, 70–71; builds road over Indian territory, 72; extermination policy in Tibet, 76; asks Dalai Lama to denounce Khambas, 89; makes peace overtures to Khambas, 92; promises to postpone 'reforms', 93; erodes Dalai Lama's power, 100–101; fails to crush rebellion (1958), 109; oppressive measures against Khambas, 110–12; admits Dalai Lama has fled to India, 149; reaction to Lhasa revolt, 160–63; military budget for Tibet, 170; claims to central Asia, 179–80; at odds with Russia, India and Nepal, 179–82; Sino-Indian war, 194–9; admits guerrilla activity, 225;